THE COMPLETE GOLFER

THE
COMPLETE GOLFER

BY

HARRY VARDON

OPEN CHAMPION, 1896, 1898, 1899, 1903
AMERICAN CHAMPION, 1900

WITH SIXTY-SIX ILLUSTRATIONS

ARNO PRESS
A New York Times Company
New York • 1977
A Golf Digest Classics Book

Reprint Edition 1977 by Arno Press Inc.
Reprinted from copy in the Harvard College Library.

Library of Congress Cataloging in Publication Data
Vardon, Harry, 1870-
    The complete golfer.
    "A Golf digest classics book."
    Reprint of the 1905 ed. published by McClure,
Phillips, New York.
    1. Golf. I. Title.
GV965.V3   1976   796.352'3   76-27206
ISBN 0-405-09371-3

Manufactured in the United States of America

Distributed by:
Golf Digest Inc.
495 Westport Avenue
Norwalk, Connecticut 06856

Harry Vardon

PREFACE

MANY times I have been strongly advised to write a book on golf, and now I offer a volume to the great and increasing public who are devoted to the game. So far as the instructional part of the book is concerned, I may say that, while I have had the needs of the novice constantly in mind, and have endeavoured to the best of my ability to put him on the right road to success, I have also presented the full fruits of my experience in regard to the fine points of the game, so that what I have written may be of advantage to improving golfers of all degrees of skill. There are some things in golf which cannot be explained in writing, or for the matter of that even by practical demonstration on the links. They come to the golfer only through instinct and experience. But I am far from believing that, as is so often said, a player can learn next to nothing from a book. If he goes about his golf in the proper manner he can learn very much indeed. The services of a competent tutor will be as necessary to him as ever, and I must not be understood to suggest that this work can to any extent take the place of that compulsory and most invaluable tuition. On the other hand, it is next to impossible for a tutor to tell a pupil on the links everything about any particular stroke while he is playing it, and if he could it would not be remembered. Therefore I hope and think that, in conjunction with careful coaching by those who are qualified for the task, and by immediate and constant practice of the methods which I set forth, this book may be of service to all who aspire to play a really good game. If any player of the first degree of skill should take exception to any of these methods, I have only one answer to make, and that is that, just as they are explained in the following pages, they are precisely those which helped me to win my five championships. These and no others I practise every day upon the links. I attach great importance to the photographs and the accompanying diagrams, the objects of which are simplicity and lucidity. When a golfer is in difficulty with any particular stroke—and the best of us are constantly in trouble with some stroke or other—I think that a careful examination of the pictures relating to that stroke will frequently put him right, while a glance at the companion in the "How not to do it" series may reveal to him at once the error into which he has fallen and which has hitherto defied detection. All the illustrations in this volume have been prepared from photographs of myself in the act of playing the different strokes on the Totteridge links last autumn. Each stroke was carefully studied at the time for absolute exactness, and the pictures now reproduced were finally selected by me from about two hundred which were taken. In order to obtain complete satisfaction, I found it necessary to have a few of the negatives repeated after the winter had set in, and there was a slight fall of snow the night before the morning appointed for the purpose. I owe so much—everything—to the great game of golf, which I love very dearly, and which I believe is without a superior for deep human and sporting interest, that I shall feel very delighted if my "Complete Golfer" is found of any benefit to others who play or are about to play. I give my good wishes to every golfer, and express the hope to each that he may one day regard himself as complete. I fear that, in the playing sense, this is an impossible ideal. However, he may in time be nearly "dead" in his "approach" to it.

I have specially to thank Mr. Henry Leach for the invaluable services he has rendered to me in the preparation of the work.

H. V.

TOTTERIDGE, *May* 1905.

CONTENTS

CHAPTER I

CHAPTER II

CHAPTER III

CONTENTS

easy—Cautious play in medal rounds—Risks to be taken—The
bold game in match play—Studying the course—Risks that are
foolishly taken—New clubs in competitions—On giving them a
trial—No training necessary—As to the pipe and glass—How to be
at one's best and keenest—On playing in the morning—In case of
a late draw—Watch your opponents.

CHAPTER XVII

The four-ball foursome—Its inferiority to the old-fashioned game—
The case of the long-handicap man—Confusion on the greens—
The man who drives last—The old-fashioned two-ball foursome
—Against too many foursomes—Partners and each other—Fitting
in their different games—The man to oblige—The policy of the
long-handicap man—How he drove and missed in the good old
days—On laying your partner a stymie—A preliminary consideration of the round—Handicapping in foursomes—A too delicate
reckoning of strokes given and received—A good foursome and
the excitement thereof — A caddie killed and a hole lost — A
compliment to a golfer.

CHAPTER XVIII

As to its being a ladies' game—A sport of freedom—The lady on the
links—The American lady golfer—English ladies are improving—
Where they fail, and why—Good pupils—The same game as the
man's—No short swings for ladies—Clubs of too light weight—
Their disadvantages—A common fault with the sex—Bad backward swings—The lady who will find out for herself—Foundations
of a bad style—The way to success.

CHAPTER XIX

Necessity for thought and ingenuity—The long-handicap man's
course—The scratch player's—How good courses are made—The
necessary land — A long nine-hole course better than a short
eighteen—The preliminary survey—A patient study of possibilities
—Stakes at the holes — Removal of natural disadvantages—
" Penny wise and pound foolish "—The selection of teeing grounds
—A few trial drives—The arrangement of long and short holes—
The best two-shot and three-shot holes—Bunkers and where to

CONTENTS

CHAPTER XXII

CHAPTER XXIII

LIST OF ILLUSTRATIONS

LIST OF ILLUSTRATIONS

THE COMPLETE GOLFER

CHAPTER I

GOLF AT HOME

The happy golfer—A beginning at Jersey—The Vardon family—An anxious
tutor—Golfers come to Grouville—A fine natural course—Initiation as a
caddie—Primitive golf—How we made our clubs—Matches in the moonlight—Early progress — The study of methods—Not a single lesson—I
become a gardener—The advice of my employer—"Never give up golf"
—A nervous player to begin with—My first competition—My brother Tom
leaves home—He wins a prize at Musselburgh—I decide for professionalism
—An appointment at Ripon.

I HAVE sometimes heard good golfers sigh regretfully,
after holing out on the eighteenth green, that in the
best of circumstances as to health and duration of life they
cannot hope for more than another twenty, or thirty, or forty
years of golf, and they are then very likely inclined to be a
little bitter about the good years of their youth that they
may have "wasted" at some other less fascinating sport.
When the golfer's mind turns to reflections such as these,
you may depend upon it that it has been one of those days
when everything has gone right and nothing wrong, and the
supreme joy of life has been experienced on the links. The
little white ball has seemed possessed of a soul—a soul full
of kindness and the desire for doing good. The clubs have
seemed endowed with some subtle qualities that had rarely
been discovered in them before. Their lie, their balance,
their whip, have appeared to reach the ideal, and such com-

mand has been felt over them as over a dissecting instrument
in the hands of a skilful surgeon.   The sun has been shining
and the atmosphere has sparkled when, flicked cleanly from
the tee, the rubber-cored ball has been sent singing through
the air.   The drives have all been long and straight, the
brassy shots well up, the approaches mostly dead, and the
putts have taken the true line to the tin.   Hole after hole has
been done in bogey, and here and there the common enemy
has been beaten by a stroke.   Perhaps the result is a record
round, and, so great is the enthusiasm for the game at this
moment, that it is regarded as a great misfortune that the
sun has set and there is no more light left for play.   These
are the times when the golfer's pulse beats strong, and he
feels the remorse of the man with the misspent youth because
he was grown up and his limbs were setting before ever he
teed a ball.

Well, at least I can say that I have not missed much of
the game that I love with a great fondness, for I played a
kind of prehistoric golf when I was a bad boy of seven, and off
and on I have played it ever since.   It was fortunate for me
that the common land at Jersey was years ago the ideal
thing for a golfing links, and that golfers from abroad found
out its secret, as they always do.   If they had failed to do so
in this case, I might still have been spending my life in horti-
cultural pursuits.   For I was born (on May 9, 1870) and bred
in Jersey, at that little place called Grouville, which is no
more than a collection of scattered cottages and farmhouses
a few miles from St. Heliers.   Both my parents were natives
of Jersey, and my father, who was seventy-four on the 5th of
last November, has been a gardener there all his life, holding
the proud record of having changed his place of employment
only once during the whole period.   There was a big family
of us—six boys and two girls—and all, except one of my
sisters, are still alive.   My brothers were George, Phil,
Edward, Tom, and Fred, and I came fourth down the list,
after Edward.   As most golfers know, my brother Tom, to

whom I owe very much, is now the professional at the Royal
St. George's Club at Sandwich, while Fred is a professional
in the Isie of Man. In due course we all went to the little
village school; but I fear, from all that I can remember, and
from what I have been told, that knowledge had little attrac-
tion for me in those days, and I know that I very often
played truant, sometimes for three weeks at a stretch. Consequently my old schoolmaster, Mr. Boomer, had no particular reason to be proud of me at that time, as he seems to
have become since. He never enjoys a holiday so much in
these days as when he comes over from Jersey to see me
play for the Open Championship, as he does whenever
the meeting is held at Sandwich. But when I did win a
Championship on that course, he was so nervous and excited
about my play and my prospects that he felt himself unequal
to watching me, and during most of the time that I was
doing my four rounds he was sitting in a fretful state upon
the seashore. I was a thin and rather delicate boy with not
much physical strength, but I was as enthusiastic as the
others in the games that were played at that time, and my
first ambition was to excel at cricket. A while afterwards I
became attached to football, and I retained some fondness
for this game long after I took up golf. Even after my
golfing tour in America a few years ago, when quite at my
best, I captained the Ganton football team and played
regularly in its matches.

One day, when I was about seven years of age, a very
shocking thing happened at Grouville. All the people there
lived a quiet, undisturbed life, and had a very wholesome
respect for the sanctity of the Sabbath day. But of all days
of the week it was a Sunday when a small party of strange
gentlemen made their appearance on the common land, and
began to survey and to mark out places for greens and tees.
Then the story went about that they were making preparations to play a game called golf. That was enough to excite
the wrathful indignation of all the tenant-farmers round

about, and without delay they began to think out means for
expelling these trespassers from the common land. A tale
of indignation spread through Grouville, and these golfers, of
whom I remember that Mr. Brewster was one, were not at
first regarded in the light of friendship. But they soon made
their position secure by obtaining all necessary authority and
permission for what they were about to do from the constable
of the parish, and from that day we had to resign ourselves
to the fact that a new feature had entered into the quiet life
of Jersey. The little party went ahead with the marking
out of their course, though indeed the natural state of the
place was so perfect from the golfer's point of view that very
little work was necessary, and no first-class golf links was
ever made more easily. There were sand and other natural
hazards everywhere, the grass was short and springy just as
it is on all good sea-coast links, and all that it was necessary
to do was to put a flag down where each hole was going to
be, and run the mower and the roller over the space selected
for the putting green. Rooms were rented at a little inn
hard by, which was forthwith rechristened the Golf Inn, and
the headquarters of the Jersey golfers are still at the same
place, though a large club-room has been added. That was
the beginning of the Royal Jersey Golf Club. The links as
they were when they were first completed were really
excellent—much better than they are to-day, for since then,
in order to prevent the sand being blown all over the course
by the strong winds which sweep across the island, the
bunkers have in most cases been filled with clay, which has
to a great extent spoiled them.

When everything was ready, more of these golfers came
across from England to play this new game which we had
never seen before, and all the youngsters of the locality were
enticed into their service to carry their clubs. I was among
the number, and that was my first introduction to the game.
We did not think much of it upon our first experience; but
after we had carried for a few rounds we came to see that

it contained more than we had imagined. Then we were
seized with a desire to play it ourselves, and discover what
we could do. But we had no links to play upon, no clubs,
no balls, and no money. However, we surmounted all these
difficulties. To begin with, we laid out a special course of
our very own. It consisted of only four holes, and each one
of them was only about fifty yards long, but for boys of
seven that was quite enough. We made our teeing grounds,
smoothed out the greens, and, so far as this part of the
business was concerned, we were soon ready for play. There
was no difficulty about balls, for we decided at once that the
most suitable article for us, in the absence of real gutties, was
the big white marble which we called a taw, and which was
about half the size of an ordinary golf ball, or perhaps a little
less than that. But there was some anxiety in our juvenile
minds when the question of clubs came to be considered, and
I think we deserved credit for the manner in which we disposed of it. It was apparent that nothing would be satisfactory except a club fashioned on the lines of a real golf
club, and that to procure anything of the sort we should have
to make it ourselves. Therefore, after several experiments,
we decided that we would use for the purpose the hard wood
of the tree which we called the lady oak. To make a club
we cut a thick branch from the tree, sawed off a few inches
from it, and then trimmed this piece so that it had a faint
resemblance to the heads of the drivers we had seen used on
the links. Any elaborate splicing operations were out of the
question, so we agreed that we must bore a hole in the
centre of the head. The shaft sticks that we chose and
trimmed were made of good thorn, white or black, and when
we had prepared them to our satisfaction we put the poker
in the fire and made it red hot, then bored a hole with it
through the head, and tightened the shaft with wedges until
the club was complete. With this primitive driver we could
get what was for our diminutive limbs a really long ball, or
a long taw as one should say. In these later days a patent

has been taken out for drivers with the shaft let into the head, which are to all intents and purposes the same in principle as those which we used to make at Grouville.

By and by some of us became quite expert at the making of these clubs, and we set ourselves to discover ways and means of improving them. The greater elaboration of such brassies as we had seen impressed us, and we also found some trouble with our oak heads in that, being green, they were rather inclined to chip and crack. Ultimately we decided to sheathe the heads entirely with tin. It was not an easy thing to make a good job of this, and we were further troubled by the circumstance that our respective fathers had no sympathy with us, and declined upon any account to lend us their tools. Consequently we had no option but to wait until the coast was clear and then surreptitiously borrow the tools for an hour or two. We called these tin-plated drivers our brassies, and they were certainly an improvement on our original clubs. Occasionally a club was made in this manner which exhibited properties superior to those possessed by any other, as clubs will do even to-day. Forthwith the reputation of the maker of this club went up by leaps and bounds, and he was petitioned by others to make clubs for them, a heavy price in taws and marbles being offered for the service. The club that had created all this stir would change hands two or three times at an increasing price until it required the payment of four or five dozen marbles to become possessed of it. But the boy who owned the treasure was looked upon as the lord of the manor, and odds were demanded of him in the matches that we played.

We practised our very elementary kind of golf whenever we could, and were soon enthusiastic. I remember particularly that many of our best matches were played in the moonlight. The moon seemed to shine more clearly at Jersey than in England, and we could see splendidly. Four of us would go out together on a moonlight night to play, and our little competition was arranged on the medal system by scores. Usually a few marbles were at stake. To prevent the loss of taws one of us was sent ahead to watch for their coming and listen for the faint thud of their fall, while the other three drove from the tee. Then the three came forward while the watcher went back to drive, and I am sorry to say that our keenness in those days led us to disregard certain principles of the sportsman's code of honour which we appreciated better as we grew up. What I mean is that the watcher was often handicapped in a way that he little suspected, for when he went back to the tee, and we went forward and found that our balls were not always so well up as we had hoped, we gave them a gentle kick forwards; for in the dim light we were able to do this unknown to each other. But in legitimate play we often got a 3 at these fifty-yard holes, and with our home-made clubs, our little white taws, our lack of knowledge, and our physical feebleness all taken into consideration, I say we have often done less creditable things since then.

After such beginnings, we progressed very well. We began to carry more and more for the golfers who came to Grouville; we found or were given real balls that took the place of the taws, and then a damaged club occasionally came our way, and was repaired and brought into our own service. Usually it was necessary to put in new shafts, and so we burnt holes in the heads and put in the sticks, as we did with clubs of our own make; but these converted clubs were disappointing in the matter of durability. It happened once or twice that golfers for whom we had been carrying gave us an undamaged club as a reward for our enthusiasm, and we were greatly excited and encouraged when such a thing happened. I used to carry clubs about twice a week. I remember that Mr. Molesworth and Dr. Purves, both well known in the golfing world, were two players for whom I very often carried, and only the other day when I saw the former at the Professional Tournament at Richmond, watching the play, I was able to remind him of those times and of a particular shot he once played. We young caddies were very eager to learn the game thoroughly, and we were in the habit of watching these golfers very closely, comparing their styles, and then copying anything from them that seemed to take our fancy. I may say at once, in reply to a question that I am often asked, and which perhaps my present readers may themselves be inclined to put, that I have never in my life taken a single golfing lesson from anyone, and that whatever style I may possess is purely the result of watching others play and copying them when I thought they made a stroke in a particularly easy and satisfactory manner. It was my habit for very many years after these early days, until in fact I had won the Open Championship, to study the methods of good golfers in this way, and there are few from whom one is not able to learn something. I cannot say that the play of any one man particularly impressed me; I cannot point to any player, past or present, and declare that I modelled my style on his. It seemed to me that I took a little from one and a little from another until my swing was a composition of the swings of several players, and my approach shots likewise were of a very mixed parentage. Of course when I took a hint from the play of anyone I had been watching it required much subsequent practice properly to weld it into my own system; but I think that this close watching of good players, and the borrowing from their styles of all information that you think is good, and then constantly practising the new idea yourself, is an excellent method of improving your golf, though I do not recommend it as the sole method of learning, despite the success which I personally have achieved. However, this is a matter for later consideration.

As we were such a large family and my father's means were very limited, there was the necessity which is common in such cases for all of the boys to turn out early in life and do something towards helping the others, and accordingly

I went to work when I was thirteen.   Some time afterwards
I became gardener to the late Major Spofforth of Beauview,
who was himself a very keen golfer, and who occasionally
gave me some of his old clubs.   Now and then, when he was
in want of a partner, he used to take me out to play with
him, and I shall never forget the words he spoke to me one
day after we had played one of these matches.   " Henry, my
boy," he said, " take my advice, and never give up golf.   It
may be very useful to you some day."   Certainly his words
came true.   I can only remember about these games that I
was in the habit of getting very nervous over them, much
more so than I did later on when I played matches of far
more consequence.   I joined a working men's golf club that
had been formed, and it was through this agency that I won
my first prize.   A vase was offered for competition among
the members, the conditions being that six medal rounds
were to be played at the rate of one a month.   When we
had played five, I was leading by so very many strokes that
it was next to impossible for any of the others to catch me
up, and as just then my time came for leaving home and
going out into the greater world of golf, the committee
kindly gave me permission to play my last round two or
three weeks before the proper time.   It removed all doubt
as to the destination of the prize, which has still one of the
most honoured places on my mantelpiece.   At that time my
handicap for this club was plus 3, but that did not mean
that I would have been plus 3 anywhere else.   As a matter
of fact, I should think I must have been about 8 or 10.

By this time my younger brother Tom had already
gone away to learn club-making from Lowe at St. Anne's-
on-Sea.   He played very much the same game of golf as I
did at that time, and it was his venture and the success that
waited upon it that made me determine to strike out.
While Tom was at St. Anne's he went on a journey north
to take part in a tournament at Musselburgh, where he
captured the second prize.   Thereupon I came to the con-

clusion that, if Tom could do that, then I too with a little patience might do the same. Indeed, I was a very keen golfer just then. At last Lowe was summoned to Lord Ripon's place at Ripon, near Harrogate, to lay out a new nine-holes course, and Tom wrote to me saying that they would be wanting a professional there, and if I desired such an appointment I had better apply for it without delay. I did so, and was engaged. I was twenty years of age when I left home to assume these duties.

CHAPTER II

SOME REMINISCENCES

Not enough golf—"Reduced to cricket"—I move to Bury—A match with Alexander Herd—No more nerves—Third place in an open competition—I play for the Championship—A success at Portrush—Some conversation and a match with Andrew Kirkaldy — Fifth for the Championship at Sandwich—Second at the Deal tournament—Eighth in the Championship at St. Andrews—I go to Ganton—An invitation to the south of France—The Championship at Muirfield—An exciting finish—A stiff problem at the last hole—I tie with Taylor—We play off, and I win the Championship—A tale of a putter—Ben Sayers wants a "wun'"—What Andrew thought of Muirfield—I win the Championship again at Prestwick—Willie Park as runner-up — My great match with Park — Excellent arrangements — A welcome victory—On money matches in general—My third Championship at Sandwich—My fourth at Prestwick—Golf under difficulties.

NO true golfer is satisfied with a little of the game, if there is no substantial reason why he should not have much of it. I was greenkeeper as well as professional to the Studley Royal Golf Club, Ripon; but golf did not seem to have taken a very deep root there up to that time. There was so little of it played that I soon found time hang heavily upon my hands, and in the summer I was reduced to playing cricket, and in fact played more with the bat than I did with the driver. There were one or two good players on the links occasionally, and now and then I had some good games with visitors to the place. One day after such a match my opponent remarked very seriously to me, "Harry, if you take my advice you will get away from here as quickly as you can, as you don't get half enough golf to bring you out." I took the advice very much to heart. I was not unduly conceited about my golf in those days, and the possibility of being Champion at some future time had taken no definite shape in my mind; but I was naturally ambitious and disinclined to waste any opportunities that might present themselves. So, when I saw that the Bury Golf Club were advertising for a professional, I applied for the post and got it. It was by no means a bad nine-holes course that I found at Bury, and I was enabled to play much more golf than at Ripon, while there were some very good amateurs there, Mr. S. F. Butcher being one of the best. I was now beginning to play fairly well, and the first professional match of my life was arranged for me, Alexander Herd of Huddersfield being my opponent in this maiden effort, upon the result of which a stake of a few pounds a side depended. Herd was by that time a famous player and accomplishing some very fine golf, so that on paper at all events the unknown Bury professional had no chance whatever. So indeed it proved. It was fixed that we were to play thirty-six holes, home and home, Herd having the privilege of playing on his own course first. I forget how many he was up at Huddersfield, but it was so many that I had practically no chance of wiping out the difference when I brought my opponent to Bury, and in the end he won quite easily. "Sandy" Herd, as we all call him, and I have had many great matches since then, and many of them of far greater consequence than this, but I shall never forget this beginning. Neither in those days, nor in the others that soon followed, when it became clear that I had a chance of becoming Champion, was I ever in the least troubled with nervousness. I was completely cured of my early complaint. Moreover, I have not known what it is to be nervous even in a Championship round when my fate depended upon almost every stroke, and particularly on those at the last few holes. The feeling that was always uppermost in my mind was that I had everything to gain and nothing to lose. It is only when a man has everything to lose and nothing to gain that he should become uneasy about his game. When you have won a few prizes and there are critical eyes upon you, there may be some excuse for nerves, but not before. All young players should grasp the simple truth of this simple statement; but it is surprising how many fail to do so. No stroke or game ever seemed to cause me any anxiety in those young days, and my rapid success may have been in a large measure due to this indifference.

In 1893 I decided that I would enter for the Open Championship, which in that year was played for at Prestwick, and I went north in company with my brother Tom, stopping on our way to take part in the tournament at Kilmalcolm, which was attended by most of the other professionals. I did fairly well in this, the first open competition for which I entered, being bracketed with poor Hugh Kirkaldy for third place. But I failed in the Championship competition, as, of course, I fully expected to do. That was Willie Auchterlonie's year, and I was some way down the list. I started in great style, and, though I broke down badly later on, there was just the consolation left for me that after all I did better than my partner, Willie Campbell.

There were some curious circumstances attending the first big success of any kind that I achieved. This was at Portrush in Ireland, shortly after the Championship meeting, and the competition was a professional tournament. I was drawn against Andrew Kirkaldy in the first round, and his brother Hugh was one of the next pair, so it seemed that the two Kirkaldys would meet in the second round. Andrew assumed that that would happen, as he had every right to do, and he was heard to remark that it was rather hard luck that the brothers should be set against each other in this manner so early in the competition. The night before the match-play part of the business commenced, I was walking down one of the streets of Portrush when I encountered Andrew himself, and in his own blunt but good-humoured way he remarked, " Young laddie, d'ye think y're

gaun to tak the money awa' with ye? Ye've no chance,
ye ken." I said nothing in reply, because I felt that he
spoke the truth. Next day a heavy gale was blowing, and
I started very cautiously. The first hole was on the side of
a hill, and when my ball lay a yard from the flag and I had
the next stroke for the hole, it was trembling in the wind and
threatening every moment to start rolling. So I waited for
it to steady itself, and my waiting exasperated Andrew
to such an extent that at length he exclaimed, " Man, d'ye
ken I'm cauld? Are ye gaun to keep me waiting here a'
nicht?" Then I took the putt and missed it, so the hole
was halved. However, I set about my opponent after that
and had begun to enjoy the game immensely by the time we
reached the turn. At this point two of the holes ran parallel
to each other, and as we were playing one of them we passed
Hugh and his partner going up to the other. " Man,
Andrew, hoo's the game?" called out brother Hugh. " Man
alive, I'm five doon!" Andrew replied in tones of distress.
" Ma conscience!" muttered Hugh as he passed along.
Andrew was more than five down at the finish of that game,
and in the second round I had the satisfaction of removing
the remaining member of the Kirkaldy family from the
competition, while in the semi-final I beat an old Open
Champion, D. Brown. But in the final, Herd defeated me
on the last green, and so I had to be content with the prize
given for runner-up. Shortly afterwards I won another prize
in a tournament at Ilkley, this time accounting for Herd as
well as my brother Tom and many other well-known players.
Tom was professional at Ilkley, and the course there was
a very difficult nine holes.

I did better in the competition for the Open Championship in the following year when the meeting was held at
Sandwich, playing a particularly good game on the second
day, when my 80 and 81 were one of the two lowest combined returns. At the finish I was fifth, and felt very pleased
to occupy the position, for the excellence of the golf that I

witnessed was a surprise to me. From Sandwich the professionals went on to Deal, where a tournament was held, in which I managed to secure second place. It was Herd who beat me once again. At St. Andrews in the 1895 Competition, I returned the lowest score in the first round, but could only tie for the ninth place at the finish. My old friend, J. H. Taylor, who made his first essay to capture the blue ribbon of golf at Prestwick at the same time that I did, was the winner at both this and the previous Championship meeting. A few months later I left Bury for Ganton; Tom, who had been over there with some Ilkley players at the Yorkshire meeting, having heard that they were in need of a new professional, and written to me at once with advice to apply. Between leaving Bury and going to Ganton I had three weeks of good golf at Pau, in the south of France, the great and unexpected honour being paid me of an invitation to form one of a small party of professionals for whom a series of matches and competitions had been arranged there. Taylor, Herd, Archie Simpson, Willie Auchterlonie, and Lloyd, the local professional, were the others. Professional golfers when they are out together usually manage to have a pretty good time, and this occasion was no exception. Knowing a little French, I was once appointed cashier and paymaster for the party, but I did not know enough of the language to feel quite at home when large figures were the subject of discussion, and I remember that the result was an awkward incident at Bordeaux on the return journey. We were called upon to pay excess fare for the luxury of travelling in the express, and, failing to understand the ticket collector, I was filling his hand with francs, one by one, waiting for him to tell me when he was in possession of the required amount. But he needed more and more, and the situation was becoming embarrassing, when the guard whistled and the train moved off. If it had not been for that intervention we might still have been paying him excess fare. I went to Ganton immediately on my return, and in the spring of that year, 1896, a match between Taylor and myself was arranged on my new course, when I had the satisfaction of winning.

I was looking forward very keenly to the Open Championship that year. It was at Muirfield, and it took place only four or five weeks after this encouraging victory over Taylor. In the meantime I had been a little off my game, and when I teed my first ball at Muirfield it seemed to me that I was as likely to make a bad drive as a good one, and I was equally uncertain with all the other clubs in my bag. But as it happened I was fortunate enough to be playing well during the competition, and was close up at the end of the first day, with Taylor in the next place above me. The next day I was again playing well, and the result was exciting. Taylor was doing his rounds only a few holes in front of me, and late in the contest it became apparent that the issue would be left between us. I did not know exactly what I had to do to win until about four holes from the finish, when someone, who had seen Taylor putt out at the last green, came up to me and told me what number of strokes was still left to me to play if I were to tie with him. When I came to the last hole I had set me what I think was the most anxious problem that has ever come my way since I first took up golf. I had five strokes left to play in order to tie with Taylor and give me the right to play off with him for the Championship, and four left with which to win it outright. It is a fairly long hole—a drive and a good brassy, with a very nasty bunker guarding the green. Thus, while it was an easy 5, it was a difficult 4, and the bold golfer who made his bid for the low figure might possibly be punished with a 6. My drive was good, and then I had to make my choice between the bold game and the sure one. A Championship hung upon the decision. The prospect of being the winner in less than five minutes was tempting. The brassy would give me the Championship or nothing. The iron would admit me to the

privilege of playing off with Taylor another day. I hesitated.
I think I would have taken the iron in any case; but just
when I was longing for an inspiration, my eye wandered
among the spectators some sixty or seventy yards in front
of me, and I caught sight of my friend James Kay of Seaton
Carew making frantic efforts to attract my attention, and
pointing with his hand to the ground on the near side of the
bunker as a hint to play short. That settled it. I played
short, got my 5, and tied with Taylor with a total score
of 316.

The play-off was full of interest and excitement. Taylor
and I were granted permission to take part in a tournament
at North Berwick before we settled the question between us.
When at length we teed up again at Muirfield, I felt as
though I were fit to play for anything, and started in a way
that justified my confidence, for I picked up a useful lead of
five strokes in the first half-dozen holes. After that Taylor
settled down to most brilliant golf, and brought my lead
down to a single stroke; but at the end of the first round
I was two to the good. To my exasperation, this lead disappeared with the very first stroke that I made after lunch.
There is a wood running along the left-hand side of the line
of the first hole on this course. With my cleek shot from
the tee I pulled the ball into this dismal place, and by the
rule in force at the time I lost two strokes and played again
from the tee, Taylor holing out in 3 to my 5. However, at
this crisis I came out again and won a stroke at each of the
next three holes, and only lost one of them from that point
to the seventeenth. Two strokes to the good and two holes
to go—that at least seemed good for the Championship.
On the seventeenth green, my brother Tom, who was carrying
my clubs for me, took a lot of trouble to point out the line
of a putt the whole length of the green, but something
prompted me to take an entirely different course, and I
holed the putt, gaining another stroke. There we were,
Taylor and I, at that last hole again, but this time we were

together, and I had a big advantage over my good friend on this occasion. There was more mental golf to be played, and though Taylor's ordeal was the more trying, neither of us had any difficulty in coming to a decision. My course was clear. With a lead of three strokes I had to play for a 5, as on the previous occasion, because it was certain to give me the Championship. Taylor's only chance was to blaze away with both his driver and his brassy, and trust to getting his second shot so well placed on the green as to secure a 3, which, in the event of my dropping a stroke through an accident in the bunker or elsewhere and taking 6, would enable him to tie. I obtained my 5 without difficulty, but Taylor's gallant bid for 3 met with an unhappy fate, for his second shot was trapped in the bunker, and it took him 6 to hole out. And so with a score of 157 to Taylor's 161, I was Open Champion at last, and for the first time in my life I felt some emotion as a golfer. I was too dazed to speak, and it seemed as if my feet had taken root on the eighteenth green, for I don't think I moved for several minutes.

There is a little tale I want to tell about that Championship, illustrating the old saying that golf is a very funny game, and giving some point to a recommendation that I shall have to make later on. Never in my life have I putted better than I did in those two rounds. If, when I had a putt the whole length of the green, I did not actually rattle it into the tin, I laid it stone dead on the lip of the hole; on no green did I take more than two putts. Yet in the various rounds I had played on several days before my putting had been very indifferent. How came this remarkable change? It seems to me that it was entirely due to a chance visit that I paid to Ben Sayers's shop when I was at North Berwick in the interval between tieing with Taylor and playing the deciding rounds. I told the clubmaker who was in charge that I was off my putting, and wanted a new putter. Hitherto I had been playing with one of the bent-necked variety. While I was looking about the shop my eye was attracted by an old cleek that lay in a corner—a light and neglected club, for which nobody seemed to have any use. The strange idea occurred to me that this would make a grand putter, and so I told the man to take out the old shaft and put a new and shorter one in, and when this process had been completed I determined to experiment with it in the play-off with Taylor. I fancied this new discovery of mine and had confidence in it, and that was why I got all those long putts down and achieved the golfer's greatest ambition. But though I keep it still and treasure it, I have never played with that putter since. It has done its duty.

I must tell just one other story concerning this Muirfield Championship. Among the favourites at the beginning of operations were Ben Sayers and Andrew Kirkaldy, and a victory on the part of either of them would have been most popular in the North, as it would have settled the cup on the other side of the Tweed. Ben was rather inclined to think his own prospects were good. Someone asked him the day before the meeting who was the most likely Champion. "Jist gie me a wun' an' I'll show ye wha'll be the Champion," he replied, and he had some reason for the implied confidence in himself, for he knew Muirfield very well, and no one had better knowledge of how to play the strokes properly there when there was a gale blowing over the course, and pulling and slicing were constantly required. But neither Ben nor Andrew was as successful as was wished, and not unnaturally they thought somewhat less of Muirfield than they had done before. Therefore it was not fair to ask Kirkaldy, after the competition had been completed, what he really considered to be the merits of the course. I was standing near him when a player came up and bluntly asked, "What d'ye think o' Muirfield now, Andrew?" Andrew's lip curled as he replied, "No for gowff ava'. Just an auld watter meedie, I'm gled I'm gaun hame." But the inquirer must needs ejaculate, "Hooch ay, she would be ferry coot whateffer if you had peen in Harry Fardon's shoes."

There was an exciting finish also to the 1898 Champion-ship, which was held at Prestwick. The final struggle was left to Willie Park and myself, and at the end of the third round, when Willie was three strokes to the good, it seemed a very likely victory for him. In the last round I was play-ing a hole in front of him, and we were watching each other as cats watch mice the whole way round the links. I made a reckoning when we reached the turn that I had wiped out the three strokes deficit, and could now discuss the remainder of the game with Park without any sense of inferiority. I finished very steadily, and when Park stood on the last tee just as I had holed out, he was left to get a 3 at this eighteenth hole to tie. His drive was a beauty, and plop came the ball down to the corner of the green, making the 3 seem a certainty. An immense crowd pressed round the green to see these fateful putts, and in the excitement of the moment, I, the next most concerned man to Park himself, was elbowed out. I just saw his long putt roll up to within about a yard of the hole, which was much too dead for my liking. Then, while Park proceeded to carry out his ideas of accomplishing a certainty, I stood at the edge of the crowd, seeing nothing and feeling the most nervous and miserable man alive. Never while playing have I felt so uncomfortable as during those two or three minutes. After what seemed an eternity there rose from all round the ring one long disappointed " O-o-o-h!" I didn't stop to look at the ball, which was still outside the hole. I knew that I had won the Championship again, and so I hastened light-heartedly away. I must admit that Park was playing an exceedingly fine game at that time, and it was only the fact that I was probably playing as well as ever I did in my life that enabled me to get the better of him. The day after winning the Championship I gained the first prize in a tournament at the adjoining course of St. Nicholas, and thereafter I frequently took part in competitions, winning much more often than not.

But the most important event, and the biggest match I ever had with anyone, was my engagement with Willie Park, who, not altogether satisfied at having missed the Championship by a putt, challenged me to play him home and home matches, thirty-six holes each time, for £100 a side. There was some difficulty in arranging final details, but eventually we agreed to play at North Berwick and Ganton, North Berwick first. I have never seen such a golfing crowd as there was at North Berwick the day we played there. All golfing Scotland seemed to be in attendance, and goodness knows how many people would have been watching the play if it had not happened that the lukewarm golfers went instead to Edinburgh to see the Prince of Wales, who was visiting the capital that day. As it was, there were fully seven thousand people on the links, and yet this huge crowd—surely one of the very biggest that have ever watched a golf match—was perfectly managed, and never in the least interfered with a single stroke made by either Park or myself. The arrangements, indeed, were admirable. In order to keep the crowd informed of the state of the game at each hole, two flags were made, one being white with a red "P" on it, and the other red with a "V" worked on in white. When Park won a hole the flag with his initial was hoisted, and the "V" was sent up when I won a hole, both flags being waved when it was a half. At each teeing ground a rope three hundred yards long was stretched, and fourteen constables and a like number of honorary officials took control of it. In order to prevent any inconvenience at the dyke on the course, a boarding, forty feet wide and fifty yards out of the line from the tee to the hole, was erected, so that the crowd could walk right over. Mr. C. C. Broadwood, the Ganton captain, acted as my referee, and Lieutenant "Freddy" Tait served in the same capacity on behalf of Park. One of the most laborious tasks was that undertaken by the two Messrs. Hunter, who acted as forecaddies, and did their work splendidly. In two practice rounds that I played before the great encounter opened I did 76 each time, and I felt very fit when we teed up on the eventful morning. And I played very steadily, too, though my putting was sometimes a little erratic, and Park is one of the greatest putters who have ever lived. The early part of the game was very extraordinary in that the first ten holes were halved in 4, 5, 4, 4, 4, 4, 4, 5, 4, 4. Then Park drew first blood, but in the end I finished two up on the day's play. When Park came to Ganton three weeks later, I beat him on the two matches by 11 up with 10 to play. Naturally he was disappointed, but he was very sportsmanlike. He was acknowledged to be the greatest match-player of his time. I do not care for myself to lay any more stress on the importance of this match, or of the value of my own achievement; but those who have taken up golf quite lately can have no conception of the stir that it caused. It was the event of my lifetime.

The remembrance of this encounter brings forward the question of big money matches generally, which several people have declared they would like to see renewed. Fifty years ago they were common enough, and there are great stories told of foursomes between Allan Robertson and Tom Morris on the one side and the brothers Dunn on the other for a stake of £400, and so on. The sightseers of golf ask why there are no such matches now. I think it is because golf professionals have to work too hard for the money they earn, and they do not care for the idea of throwing it away again on a single match. They do not receive large " benefits " or gate money, as do professionals in other branches of sport. So they deem it best to be careful of their savings. Besides, such matches tend to create bad feeling among the players, and we professionals are such a happy family that we distrust any scheme with such a tendency. Moreover, golf at the present time is a delightfully pure game, so far as gambling is concerned—purer than most others—and such matches would very likely encourage the gambling idea.

That would be a misfortune. I contend that after all, for the best and fairest and most interesting trial of strength there is nothing like a good tournament where each player has to test himself against all comers. Every man plays to win, the golf is generally good, and what more is wanted?

When I won the Championship again in the following year at Sandwich, my success was chiefly due to my brassy play, which was better than it ever was before or has been since. From my brassy strokes the ball was often enough laid dead near the hole; certainly my second shots were always the winning shots. The game seemed very easy to me then, and I gained the Championship for the third time with less difficulty than on either of the two previous occasions. In 1900 I made a long tour in America, and won the American Championship. Concerning these events I desire to write at some length in a later chapter. The greatest success which I have ever achieved in face of difficulties was when I again became Open Champion at Prestwick in 1903. For some time beforehand I had been feeling exceedingly unwell, and, as it appeared shortly afterwards, there was serious trouble brewing. During the play for the Championship I was not at all myself, and while I was making the last round I was repeatedly so faint that I thought it would be impossible for me to finish. However, when I holed my last putt I knew that I had won. My brother Tom was runner-up, six strokes behind, and, glad as I was of the distinction of having equalled the record of the two Morrises in having won the Championship four times, I could have wished, and did wish, that Tom had been the victor. In all the circumstances I was very much surprised that I did so well. The last day's work was an enormous strain, yet on the following day I played in a tournament at Irvine, won the first prize, and broke the record of the course. It is wonderful what golf can be played when one's mind is given to the task, whatever the adverse factors in the case may be.

However, these are the events of recent golfing history, and I have no desire to inflict upon my readers a narrative of any more of them. As nearly as I can reckon, I have up to date won the first prize in forty-eight first-class tournaments, and by being four times British Open Champion and once American have still that record to my credit. And I hope to play many of my best games in the future, for it takes longer to kill the golf in a man than it does to breed it.

CHAPTER III

THE WAY TO GOLF

The mistakes of the beginner—Too eager to play a round—Despair that follows—A settling down to mediocrity—All men may excel—The sorrows of a foozler—My advice—Three months' practice to begin with—The makings of a player—Good golf is best—How Mr. Balfour learned the game—A wise example—Go to the professional—The importance of beginning well—Practise with each club separately—Driver, brassy, cleek, iron, mashie, and putter—Into the hole at last—Master of a bag of clubs—The first match—How long drives are made—Why few good players are coming on—Golf is learned too casually.

THERE are different ways of learning to play the great game of golf, each of which enjoys its share of patronage. Here as elsewhere, there are, of course, the two broad divisions into which the methods of doing all things are in the first instance classed—the right way and the wrong way—and, generally speaking, the wrong way has proved the more popular and is accountable for much of the very bad golf that one sees almost every day upon the links. There are two mistakes to which the beginner is much addicted, and to them is due the unhappy circumstance that in so many cases he never gets his club handicap down to single figures. Before he has ever played golf in his life, but at that interesting period when he has made up his mind to do so, and has bought his first set of clubs, he is still inclined to make the same error that is made by so many people who know nothing of the game, and loftily remark that they do not want to know anything—that it is too absurdly simple to demand serious thought or attention, and can surely need no special pains in learning to play. Is not the ball quite still on the tee before you, and all that is necessary being to hit it, surely the rest is but a question of strength and accuracy of aim? Well, we need not waste time in discussing the opinions of the scoffers outside, or in submitting that there never was a game less easy to learn than golf. But the man who has been converted to golf most frequently has a vestige of this superstition of his heathen days lingering with him, and thus at the outset he is not inclined to waste any time, as he would say, in tuition, particularly as it happens that these new converts when quite fresh are invariably most delightfully enthusiastic. They have promised themselves a new sensation, and they are eager to get on to the links and see how much further than the two hundred yards that they have heard about they can drive at the first attempt or two. Then comes the inevitable disappointment, the despair, the inclination to give it up, and finally the utter abject despondency which represents the most miserable state on earth of the golfer, in which he must be closely watched lest he should commit murder upon the beautiful set of clubs of which at the beginning he was so proud, and which he spent his evenings in brightening to the degree that they resembled the family plate. Then after this passage through purgatory come the first gleams of hope, when two holes in succession have been done in only one over bogey, and a 24 handicap man has actually been beaten by 3 up and 2 to play—a conquest which, if it is the first one, is rarely forgotten in the golfer's lifetime. After that there is a steady settling down to mediocrity. There is afterwards only an occasional fit of despair, the game is for the most part thoroughly enjoyed, there are times when, after a round in which driving and putting have been rather better than usual, the golfer encourages himself over his cup of tea with the fancy that after all he may some day win a medal and become a senior; but in the main the conviction forces itself upon him that it is impossible that he can ever become a really fine player. He argues that this is not at all his own fault. He points out to himself that circumstances are too strong for him. He considers that he is not very young—at least not so young as many of the experts of his club who have been golfing ever since they were boys. His limbs have not that suppleness which makes the scratch player. His eye is not so keen as theirs. Besides, he is a business man who has to give up so much of his time to the earning of his daily bread that it is impossible he should ever devote himself to the game with that single-mindedness which alone can ensure proficiency. He must take himself as he finds himself, and be satisfied with his 18 handicap. These are the somewhat pathetic excuses that he makes in this mood of resignation. Of course he is wrong—wrong from the beginning to the end—but there is little satisfaction in that for the earnest lover of the game who would see all men excel, and who knows only too well that this failure is but a specimen of hundreds of his kind—good golfing lives thrown away, so to speak. If a man is not a cripple, if he suffers from no physical defect, there is no reason why he should not learn to play a good game of golf if he goes about it in the right way. There is indeed a one-armed golfer who plays a very fair game, and one may admit all these things without in any way suggesting that golf is not a game for the muscles and the nerves and all the best physical qualities of a well-grown man. No great amount of brute force is necessary, and fleetness of foot, which men lose as they grow old, is never wanted; but still golf is a game for manly men, and when they take it up they should strive to play it as it deserves to be played.

Now I know what severe temptation there will be to all beginners to disregard the advice that I am about to offer them; but before proceeding any further I will invite them to take the opinion of any old golfer who, chiefly through a careless beginning (he knows that this is the cause), has missed his way in the golfer's life, and is still plodding away as near the limit handicap as he was at the beginning. The beginner may perhaps be disposed to rely more upon the statement of this man of experience and disappointment than on that of the professional, who is too often suspected of having his own ends in view whenever he gives advice. Let the simple question be put to him whether, if he could be given the chance of doing it all over again from the beginning, he would not sacrifice the first three or six months of play to diligent study of the principles of the game, and the obtaining of some sort of mastery over each individual shot under the careful guidance of a skilled tutor, not attempting during this time a single complete round with all his clubs in action, and refusing all temptations to play a single match—whether he would not undergo this slow and perhaps somewhat tedious period of learning if he could be almost certain of being able at the end of it to play a really good game of golf, and now at this later period of his career to have a handicap much nearer the scratch mark than his existing one is to the border-line between the senior and the junior? I am confident that in the great majority of cases, looking back on his misspent golfing youth, he would answer that he would cheerfully do all this learning if he could begin again at the beginning. Now, of course, it is too late, for what is once learned can only with extreme difficulty be unlearned, and it is almost impossible to reform the bad style and the bad habits which have taken root and been cultivated in the course of many years; and if it were possible it would be far more difficult than it would have been to learn the game properly at the beginning.

My earnest advice to the beginner is to undergo this slow process of tuition for nothing less than three months, and preferably more. It is a very long time, I know, and it may seem painfully tedious work, simply knocking a ball backwards and forwards for all those months; but if he does not accept my suggestion he will have harder things to try his patience during many years afterwards, while, if he takes my advice, he may be down very near to scratch at the end of his first year, and he will be very thankful that he spent the period of probation as he did. He will constantly be giving a half to players who have been playing for more years than he has months, and he will be holding his own in the very best golfing company. He will be getting the finest delight out of the game that it is possible to get. It is said that the long handicap man gets as much pleasure out of the game as the short handicap man. As the former has never been a short handicap man he is evidently not qualified to judge. The scratch man, who has been through it all, would never change his scratch play for that of his old long-handicap days—at least I have never yet met the scratch man who would. No doubt the noble army of foozlers derive an immense amount of enjoyment from the practice of their game, and it is my earnest prayer that they may long continue to do so. It is one of the glorious advantages of golf that all, the skilled and the unskilled, can revel in its fascinations and mysteries; but there is no golfing delight so splendid as that which is obtained from playing the perfect game, or one which nearly approaches it. The next best thing to it is playing what one knows to be an improving game, however bad, and the golfer whose play has been incorrectly established has not often even the knowledge that his game is improving. He declares more often than not that it gets worse, and one is frequently inclined to believe him.

Now the middle-aged man may say that he is too old to go in for this sort of thing, that all he wants is a little fresh air and exercise, and as much enjoyment as he can get out of playing the game in just the same sort of way that the "other old crocks" do. He would rather play well, of course, if it were not too late to begin; but it is too late, and there is an end of it. That is the way in which he puts it. So large a proportion of our new converts to golf belong to this middle-aged class, that it is worth while giving a few special words of advice to them. Mr. Forty and Mr

Forty-Five, you are not a day too old, and I might even make scratch men of you, if I were to take you in hand and you did all the things I told you to do and for as long as I told you. Given fair circumstances, there is no reason why any man should despair of becoming either a scratch player or one who is somewhere very near it, and it is as easy to learn to play well as it is to learn to play badly.

So I advise every golfer to get hold of the game stroke by stroke, and never be too ambitious at the commencement. I have heard it stated on very good authority that when Mr. Balfour first began to play he submitted himself to very much the same process of tuition as that which I am about to advise, and that under the guidance of Tom Dunn he actually spent a miserable fortnight in bunkers only, learning how to get out of them from every possible position. The right honourable gentleman must have saved hundreds of strokes since then as the result of that splendid experience, trying as it must have been. He is in these days a very good and steady player, and he might be still better if parliamentary cares did not weigh so heavily upon him. I may humbly suggest that the way in which he began to play golf was characteristic of his wisdom.

Therefore, when the golfer has become possessed of his first set of clubs, let him proceed to the shop of a good professional player—presumably it will be the shop where he bought his clubs—and let him place himself unreservedly in the hands of this expert in the game. Most professionals are good players and good teachers, and the golfer cannot go far wrong in this matter if he allows himself to be guided by his own instincts. I say that he should place himself unreservedly in this man's hands; but in case it should be necessary I would make one exception to this stipulation. If he thinks well of my advice and desires to do the thing with the utmost thoroughness from the beginning, he may request that for the first lesson or two no ball may be put upon the ground at which to practise swings. The professional is sure to agree that this is the best way, though he encounters so few beginners who are prepared to make all the sacrifices that I have suggested, that he might have hesitated in recommending this course of procedure himself.

A golfer's swing is often made for good or ill in the first week of his experience. His first two days of practice may be of the greatest importance in fashioning his style. If, when he takes his first lesson or two and makes his first few swings, he has a ball on the ground before him which he is trying to hit, all his thoughts will be concentrated on what appears to him to be the necessity of hitting it—hitting it at any cost. No matter what he has been told about the way to swing, he will forget it all in this moment of anxiety, and swing anyhow. In such circumstances a really natural and proper swing is rarely accomplished, and, before the golfer is aware of the frightful injustice he has done himself, his future prospects will probably have been damaged. But if he has no ball before him he will surely learn to swing his club in exactly the way in which it ought to be swung. His whole mind will be concentrated upon getting every detail of the action properly regulated and fixed according to the advice of his tutor, and by the time he has had two lessons in this way he will have got so thoroughly into the natural swing, that when he comes to have a ball teed up in front of him he will unconsciously swing at it in the same manner as he did when it was absent, or nearly so. The natural swing, or some of its best features, will probably be there, although very likely they will be considerably distorted.

At the same time the young golfer must not imagine because he has mastered the proper swing when there is no ball before him, that he has overcome any considerable portion of the difficulties of golf, for even some of the very best players find that they can swing very much better without a ball than with one. However, he may now taste the sweet pleasure of driving a ball from the tee, or of doing his best with that object in view. His initial attempts may not be brilliant; it is more than likely that they will be sadly disappointing. He may take comfort from the fact that in ninety-nine cases out of a hundred they are so. But by and by a certain confidence will come, he will cease, under the wise advice of his tutor, to be so desperately anxious to hit the ball anyhow so long as he hits it, and then in due course the correctness of swing which he was taught in his first two days will assert itself, and the good clean-hit drives will come. There will be duffings and toppings and slicings, but one day there will be a long straight drive right away down the course, and the tyro will be told that the professional himself could not have done it better. This is one of the most pleasurable moments in life.

His system of practice thereafter should be upon the following lines. He should continue to practise diligently with his driver until he gets these good, long balls nearly every time, sternly resisting the temptation even to so much as look at any of the other nice new clubs that he has got in his bag, and whose mysteries he is exceedingly curious to investigate. It may take him a week or a fortnight or a month to master the driver; but he should do it before he gives a thought to any other club. When he can use the driver with confidence, he may take out his new brassy and go through the same process with that, until he feels that on a majority of occasions, from a fairly decent lie, he could depend upon making a respectable brassy shot. He will find unsuspected difficulties in the brassy, and in doing his best to overcome them he will probably lose to some extent the facility for driving which he had acquired. Therefore, when he has become a player with his brassy, he should devote a short space of time to getting back on to his drive. It will not take him long, and then he should take out both the clubs he has been

practising with and hammer away at the two of them
together, until after a large amount of extra practice he finds
that he is fairly reliable in driving a ball from the tee to
begin with, and putting in a creditable second shot with his
brassy from the lie upon which he found his ball.

During this second stage of learning he must deny himself the pleasure of trying his iron clubs just as rigorously as
he restrained himself from the brassy when he was practising
drives only; but when the driver and the brassy are doing
well, he may go forward with the cleek. He will not find
this learning such dull work after all. There will be something new in store for him every week, and each new club
as it is taken out of the bag will afford an entirely new set
of experiences. After the driver and the brassy it will
be like a new game when he comes to try cleek shots, and in
the same way he will persevere with the cleek until it is
evident that he really knows how to use it. The driver,
the brassy, and the cleek may then be practised with on the
same occasion, and if he has made the best use of his time
and is an apt pupil, he will find himself now and then,
with these three shots taken in turn, getting beyond the
green at some of the longest holes. Next it will be the
turn of the iron, and so in due season he will be able to
practise with the driver, the brassy, the cleek, and the iron.
The mashie will follow, and then the five of them together,
and at last he may have an afternoon on the green trying
his skill with a putter, and listening for the first time to the
music of the ball—no such music as this to the golfer's ear,
though it consists of but a single note—as it drops into the
tin and is holed out at last.

He is at work now with all the clubs that are usually
necessary to play a hole; but at the risk of seeming over
careful I would warn him once more against going along
too fast, and thinking that even at this stage he is able to
embark on match play with all the days of studentship
left behind. When he takes out his full set of clubs, he

will find, in using them as occasion demands, that he is strangely erratic all of a sudden with one or two of them. Let him have half an hour's practice once more alone with these troublesome fellows until the old order of things has been restored. Let him treat all other offenders in the same manner. He must be determined that there shall not be a club in his bag that shall be allowed to play these tricks with him. Let one day's hard labour be the invariable penalty, until at last they are all obedient in his hands, and the joyful day comes when he feels that he can pick any tool out of his golfing bag and use it skilfully and well, and that after examining a ball in any lie, at any distance from the hole, or with any hazard before him, he knows exactly how it should be played, and feels that he has a very reasonable chance of playing it in that way and achieving the success that such a shot deserves. Such a stroke will not be brought off correctly every time; the golfer has not yet been born who always does the right thing in the right way. But the more one practises the more frequently will he succeed. Following Mr. Balfour's good example, the beginner may do worse than spend a few days trying the most difficult strokes he can discover on his links, for in actual play he will find himself in these difficult places often enough to begin with, and a little special study of such shots at the outset will prove a very valuable investment of time. The ball should be thrown down carelessly at different places, and should be played from the spot at which it settles, however uninviting that spot may be.

When he has secured a fair command over all his clubs, from the driver to the niblick, the golf student may play a round of the links; but he should do so only under the watchful eye of the professional, for he will find that in thus marching on from hole to hole, and perhaps getting a little excited now and then when he plays a hole more than usually well, it is only too easy to forget all the good methods in which he has been so carefully trained, and all the wise maxims he knows so well by heart that he could almost utter them in his sleep. Let him play a few rounds in this way, and in between them devote himself as assiduously as ever to practise with individual clubs, before he thinks of playing his first match. He must settle his game on a secure foundation before he measures his strength against an opponent, for unless it is thus safeguarded it is all too likely that it will crumble to ruins when the enemy is going strongly, and the novice feels, with a sense of dismay, that he is not by any means doing himself justice. Of course I am not suggesting that he should wait until he has advanced far towards perfection before he engages in his first match. When he has thoroughly grasped the principles and practice of the game, there is nothing like match play for proving his quality, but he should not be in haste thus to indulge himself. Any time from three to six months from the day when he first took a club in hand will be quite soon enough, and if he has been a careful student, and is in his first match not overcome with nerves, he should render a good account of himself and bring astonishment to the mind of his adversary when the latter is told that this is the first match of a lifetime.

During the preparatory period the golfer will be wise to limit his practices to three or four days a week. More than this will only tire him and will not be good for his game. I have only now to warn him against a constant attempt, natural but very harmful, to drive a much longer ball every time than was driven at the previous stroke. He must bring himself to understand that length comes only with experience, and that it is due to the swing becoming gradually more natural and more certain. He may see players on the links driving thirty or forty yards further than he has ever driven, and, wondering why, he is seized with a determination to hit harder, and then the old, old story of the foozled drive is told again. He forgets that these players are more experienced than he is, that their swing is more natural to them, and that they are more certain of it. In these circumstances the extra power which they put into their stroke is natural also. To give him an exact idea of what it is that he ought to be well satisfied with, I may say that the learner who finds that he is putting just two or three yards on to his drive every second week, may cease to worry about the future, for as surely as anything he will be a long driver in good time.

In the course of this volume there are several chapters describing the way in which the various strokes should be played, but I am no believer in learning golf from books alone. I do not think it likely that the professional teacher who is giving the pupil lessons will disagree with any of the chief points of the methods that I explain, and, read in conjunction with his frequent lessons at the beginning of his golfing career, and later on studied perhaps a little more closely and critically, I have hope that they will prove beneficial. At all events, as I have already suggested, in the following pages I teach the system which has won Championships for me, and I teach that system only.

It is perhaps too much to hope, after all, that any very large proportion of my readers will make up their minds to the self-sacrificing thoroughness which I have advocated, and undertake a careful preparation of from three to six months' duration before really attempting to play golf. If they all did so we should have some fine new players. It is because they do not learn to play in this way that so few good players are coming to the fore in these days. One is sometimes inclined to think that no new golfer of the first class has come forward during the last few years. In my opinion it is all due to the fact that nowadays they learn their game too casually.

CHAPTER IV

THE CHOICE AND CARE OF CLUBS

Difficulties of choice—A long search for the best—Experiments with more than a hundred irons—Buy few clubs to begin with—Take the professional's advice—A preliminary set of six—Points of the driver—Scared wooden clubs are best—Disadvantages of the socket—Fancy faces—Short heads—Whip in the shaft—The question of weight—Match the brassy with the driver—Reserve clubs—Kinds of cleeks—Irons and mashies—The niblick—The putting problem—It is the man who putts and not the putter—Recent inventions—Short shafts for all clubs—Lengths and weights of those I use—Be careful of your clubs—Hints for preserving them.

THE good golfer loves his clubs and takes a great and justifiable pride in them. He has many reasons for doing so. Golf clubs are not like most other implements that are used in sport. A man may go to a shop and pick out a cricket bat or a billiard cue with which he may be tolerably certain he will be able to play something approaching to his best game when he is in the mood for playing it. The acquaintance which is begun in the shop is complete a few days later. But a man may see a golf club which he strongly fancies and buy it, and yet find himself utterly incapable of using it to good advantage. He may purchase club after club, and still feel that there is something wanting in all of them, something which he cannot define but which he knows ought to exist if his own peculiar style of play is to be perfectly suited. Until he finds this club he is groping in the dark. One driver may be very much like another, and even to the practised eye two irons may be exactly similar; but with one the golfer may do himself justice, and with the other court constant failure. Therefore, the acquisition of a set of clubs, each one of which enjoys the complete confidence of its owner, is not the task of a week or even a year. There are some golfers who do not accomplish it in many years, and happy are they when at last they have done so. Then they have a very sincere attachment to each one of these instruments, that have been selected with so much difficulty. It is not always possible to give reasons for their excellence, for the subtle qualities of the clubs are not visible to the naked eye. Their owners only know that at last they have found the clubs that are the best for them, and that they will not part with them for any money—that is, if they are golfers of the true breed. In these days I always play with the same set of irons. They are of different makes, and to the average golfer they appear quite ordinary irons and very much like others of their class. But they are the results of trials and tests of more than one hundred clubs.

Therefore no golfer in his early days should run away with the idea that he is going to suit himself entirely with a set of clubs without much delay, and though his purse may be a small one, I feel obliged to suggest that money spent in the purchase of new clubs which he strongly fancies, during his first few years of play, is seldom wasted. Many of the new acquisitions may be condemned after a very short trial; but occasionally it will happen that a veritable treasure is discovered in this haphazard manner. With all these possibilities in view, the beginner, knowing nothing of golf, and being as yet without a style to suit or any peculiar tastes that have to be gratified, should restrain himself from the desire to be fully equipped with a " complete outfit " at the very beginning of his career. Let him buy as few clubs as possible, knowing that it is quite likely that not one of those which he purchases at this stage will hold a place in his bag a year or two later. As he can have no ideas at all upon the subject, he should leave the entire selection of his first bag to some competent adviser, and he will not generally find such an adviser behind the counter at a general athletic outfitting establishment in the town or city, which too often is the direction in which he takes his steps when he has decided to play the game. In these stores the old and practised golfer may often pick up a good club at a trifling cost; but the beginner would be more likely to furnish himself with a set which would be poor in themselves and quite unsuited for his purpose.

The proper place for him to go to is the professional's shop which is attached to the club of which he has become a member. Nearly all clubs have their own professionals, who are makers and sellers of clubs, and I know no professional who is not thoroughly conscientious in this part of his business. It pays him to give the completest satisfaction to his clients, and particularly to the members of his own club. This professional is also a first-class golfer, who knows all, or nearly all, that there is to be known about the game, and who in his time has had imposed upon him the difficult task of teaching hundreds of beginners their first steps in golf. Thus he knows better than any man the erratic tendencies of the golfing initiate and the best means of counteracting them. Experience has given him the faculty for sizing up the golfing points of the tyro almost at the first glance, and therefore he can supply him at the beginning with those clubs with which certainly he will have most chance of success. He will suit his height and his build and his reach, and he will take care that the clubs in the set which he makes up are in harmony with each other and will have that lie which will best suit the player who is to use them. And even though, when the beginner gathers knowledge of the game and finds out his own style —which neither he nor the professional can determine in advance—some of them may gradually become unsuitable to him, they are nevertheless likely to be in themselves good clubs.

A beginner may at the outset limit himself to the pur-

chase of six new clubs. He must have a driver, a brassy, a
cleek, an iron, a mashie, and a putter. At an early opportunity he may add a niblick to this small set, but there is
no need to invest in it at the outset, and as this club is one
which is least likely to require change, it is best that it
should not be bought until the player has some ideas of his
own as to what is wanted. By way of indicating what will
be needful to make this set complete for the purposes of
good golf, when the player has obtained a fairly complete
experience, I may mention the instruments that I take out
when playing an important match. I have two drivers, one
brassy, a baffy or spoon, two cleeks (one shorter than the
other), an iron, sometimes one mashie, sometimes two (one
for running up and the other for pitch shots), a niblick, and
sometimes two putters (one for long running-up putts and the
other for holing out). This selection may be varied slightly
according to the course on which the match is to be played
and the state of the weather, but in general principles the
constitution of the bag remains the same, and a player who is
equipped with such a set ought to be able to play any hole
in any way, and if he cannot do so it is his own skill that
is lacking and not an extra club. We may now consider in
order a few of the points of these clubs. I shall have occasion, when dealing with the method of play with each of them,
to call attention to many points of detail which can only be
properly explained when indicating particular objects which
it is desired to achieve with them, so for the present I shall
confine myself chiefly to general features.

Take the driver to begin with, and the preliminary word
of advice that I have to offer concerning the choice of this
club is at variance with the custom of the present moment,
though I am confident that before long the golfing world
will again come round to my view of the matter—not my
view only, but that of many of the leading amateur and
professional players. One of the problems which agitate the
mind of the golf-club maker deals with the best and most

effectual method of attaching the head of the club to the shaft. For a very long period this was done by what we call scaring or splicing, the neck of the club having a long bevel which was spliced with the shaft and bound round for several inches with black twine. Latterly, however, a new kind of club has become the fashion with all but the oldest and most experienced players, and it is called the socket driver. The continuation of the neck of this club is shorter than in the case of the spliced driver, and instead of there being any splicing at all, a hole is bored vertically into the end of the neck and the shaft fitted exactly into it, glued up, and finally bound round for less than an inch. This club certainly looks neater than the old-fashioned sort, and the man who is governed only by appearances might very easily imagine that it is really more of one piece than the other, that the union of the shaft with the head has less effect upon the play of the club, and that therefore it is better. But experience proves that this is not the case. What we want at this all-important part of the driver is spring and life. Anything in the nature of a deadness at this junction of the head with the shaft, which would, as it were, cut off the one from the other, is fatal to a good driver. I contend that the socket brings about this deadness in a far greater degree than does the splice. The scared or old-fashioned drivers have far more spring in them than the new ones, and it is my experience that I can constantly get a truer and a better ball with them. When the wood of the shaft and the wood of the neck are delicately tapered to suit each other, filed thin and carefully adjusted, wood to wood for several inches, and then glued and tightened up to each other with twine for several inches, there is no sharp join whatever but only such a gradual one as never makes itself felt in practice. Moreover, these clubs are more serviceable, and will stand much more wear and tear than those which are made with sockets. Sometimes they give trouble when the glue loosens, but the socketed club is much easier to break. On club links generally in these days you will probably see more socketed drivers and brassies (for these remarks apply to all wooden clubs) than those that are spliced; but this is simply the result of a craze or fashion with which neat appearance has something to do; and if you desire to convince yourself that I am right, take note of the styles of the drivers used by the best players at the next first-class amateur or professional tournament that you witness. The men who are playing on these occasions are ripe with experience, and so long as they get the best results they do not care what their clubs look like.

The head of the club should be made of persimmon or dogwood—both very hard and full of driving power. Usually the bare face of such a club is good enough for contact with any ball on any tee, but the time will come when the golfer, developing innumerable fads and fancies, will reach the conclusion that he must have an artificial face of some kind fitted on at the place of contact with the ball. Or such an artificial face may become necessary by reason of the wear and tear on the face of the driver. Why forsake the old leather face? There is an idea abroad in these days that it is too soft and dead for the purposes of the new rubber-cored ball; and the impression that the latter likes the very hardest surface it is possible to apply to it has resulted in horn, vulcanite, and even steel faces being fitted to drivers and brassies. I do not think that in actual practice they are any better than leather, though some golfers may persuade themselves that they are. If a man, who is a good and steady driver, makes several drives from the tee with a club which has a leather face, and several more with another possessing a steel or vulcanite face, I am confident that he will on the average get at least as far with the leather as with the other, and I shall be surprised, if the test is fair and reliable, if he does not get further. I have leather faces on my drivers, and I think that latterly I have been driving further than I ever did. A point of objection to the harder surfaces, which at times is very serious, is that the ball is very much more liable to skid off them than off others, and thus the golfer may often blame himself for shots that look like a mixture of foozle and slice when the fault is not his at all, but that of the peculiarity of the club with which he is so much in love. On the other hand, it must be admitted that he scores over his opponent with the leather-faced club when the weather is wet, for the leather is then liable to soften and becomes very dead.

Never select a club because it has a long head, but let your preference be in favour of the shorter heads. The beginner, or the player of only moderate experience, puts it to himself that it is a very difficult thing always to strike the ball fairly on the face of the club, and that the longer the face is the more room he has for inaccuracy of his stroke. But he is wrong. Whatever the length of the face, unless the ball is hit fairly and squarely in the centre, it will not travel properly, and the effect is really worse when the point of contact is a little off the centre in a long-faced club than when it is the same distance removed from the centre of a short face. Moreover, despite this fact, which will soon become apparent to the golfer, the knowledge that he has a long-faced driver may very easily get him into a loose way of playing his tee shots. He may cease to regard exactness as indispensable, as it always is. The tendency of late years has been to make the heads of wooden clubs shorter and still shorter, and this tendency is well justified.

The question of the whip or suppleness of the shaft must generally be decided by individual style and preference; but I advise the beginner against purchasing a whippy driver to start with, whatever he may do later on. He should rather err on the side of stiffness. When a man is well on his drive, has a good style, and is getting a long ball from the tee every time, it is doubtless true that he obtains better results from a shaft with a little life in it than from a stiff one. But the advantage is not by any means so great as might be imagined, and many fine players drive their best balls with stiff clubs. It must always be remembered that when the stroke is not made perfectly there is a much greater tendency to slice with a supple shaft than with a stiff one, and the disadvantages of the former are especially pronounced on a windy day. It is all a matter of preference and predilection, and when these are absent the best thing to do is to strike the happy medium and select a shaft that is fairly supple but which still leaves you in the most perfect command of the head of the club, and not as if the latter were connected with your hands by nothing more than a slender rush.

Weight again is largely a matter of fancy, and there is no rule to the effect that a slender player should use a light club and one of powerful build a heavy one; indeed, one constantly finds the slim men employing the most ponderous drivers, as if, as it were, to make up for their own lightness, while heavy men will often prefer clubs that are like pen-holders to them. Once more I suggest the adoption of the medium as being generally the most satisfactory. I have a strong dislike to drivers that are unusually light, and I do not think that anyone can consistently get the best results from them. They entail too much swinging, and it is much harder to guide the club properly when the weight of the head cannot be felt. Of course a club that is strongly favoured by a golfer and suits him excellently in all respects save that it errs on the side of lightness, can easily be put right by the insertion of a little lead in the sole.

Little need be said in this place about the selection of the brassy. Whatever may be the amount of whip in the shaft of the driver, the brassy should not possess any undue suppleness, for it has heavier and rougher work to do than the club which is used for the tee shots, and there must be very little give in the stick if satisfactory results are to be obtained when the ball is lying at all heavily. The head and the face should be small; but in other respects the pattern of the driver should be closely adhered to, for it is one of the principles of my tuition that when the golfer takes his brassy in his hand to play his second shot, he should be brought to feel as nearly as possible that he is merely doing the drive over again. Many authorities recommend that the shaft of the brassy shall be an inch or so shorter than that of the driver; but I can see no necessity for its being shorter; and, on the other hand, for the reason I have just stated, I think it is eminently desirable that it should be exactly the same length. On this point I shall have more to say in another chapter. Care should be taken that both the brassy and the driver have exactly the same lie, that is to say, that when the soles of both clubs are laid quite flat upon the ground the shafts shall be projecting towards the golfer at precisely the same angle. If they have not the same lie, then, if the player takes up the same stance at the same distance from the ball when making a brassy shot as when he struck the ball from the tee with his driver, the sole of the club will not sweep evenly along the turf as it comes on to the ball, and the odds will be against a good shot being made.

I am a strong believer in having reserve drivers and brassies, even if one is only a very moderate golfer. Everybody knows what it is to suffer torture during the period when one is said to be "off his drive," and I think there is no remedy for this disease like a change of clubs. There may be nothing whatever the matter with the club you have been playing with, and which at one time gave you so much delight, but which now seems so utterly incapable of despatching a single good ball despite all the drastic alterations which you make in your methods. Of course it is not at all the fault of the club, but I think that nearly everybody gets more or less tired of playing with the same implement, and at length looks upon it with familiar contempt. The best thing to do in such circumstances is to give it a rest, and it will soon be discovered that absence makes the heart grow fonder in this matter as in so many others. But the reserve clubs which are taken out while the first string are resting should be in themselves good and almost as exactly suitable to the player's style as the others. It is a mistake to take up a club which has been regarded as a failure, and in which one has no confidence. Therefore, I suggest that so soon as the golfer has really found his style and is tolerably certain about it, and the exact kind of club that he likes best, he should fit himself up with both a spare driver and a spare brassy, and give them each a turn as occasion demands. It is hardly necessary to add that whenever an important game is being played, considerable wisdom will be exercised if the reserves are taken out in the bag along with the clubs with which it is intended to play, for though breakages are not matters of everyday occurrence, they do happen sometimes, and nothing would be more exasperating in such a contingency than the knowledge that for the rest of the game you would be obliged to play your tee shots with your brassy or your brassy shots with your cleek.

The driving cleek, for long shots, should have a fairly straight face with very little loft upon it. It should have a thick blade, should be fairly heavy, and its shaft should be stout and stiff. This makes a powerful club, with which some fine long work can be accomplished. I am inclined to think that one reason why so many players find it extremely difficult to get good work out of their cleeks, is that they use them with heads too thin and light. A large proportion of the cleeks one sees about are too delicate and ladylike. It is sometimes expected of a cleek that it will despatch a ball for, say, a hundred and sixty yards, and no club will do that, no matter how skilful the golfer who wields it may be, unless there is sufficient weight in it. A second cleek, which will be found in the bag of the experienced golfer, will have a thinner blade and much more loft upon it, but in other respects will be very much like the other one, though not nearly so heavy. This instrument is for the shorter cleek-shot distances, which are just so long that an iron cannot reach them.

There is great diversity in irons, and the player may be left in the first place in the hands of his professional adviser, and afterwards to his own taste, with the single hint from me that undue lightness should at all times be avoided. Of the two mashies which the complete golfer will carry out with him on to the links, one, for pitching the ball well up with very little run to follow, will have a deep face, will be of medium weight, and be very stiff in the shaft. I emphasise the deep face and the rigidity of the shaft. This mashie will also have plenty of loft upon it. The other one, for use chiefly in running up to the hole, will have a straighter face, but will otherwise be much the same. However, not all golfers consider two mashies to be necessary, and I myself depend chiefly upon one. Of the niblick it need only be said that it must be strong, heavy, and well lofted.

I have stated that the golfer may carry two putters in his bag; but I mean that he should do so only when he has a definite and distinct purpose for each of them, and I certainly do not advise his going from one kind to the other for the same sort of putt. There is great danger in such a practice. If he is doing very poor putting with one club, he will naturally fly for help to the other one, and the probability is that he will do just as badly with that. Then he returns to the first one, and again finds that his putts do not come off, and by this time he is in a hopeless quandary. If he has only one putter he will generally make some sort of a success of it if he can putt at all, and my private belief is that the putter itself has very little to do with the way in which a golfer putts. It is the man that counts and not the tool. I have tried all kinds of putters in my time, and have generally

gone back to the plainest and simplest of all. I have occasionally used the aluminium putter. It has much to recommend it to those who like this style of implement, and Braid
always does very well with it. The Travis or Schenectady
putter, which was so popular for a short time after the
Amateur Championship last year, owing to the American
player having done such wonderful things with it, I do not
succeed with. When I try to putt with it I cannot keep my
eye away from its heel. But the fact is, as I have already
indicated, that you can putt with anything if you hit the ball
properly. Everything depends on that—hitting the ball
properly—and no putter that was ever made will help you
to hole out if you do not strike the ball exactly as it ought
to be struck, while if you do so strike it, any putter will hole
out for you. The philosophy of putting is simple, but is
rarely appreciated. The search for the magic putter that
will always pop the ball into the hole and leave the player
nothing to do will go on for ever.

One other observation that I have to make on clubs in
general is, that I think it is a mistake to have the shafts any
longer than is absolutely necessary. Some golfers think that
an iron or a cleek is just the right length for them when there
are still a few inches of stick projecting inwards, towards
their bodies, when they have made their grip. Why that
spare stick? It cannot possibly be of any use, and may con-
ceivably be harmful. It is surely better to have it cut off and
then to grip the club at the end of the handle. A larger
sense of power and control is obtained in this manner. My
own clubs seem to most golfers who examine them to be on
the short side, and this is a convenient opportunity for giving
a few details concerning my favourites, which may prove of
interest to the readers of these notes. I should prefix the
statement with the observation that I am 5 feet $9\frac{1}{4}$ inches in
height, and that normally I weigh $11\frac{1}{2}$ stones. Young
players who might be inclined to adapt their clubs to my
measurements should bear these factors in mind, though I

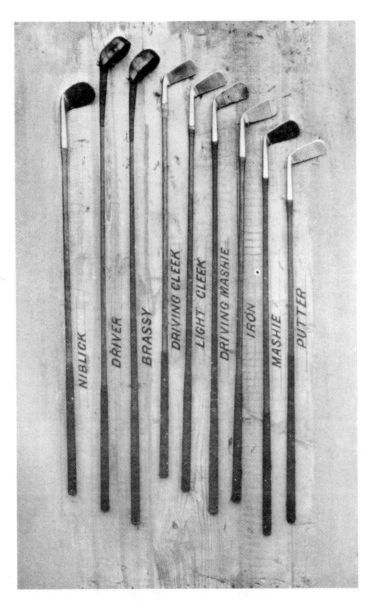

PLATE I. MY SET OF CLUBS

seem to be of something like average height and build.
Here, then, are the statistics of my bag:—

Club.				Length.		Weight.
Driver	.	.	.	. 42	inches	12¾ oz.
Brassy	.	.	.	. 42	,,	12½ ,,
Driving mashie		.	. 38		,,	14½ ,,
Driving cleek	.	.	. 37		,,	13½ ,,
Light cleek	.	.		37	,,	13½ ,,
Iron	.	.	.	. 35½	,,	15¼ ,,
Mashie	.	.	.	. 36½	,,	15¼ ,,
Niblick	.	.	.	. 37	,,	19 ,,
Putter (putting cleek)		.	33½		,,	15 ,,

Each measurement was made from the heel to the end of
the shaft.

I have two explanations to make concerning this list of
dimensions. I have included the driving mashie, of which I
have said nothing in this chapter. It is an alternative club,
and it is better that it should be discussed exclusively in its
proper place, which is when cleek shots are being considered.
Again, on making a critical examination of these measurements, the golfer of a little experience will promptly ask why
my mashie is an inch and a quarter longer than my iron.
It is longer because one has sometimes to play high lofting
shots over trees and the like, and in such cases the loft of the
mashie is necessary and a considerable amount of power as
well—hence the extra stick.

As I have said, the collection of a set of clubs that con-
form in essentials to their owner's ideal is a very slow and
often an expensive process. A club that was bought in the
shop for six shillings might have cost its owner six sovereigns
when the many unsatisfactory and discarded articles that
were bought while this one perfect gem was being searched
for are taken into account. Therefore it behoves the man
who is to any extent satisfied with his clubs to take a proper
pride in them and look well after them I like to see a
golfer play with bright irons, and shafts that give evidence

of tender and affectionate care. It jars upon one's nerves to see rusty irons and mashies which have evidently not been cleaned for months, and which are now past hope. Such a man does not deserve to have good clubs, nor to play good strokes with them. But many golfers, even when they have a tender and careful regard for the excellent merits of their favourites, seem to imagine that the beginning and end of their duty towards them is to keep their irons bright and free from the slightest semblance of rust. More often than not the shaft is never given a thought, and yet a perfect shaft that just suits the man who has to play with it is one of the rarest and most difficult things to discover. It would be difficult to replace it, and to keep it in its best condition it needs constant care and attention. An unreasoning golfer may play with his clubs on wet days, see that the irons are brightened afterwards, and store his collection in his locker without another thought concerning them. And then some time later when he is out on the links snap goes one of his shafts, and " Confound that rotten wood ! " he exclaims. But it is not a case of rotten wood at all. When shafts are constantly allowed to get wet and are afterwards merely wiped with a rag and given no further attention, all the life dries out of the wood, and they are sure to break sooner or later. It should be your invariable practice, when you have been out on a wet day, first to see that your shafts are well dried and then to give them a thoroughly good oiling with linseed oil, applied with a rag kept specially for the purpose. This will keep them in excellent condition. The tops of the club heads may be oiled in the same way ; but extreme care should be taken that not a drop of oil is allowed to touch the face of the wooden clubs. It would tend to open the grain, and then, when next you played in the wet, the damp would get inside the wood and cause it gradually to rot. I counsel all golfers when playing in wet weather to have covers or hoods attached to their bags, so that the heads of their instruments may always be kept in shelter. This will do much for their preservation, and at the same time add materially to the satisfaction of the player, for he can never feel that he has the means to do himself justice on the tee when the head of his driver is in a half soaked state.   No player, whatever his abilities as a golfer, should refrain from exercising this precautionary measure because he has seen only the very best players doing so, and because he fancies it may be regarded by his friends as affectation.   The fact that it is chiefly the best players who do these things only indicates that they know better than others what is due to their clubs and how to look after them.   There is no affectation in copying their methods in this respect.

CHAPTER V

DRIVING—PRELIMINARIES

Advantage of a good drive—And the pleasure of it—More about the driver—Tee low—Why high tees are bad—The question of stance—Eccentricities and bad habits—Begin in good style—Measurements of the stance—The reason why—The grip of the club—My own method and its advantages—Two hands like one—Comparative tightness of the hands—Variations during the swing—Certain disadvantages of the two-V grip—Addressing the ball—Freaks of style—How they must be compensated for—Too much waggling—The point to look at—Not the top of the ball but the side of it.

IT has been said that the amateur golfers of Great Britain are in these days suffering from a " debauchery of long driving." The general sense of Mr. Travis's remark is excellent, meaning that there is a tendency to regard a very long drive as almost everything in the playing of a hole, and to be utterly careless of straightness and the short game so long as the ball has been hit from the tee to the full extent of the golfer's power. A long drive is not by any means everything, and the young golfer should resist any inclination to strive for the 250-yard ball to the detriment or even the total neglect of other equally important, though perhaps less showy, considerations in the playing of a hole. But having said so much, and conveyed the solemn warning that is necessary, I am obliged to admit that the long driver has very full justification for himself, and that the wisely regulated ambition of the young player to be one is both natural and laudable. The long drive, as I say, is not everything; but to play well it is as necessary to make a good drive as to hole a short putt, or nearly so, and from the golfer who does not drive well a most marvellous excellence is required in the short game if he is to hold his own in good company, or ever be anything more than a long-handicap man. The good drive is the foundation of a good game, and just as one and one make two, so it follows that the man who drives the longer ball has the rest of the game made easier and more certain for him. This apart, there is no stroke in golf that gives the same amount of pleasure as does the perfect driving of the ball from the tee, none that makes the heart feel lighter, and none that seems to bring the glow of delight into the watching eye as this one does. The man who has never stood upon the tee with a sturdy rival near him and driven a perfect ball, the hands having followed well through and finished nicely up against the head, while the little white speck in the distance, after skimming the earth for a time, now rises and soars upwards, clearing all obstacles, and seeming to revel in its freedom and speed until at last it dips gracefully back to earth again—I say that the man who has not done this thing has missed one of the joys of life. I have heard the completest sportsmen say that there are very few things in the entire world of sport that can be compared with it, and none that is superior.

So now let us get on to our drive.

In the first place, the driver must be selected, and the hints I have already given upon the choice of clubs will serve tolerably well in this respect. Let it only be said again that the golfer should do his utmost to avoid extremes in length or shortness. One hears of the virtues of fishing-rod drivers, and the next day that certain great players display a tendency to shorten their clubs. There is nothing like the happy medium, which has proved its capability of getting the longest balls. The length of the club must, of course, vary according to the height of the player, for what would be a short driver for a six-foot man would almost be a fishing-rod to the diminutive person who stands but five feet high. Let the weight be medium also; but for reasons already stated do not let it err on the side of lightness. The shaft of the club should be of moderate suppleness. As I have said, if it is too whippy it may be hard to control, but if it is too stiff it leaves too much hard work to be done by the muscles of the golfer. Practising what I preach, my own drivers are carefully selected for this delicate medium of suppleness of shaft, and when a stick is found that is exactly perfect it is well worth great care for ever. Also I reiterate that the head of the club should not be too large; driving is not thereby made any easier, and carelessness is encouraged. The face should not be quite vertical: if it were, only the top edge and not the full face would be seen when the stance had been taken and the club head was resting upon the tee in its proper place. There must be just so much loft that the face can be seen when the golfer is ready and in position for the swing. But avoid having too much loft filed on the club as a fancied remedy for driving too low and getting into all the bunkers. You do not fail to get the ball up because there is not sufficient loft on the club, but because you are doing something wrong which can easily be remedied; while, on the other hand, be very careful of the fact that, as you add loft to the face of the driver so at the same time you are cutting off distance and losing both power and the delightful sense of it. When the weather is wet, it is a good plan to chalk the face of the club, as this counteracts the tendency of the ball to skid from it.

Tee the ball low, rejecting the very prevalent but erroneous idea that you are more certain of getting it away cleanly and well when it is poised high off the ground. The stroke that sweeps the ball well away from the low tee is the most natural and perfect, and it follows that the ball, properly driven from this low tee, is the best of all. Moreover, one is not so liable to get too much underneath the ball and make a feeble shot into the sky, which is one of the most exasperating forms of ineffectual effort in the whole range of golf. Another convincing argument in favour of the low tee is that it preserves a greater measure of similarity between the first shot and the second, helping to make the latter, with the brassy, almost a repetition of the first, and therefore simple and comparatively easy.   If you make a high tee, when you come to play your second stroke with your brassy, you will be inclined to find fault with even the most perfect brassy lies—when the ball is so well held up by the blades of grass that the best possible shot with this far-sending club should be the result.   If you are favoured with an ordinary brassy lie, you imagine the ball to be in a hole, exclaim that you are badly cupped, and call out vexatiously for an iron.   This is the regular result of playing from a high tee, whereas, when the low one is systematically adopted, the difference between the play with the driver and with the brassy from a good lie is inconsiderable, the brassy is used more frequently, and the results are regularly better.   As I have already suggested, one of the principles of my long game is to make the play with the brassy as nearly similar to that with the driver as possible, and a low tee is the first step in that direction.

There are wide variations in the stances adopted by different players, and extremes of one sort or another are usually the result of bad habits contracted in the early stages of initiation into the mysteries of the game.   Sometimes the ball is seen opposite the toe of the left foot; at others it is far away to the right.   Either of these players may get long balls constantly, but it is in spite of the stance and not because of it, for they are contending against a handicap all the time, and have unconsciously to introduce other mannerisms into their play to counteract the evil which a bad stance inevitably brings about.   It is certain that if they had driven in the easier way from their youth upwards, they would in their golfing prime have been getting longer balls than those with which they are after all apparently satisfied.   But I have already admitted generally, and here again admit in a specific instance, the dissatisfaction, and even danger, that is likely to accrue from an attempt to uproot a system of play which has been established in an individual for many years.   One can only insist upon the necessity of starting well, and plead earnestly to any readers who may not yet be far advanced in their experience of the game, to see that their play is based on wise and sure foundations.   There is nothing of my own discovery or invention in my stance for the drive.   It is simply that which is theoretically and scientifically correct, being calculated, that is, to afford the greatest freedom of movement to the arms, legs, and body in the swinging of the club, so that the strength may be exerted to the fullest advantage at the right moment and continued in its effect upon the ball for the longest possible period.

First, then, as to distance from the ball.   The player should stand so far away from it that when he is in position and the club face is resting against the teed ball, just as when ready to strike it, the end of the shaft shall reach exactly up to his left knee when the latter is ever so slightly bent.   In this position he should be able, when he has properly gripped the club, to reach the ball comfortably and without any stretching, the arms indeed being not quite straight out but having a slight bend at the elbows, so that when the club is waggled in the preliminary address to the ball, plenty of play can be felt in them.   I must now invite the player who is following me in these remarks to give his attention simultaneously to the photograph of myself, as I have taken my stance upon the tee for an ordinary drive (Plate VI.), with the object of getting the longest ball possible under conditions in all respects normal; and to the small diagram in the corner of the picture giving all the measurements necessary to a complete understanding of the position.   I may point out again that my height is 5 feet 9¼ inches, and that the length of my driver from the heel to the end of the shaft is 42 inches.   My stature being medium, the majority of players who desire to follow my suggestions will be able to do so without any altering of the measurements given in these diagrams; and, indeed, until any variation in height one way or the other becomes considerable, there is no necessity to vary them. Remember that in this and all subsequent illustrations the line marked A points to the direction in which it is desired that the ball should travel, and that the B line over which the player stands is at right angles to it. Those who wish at this moment to examine the stance in the most practical manner, and to compare it with that which they have been in the habit of playing from, need hardly be informed that at the corners of nearly every carpet there are rectangular lines either in the pattern or made by borders, which may be taken to represent those in the diagram, and a penny placed at the junction will stand for the ball. It will be observed that, for the most lucid and complete exposition of the stances, in this and all subsequent cases, the diagrams have been turned about, so that here the player has, as it were, his back to the reader, while in the photographs he is, of course, facing him. But the stances are identical. The diagrams have been drawn to scale.

It will be noticed, in the first place, that I have my toes turned well outwards. The pivoting which is necessary, and which will be described in due course, is done naturally and without any effort when the toes are pointed in this manner. While it is a mistake to place the feet too near each other, there is a common tendency to place them too far apart. When this is done, ease and perfection of the swing are destroyed and power is wasted, whilst the whole movement is devoid of grace. It will be seen that my left foot is a little, but not much, in advance of the ball. My heel, indeed, is almost level with it, being but an inch from the B line at the end of which the ball is teed. The toe, however, is $9\frac{1}{2}$ inches away from it, all measurements in this case and others being taken from the exact centre of the point of the toe. The point of the right toe is 19 inches distant from the B line, and while this toe is 27½ inches from the A line the other is 34 inches from it, so that the right foot is 6½ inches in advance of the left. After giving these measurements, there is really little more to explain about the stance, particularly as I shall show shortly how variations from it almost certainly bring about imperfect drives. Theoretically, the reason for the position is, I think, fairly obvious. The right foot is in advance of the left, so that at the most critical period of the stroke there shall be nothing to impede the follow-through, but everything to encourage it, and so that at the finish the body itself can be thrown forward in the last effort to continue the application of power. It would not be in a position to do so if the left foot were in front to bar the way. The position of the ball as between the right foot and the left is such that the club will strike it just at the time when it is capable of doing so to the utmost advantage, being then, and for the very minute portion of a second during which ball and club may be supposed to remain in contact, moving in as nearly as possible a straight line and at its maximum speed.

Now comes the all-important consideration of the grip. This is another matter in which the practice of golfers differs greatly, and upon which there has been much controversy. My grip is one of my own invention. It differs materially from most others, and if I am asked to offer any excuse for it, I shall say that I adopted it only after a careful trial of all the other grips of which I had ever heard, that in theory and practice I find it admirable—more so than any other— and that in my opinion it has contributed materially to the attainment of such skill as I possess. The favour which I accord to my method might be viewed with suspicion if it had been my natural or original grip, which came naturally or accidentally to me when I first began to play as a boy, so many habits that are bad being con- tracted at this stage and clinging to the player for the rest of his life. But this was not the case, for when I

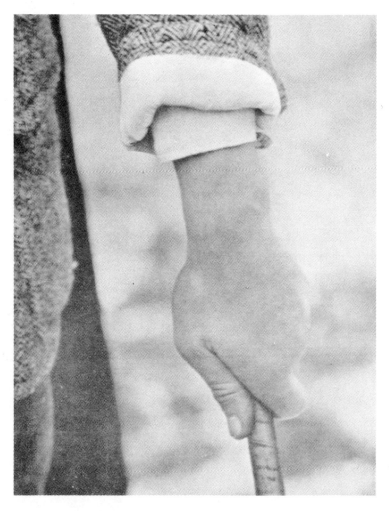

PLATE II. THE GRIP WITH THE LEFT HAND

PLATE III.   THE OVERLAPPING GRIP

PLATE V. THE OVERLAPPING GRIP

PLATE IV. THE OVERLAPPING GRIP

first began to play golf I grasped my club in what is generally regarded as the orthodox manner, that is to say, across the palms of both hands separately, with both thumbs right round the shaft (on the left one, at all events), and with the joins between the thumbs and first fingers showing like two V's over the top of the shaft. This is usually described as the two-V grip, and it is the one which is taught by the majority of professionals to whom the beginner appeals for first instruction in the game. Of course it is beyond question that some players achieve very fine results with this grip, but I abandoned it many years ago in favour of one that I consider to be better. My contention is that this grip of mine is sounder in theory and easier in practice, tends to make a better stroke and to secure a straighter ball, and that players who adopt it from the beginning will stand a much better chance of driving well at an early stage than if they went in for the old-fashioned two-V. My grip is an overlapping, but not an interlocking one. Modifications of it are used by many fine players, and it is coming into more general practice as its merits are understood and appreciated. I use it for all my strokes, and it is only when putting that I vary it in the least, and then the change is so slight as to be scarcely noticeable. The photographs (Plates II., III., IV., and V.) illustrating the grip of the left hand singly, and of the two together from different points of view, should now be closely examined.

It will be seen at once that I do not grasp the club across the palm of either hand. The club being taken in the left hand first, the shaft passes from the knuckle joint of the first finger across the ball of the second. The left thumb lies straight down the shaft—that is to say, it is just to the right of the centre of the shaft. But the following are the significant features of the grip. The right hand is brought up so high that the palm of it covers over the left thumb, leaving very little of the latter to be seen. The first and second fingers of the right hand just reach round to the thumb of the left, and the third finger completes the overlapping process, so that the club is held in the grip as if it were in a vice. The little finger of the right hand rides on the first finger of the left. The great advantage of this grip is that both hands feel and act like one, and if, even while sitting in his chair, a player who has never tried it before will take a stick in his hands in the manner I have described, he must at once be convinced that there is a great deal in what I say for it, although, of course, if he has been accustomed to the two V's, the success of my grip cannot be guaranteed at the first trial. It needs some time to become thoroughly happy with it.

We must now consider the degree of tightness of the grip by either hand, for this is an important matter. Some teachers of golf and various books of instruction inform us that we should grasp the club firmly with the left hand and only lightly with the right, leaving the former to do the bulk of the work and the other merely to guide the operations. It is astonishing with what persistency this error has been repeated, for error I truly believe it is. Ask any really first-class player with what comparative tightness he holds the club in his right and left hands, and I am confident that in nearly every case he will declare that he holds it nearly if not quite as tightly with the right hand as with the left. Personally I grip quite as firmly with the right hand as with the other one. When the other way is adopted, the left hand being tight and the right hand simply watching it, as it were, there is an irresistible tendency for the latter to tighten up suddenly at some part of the upward or downward swing, and, as surely as there is a ball on the tee, when it does so there will be mischief. Depend upon it the instinct of activity will prevent the right hand from going through with the swing in that indefinite state of looseness. Perhaps a yard from the ball in the upward swing, or a yard from it when coming down, there will be a convulsive grip of the right hand which, with an immediate acknowledgment

of guilt, will relax again.   Such a happening is usually fatal ;
it certainly deserves to be.   Slicing, pulling, sclaffing, and
the foundering of the innocent globe—all these tragedies
may at times be traced to this determination of the right
hand not to be ignored but to have its part to play in the
making of the drive.   Therefore in all respects my right
hand is a joint partner with the left.

The grip with the first finger and thumb of my right
hand is exceedingly firm, and the pressure of the little finger
on the knuckle of the left hand is very decided.   In the
same way it is the thumb and first finger of the left hand
that have most of the gripping work to do.   Again, the
palm of the right hand presses hard against the thumb of
the left.   In the upward swing this pressure is gradually
decreased, until when the club reaches the turning-point
there is no longer any such pressure; indeed, at this point
the palm and the thumb are barely in contact.   This release
is a natural one, and will or should come naturally to the
player for the purpose of allowing the head of the club to
swing well and freely back.   But the grip of the thumb and
first finger of the right hand, as well as that of the little
finger upon the knuckle of the first finger of the left hand,
is still as firm as at the beginning.   As the club head is
swung back again towards the ball, the palm of the right
hand and the thumb of the left gradually come together
again.   Both the relaxing and the re-tightening are done
with the most perfect graduation, so that there shall be
no jerk to take the club off the straight line.   The easing
begins when the hands are about shoulder high and the club
shaft is perpendicular, because it is at this time that the
club begins to pull, and if it were not let out in the manner
explained, the result would certainly be a half shot or very
little more than that, for a full and perfect swing would be
an impossibility.   This relaxation of the palm also serves to
give more freedom to the wrist at the top of the swing just
when that freedom is desirable.

I have the strongest belief in the soundness of the grip that I have thus explained, for when it is employed both hands are acting in unison and to the utmost advantage, whereas it often happens in the two-V grip, even when practised by the most skilful players, that in the downward swing there is a sense of the left hand doing its utmost to get through and of the right hand holding it back.

There is only one other small matter to mention in connection with the question of grip. Some golfers imagine that if they rest the left thumb down the shaft and let the right hand press upon it there will be a considerable danger of breaking the thumb, so severe is the pressure when the stroke is being made. As a matter of fact, I have quite satisfied myself that if the thumb is kept in the same place there is not the slightest risk of anything of the kind. Also if the thumb remains immovable, as it should, there is no possibility of the club turning in the hands as so often happens in the case of the two-V grip when the ground is hit rather hard, a pull or a slice being the usual consequence. I must be excused for treating upon these matters at such length. They are often neglected, but they are of extreme importance in laying the foundations of a good game of golf.

In addressing the ball, take care to do so with the centre of the face of the club, that is, at the desired point of contact. Some awkward eccentricities may frequently be observed on the tee. A player may be seen addressing his ball from the toe of the driver, and I have even noticed the address being made with the head of the club quite inside the ball, while in other cases it is the heel of the club which is applied to the object to be struck. The worthy golfers who are responsible for these freaks of style no doubt imagine that they are doing a wise and proper thing, and in the most effectual manner counteracting some other irregularity of their method of play which may not be discoverable, and which is in any case incurable. Yet nothing is more certain than that another irregularity must be introduced into the drive in order to correct the one made in the address. To the point at which the club is addressed it will naturally return in the course of the swing, and if it is to be guided to any other than the original place, there must be a constant effort all through the swing to effect this change in direction, and most likely somewhere or other there will be sufficient jerk to spoil the drive. In the case where the ball is addressed with the toe of the club, the player must find it necessary almost to fall on the ball in coming down, and it is quite impossible for him to get his full distance in such circumstances.

A waggle of the head of the club as a preliminary before commencing the swing is sometimes necessary after the stance and grip have been taken, but every young golfer should be warned against excess in this habit. With the stance and grip arranged, the line of the shot in view, and a full knowledge of what is required from the stroke, there is really very little more that needs thinking about before the swing is taken. One short preliminary waggle will tend to make the player feel comfortable and confident, but some golfers may be observed trying the patience of all about them by an interminable process of waggling, the most likely result of which is a duffed shot, since, when at last the stroke is made, the player is in a state of semi-catalepsy, and has no clear idea of what he is going to do or how he is going to do it.

In addressing the ball, and during the upward and downward swings until it has been safely despatched, the sight should be kept riveted, not on the top of the ball, as is customary, but upon the ground immediately to the right of it (see diagram on p. 170). To the point where the gaze is fixed the head of the club will automatically be guided. That is why you are told to keep your eye on the ball. But you do not want to hit the top of the ball. So look to the side, where you do want to hit it.

CHAPTER VI

DRIVING—THE SWING OF THE CLUB

"Slow back"—The line of the club head in the upward swing—The golfer's head must be kept rigid—The action of the wrists—Position at the top of the swing—Movements of the arms—Pivoting of the body—No swaying— Action of the feet and legs—Speed of the club during the swing—The moment of impact—More about the wrists—No pure wrist shot in golf— The follow-through—Timing of the body action—Arms and hands high up at the finish—How bad drives are made—The causes of slicing—When the ball is pulled—Misapprehensions as to slicing and pulling—Dropping of the right shoulder—Its evil consequences—No trick in long driving—Hit properly and hard—What is pressing and what is not—Summary of the drive.

NOW let us consider the upward and downward swings of the club, and the movements of the arms, legs, feet, and body in relation to them. As a first injunction, it may be stated that the club should be drawn back rather more slowly than you intend to bring it down again. "Slow back" is a golfing maxim that is both old and wise. The club should begin to gain speed when the upward swing is about half made, and the increase should be gradual until the top is reached, but it should never be so fast that control of the club is to any extent lost at the turning-point. The head of the club should be taken back fairly straight from the ball—along the A line—for the first six inches, and after that any tendency to sweep it round sharply to the back should be avoided. Keep it very close to the straight line until it is half-way up. The old St. Andrews style of driving largely consisted in this sudden sweep round, but the modern method appears to be easier and productive of better results. So this carrying of the head of the club upwards and backwards seems to be a very simple matter, capable of explanation in a very few words; but, as every golfer of a month's experience knows, there is a long list of details to be attended to, which I have not yet named, each of which seems to vie with the others in its attempt to destroy the effectiveness of the drive. Let us begin at the top, as it were, and work downwards, and first of all there is the head of the golfer to consider.

The head should be kept perfectly motionless from the time of the address until the ball has been sent away and is well on its flight. The least deviation from this rule means a proportionate danger of disaster. When a drive has been badly foozled, the readiest and most usual explanation is that the eye has been taken off the ball, and the wise old men who have been watching shake their heads solemnly, and utter that parrot-cry of the links, "Keep your eye on the ball." Certainly this is a good and necessary rule so far as it goes; but I do not believe that one drive in a hundred is missed because the eye has not been kept on the ball. On the other hand, I believe that one of the most fruitful causes of failure with the tee shot is the moving of the head. Until the ball has gone, it should, as I say, be as nearly perfectly still as possible, and I would have written that it should not be moved to the extent of a sixteenth of an inch, but for the fact that it is not human to be so still, and golf is always inclined to the human side. When the head has been kept quite still and the club has reached the top of the upward swing, the eyes should be looking over the middle of the left shoulder, the left one being dead over the centre of that shoulder. Most players at one time or another, and the best of them when they are a little off their game, fall into every trap that the evil spirits of golf lay for them, and unconsciously experience a tendency to lift the head for five or six inches away from the ball while the upward swing is being taken. This is often what is imagined to be taking the eye off the ball, particularly as, when it is carried to excess, the eye, struggling gallantly to do its duty, finds considerable difficulty in getting a sight of the ball over the left shoulder, and sometimes loses it altogether for an instant. An examination of the photograph showing the top of the swing (Plate VII.) will make it clear that there is very little margin for the moving of the head if the ball is to be kept in full view for the whole of the time.

In the upward swing the right shoulder should be raised gradually. It is unnecessary for me to submit any instruction on this point, since the movement is natural and inevitable, and there is no tendency towards excess; but the arms and wrists need attention. From the moment when the club is first taken back the left wrist should begin to turn inwards (that is to say, the movement is in the same direction as that taken by the hands of a clock), and so turn away the face of the club from the ball. When this is properly done, the toe of the club will point to the sky when it is level with the shoulder and will be dead over the middle of the shaft. This turning or twisting process continues all the way until at the top of the swing the toe of the club is pointing straight downwards to the ground. A reference to Plate VII. will show that this has been done, and that as the result the left wrist finishes the upward swing underneath the shaft, which is just where it ought to be. When the wrist has not been at work in the manner indicated, the toe of the club at the top of the drive will be pointing upwards. In order to satisfy himself properly about the state of affairs thus far in the making of the drive, the golfer should test himself at the top of the swing by holding the club firmly in the position which it has reached, and then dropping the right hand from the grip. He will thus be enabled to look right round, and if he then finds that the maker's name on the head of the club is horizontal, he will know that he has been doing the right thing with his wrists, while if it is vertical the wrist action has been altogether wrong.

During the upward swing the arms should be gradually

PLATE VI. DRIVER AND BRASSY. THE STANCE

PLATE VII. DRIVER AND BRASSY. TOP OF THE SWING

PLATE *VIII*. DRIVER AND BRASSY. TOP OF THE SWING, FROM BEHIND

PLATE IX. DRIVER AND BRASSY. FINISH OF THE SWING

let out in the enjoyment of perfect ease and freedom (without being spread-eagled away from the body) until at the top of the swing the left arm, from the shoulder to the elbow, is gently touching the body and hanging well down, while the right arm is up above it and almost level with the club. The picture indicates exactly what I mean, and a reference to the illustration showing what ought not to be the state of affairs generally when the top of the swing is reached (Plate XI.), should convince even the veriest beginner how much less comfortable is the position of the arms in this instance than when the right thing has been done, and how laden with promise is the general attitude of the player in the latter position as compared with his cramped state in the former. I think I ought to state, partly in justice to myself, and partly to persuade my readers that the best way in this case, as in all others, is the most natural, that I found it most inconvenient and difficult to make such extremely inaccurate swings as those depicted in this and other photographs of the " How not to do it " series, although they are by no means exaggerations of what are seen on the links every day, even players of several years' experience being constantly responsible for them.

In the upward movement of the club the body must pivot from the waist alone, and there must be no swaying not even to the extent of an inch. When the player sways in his drive the stroke he makes is a body stroke pure and simple. The body is trying to do the work the arms should do, and in these circumstances it is impossible to get so much power into the stroke as if it were properly made, while once more the old enemies, the slice and the pull, will come out from their hiding-places with their mocking grin at the unhappy golfer.

The movements of the feet and legs are important. In addressing the ball you stand with both feet flat and securely placed on the ground, the weight equally divided between them, and the legs so slightly bent at the knee joints as to make the bending scarcely noticeable. This position is maintained during the upward movement of the club until the arms begin to pull at the body. The easiest and most natural thing to do then, and the one which suggests itself, is to raise the heel of the left foot and begin to pivot on the left toe, which allows the arms to proceed with their uplifting process without let or hindrance. Do not begin to pivot on this left toe ostentatiously, or because you feel you ought to do so, but only when you know the time has come and you want to, and do it only to such an extent that the club can reach the full extent of the swing without any difficulty. While this is happening it follows that the weight of the body is being gradually thrown on to the right leg, which accordingly stiffens until at the top of the swing it is quite rigid, the left leg being at the same time in a state of comparative freedom, slightly bent in towards the right, with only just enough pressure on the toe to keep it in position.

To the man who has never driven a good ball in his life this process must seem very tedious. All these things to attend to, and something less than a second in which to attend to them! It only indicates how much there is in this wonderful game—more by far than any of us suspect or shall ever discover. But the time comes, and it should come speedily, when they are all accomplished without any effort, and, indeed, to a great extent, unconsciously. The upward swing is everything. If it is bad and faulty, the downward swing will be wrong and the ball will not be properly driven. If it is perfect, there is a splendid prospect of a long and straight drive, carrying any hazard that may lie before the tee. That is why so very much emphasis must be laid on getting this upward swing perfect, and why comparatively little attention need be paid to the downward swing, even though it is really the effective part of the stroke.

Be careful not to dwell at the turn of the swing. The club has been gaining in speed right up to this point, and though I suppose that, theoretically, there is a pause at the turning-point, lasting for an infinitesimal portion of a second, the golfer should scarcely be conscious of it. He must be careful to avoid a sudden jerk, but if he dwells at the top of the stroke for only a second, or half that short period of time, his upward swing in all its perfection will have been completely wasted, and his stroke will be made under precisely the same circumstances and with exactly the same disadvantages as if the club had been poised in this position at the start, and there had been no attempt at swinging of any description. In such circumstances a long ball is an impossibility, and a straight one a matter of exceeding doubt. The odds are not very greatly in favour of the ball being rolled off the teeing ground. So don't dwell at the turn; come back again with the club.

The club should gradually gain in speed from the moment of the turn until it is in contact with the ball, so that at the moment of impact its head is travelling at its fastest pace. After the impact, the club head should be allowed to follow the ball straight in the line of the flag as far as the arms will let it go, and then, having done everything that is possible, it swings itself out at the other side of the shoulders. The entire movement must be perfectly smooth and rhythmical; in the downward swing, while the club is gaining speed, there must not be the semblance of a jerk anywhere such as would cause a jump, or a double swing, or what might be called a cricket stroke. That, in a few lines, is the whole story of the downward swing; but it needs some little elaboration of detail. In the first place, avoid the tendency—which is to some extent natural—to let the arms go out or away from the body as soon as the downward movement begins. When they are permitted to do so the club head escapes from its proper line, and a fault is committed which cannot be remedied before the ball is struck. Knowing by instinct that you are outside the proper course, you make a great effort at correction, the face of the club is drawn across the ball, and there is one more slice. The arms should be kept fairly well in during the latter half of the downward swing, both elbows almost grazing the body. If they are properly attended to when the club is going up, there is much more likelihood of their coming down all right.

The head is still kept motionless and the body pivots easily at the waist; but when the club is half-way down, the left hip is allowed to go forward a little—a preliminary to and preparation for the forward movement of the body which is soon to begin. The weight is being gradually moved back again from the right leg to the left. At the moment of impact both feet are equally weighted and are flat on the ground, just as they were when the ball was being addressed; indeed, the position of the body, legs, arms, head, and every other detail is, or ought to be, exactly the same when the ball is being struck as they were when it was addressed, and for that reason I refer my readers again to the photograph of the address (No. VI.) as the most correct position of everything at the moment of striking. After the impact the weight is thrown on to the left leg, which stiffens, while the right toe pivots and the knee bends just as its partner did in the earlier stage of the stroke, but perhaps to a greater extent, since there is no longer any need for restraint.

Now pay attention to the wrists. They should be held fairly tightly. If the club is held tightly the wrists will be tight, and *vice versâ*. When the wrists are tight there is little play in them, and more is demanded of the arms. I don't believe in the long ball coming from the wrists. In defiance of principles which are accepted in many quarters, I will go so far as to say that, except in putting, there is no pure wrist shot in golf. Some players attempt to play their short approaches with their wrists as they have been told to do. These men are likely to remain at long handicaps for a long time. Similarly there is a kind of superstition that the elect among drivers get in some peculiar kind of " snap "—a momentary forward pushing movement—with their wrists at the time of impact, and that it is this wrist work at the critical period which gives the grand length to their drives, those extra twenty or thirty yards which make the stroke look so splendid, so uncommon, and which make the next shot so much easier. Generally speaking, the wrists when held firmly will take very good care of themselves; but there is a tendency, particularly when the two-V grip is used, to allow the right hand to take charge of affairs at the time the ball is struck, and the result is that the right wrist, as the swing is completed, gradually gets on to the top of the shaft instead of remaining in its proper place. The consequence is a pulled ball,—in fact, this is just the way in which I play for a pull. When the fault is committed to a still greater extent, the head of the club is suddenly turned over, and then the ball is foundered, as we say,—that is, it is struck downwards, and struggles, crippled and done for, a few yards along the ground in front of the tee. I find that ladies are particularly addicted to this very bad habit. Once again I have to say that if the club is taken up properly there is the greater certainty of its coming down properly, and then if you keep both hands evenly to their work there is a great probability of a good follow-through being properly effected.

When the ball has been struck, and the follow-through is being accomplished, there are two rules, hitherto held sacred, which may at last be broken. With the direction and force of the swing your chest is naturally turned round until it is facing the flag, and your body now abandons all restraint, and to a certain extent throws itself, as it were, after the ball. There is a great art in timing this body movement exactly. If it takes place the fiftieth part of a second too soon the stroke will be entirely ruined; if it comes too late it will be quite ineffectual, and will only result in making the golfer feel uneasy and as if something had gone wrong. When made at the proper instant it adds a good piece of distance to the drive, and that instant, as explained, is just when the club is following through. An examination of the photograph indicating the finish of the swing (No. IX.)

will show how my body has been thrown forward until at this stage it is on the outward side of the B line, although it was slightly on the other side when the ball was being addressed. Secondly, when the ball has gone, and the arms, following it, begin to pull, the head, which has so far been held perfectly still, is lifted up so as to give freedom to the swing, and incidentally it allows the eyes to follow the flight of the ball.

I like to see the arms finish well up with the hands level with the head. This generally means a properly hit ball and a good follow-through. At the finish of the stroke the arms should be as nearly as possible level with each other. At the top of the swing the right arm was noticeably above the left, but now the former has fallen somewhat. The photograph (No. IX.) indicates that the right arm is some way below the level of the shaft of the club, whereas it will be remembered that on the upward swing it was just level with it. Notice also the position of the wrists at the finish of the stroke.

Having thus indicated at such great length the many points which go to the making of a good drive, a long one and a straight one, yet abounding with ease and grace, allow me to show how some of the commonest faults are caused by departures from the rules for driving. Take the sliced ball, as being the trouble from which the player most frequently suffers, and which upon occasion will exasperate him beyond measure. When a golfer is slicing badly almost every time, it is frequently difficult for him to discover immediately the exact source of the trouble, for there are two or three ways in which it comes about. The player may be standing too near to the ball; he may be pulling in his arms too suddenly as he is swinging on to it, thus drawing the club towards his left foot; or he may be falling on to the ball at the moment of impact. When the stance is taken too near to the ball there is a great inducement to the arms to take a course

PLATE X. HOW NOT TO DRIVE

In this case the player's feet are much too close together, and there is a space between the hands as there should never be, whatever style of grip is favoured. Also the right hand is too much underneath the shaft. The result of these faults will usually be a pulled ball, but a long drive of any sort is impossible.

PLATE XI. HOW NOT TO DRIVE

In this case the left wrist instead of being underneath the handle is level with it—a common and dangerous fault. The left arm is spreadeagled outwards, and the toe of the club is not pointing downwards as it ought to be. The pivoting on the left toe is very imperfect. There is no power in this position. Sometimes the result is a pull, but frequently the ball will be foundered. No length is possible.

PLATE XII. HOW NOT TO DRIVE

This is an example of a bad finish. Instead of being thrown forward after the impact the body has fallen away. The usual consequence is a sliced ball, and this is also one of the commonest causes of short driving.

PLATE XIII. HOW NOT TO DRIVE

Here again the body has failed to follow the ball after impact. The stance is very bad, the forward position of the left foot preventing a satisfactory follow-through. The worst fault committed here, however, is the position taken by the left arm. The elbow is far too low. It should be at least as high as the right elbow. Result—complete lack of power and length.

too far outwards (in the direction of the A line) in the upward swing. The position is cramped, and the player does not seem able to get the club round at all comfortably. When the club head is brought on to the ball after a swing of this kind, the face is drawn right across it, and a slice is inevitable. In diagnosing the malady, in cases where the too close stance is suspected, it is a good thing to apply the test of distance given at the beginning of the previous chapter, and see whether, when the club head is resting in position against the teed ball, the other end of the shaft just reaches to the left knee when it is in position, and has only just so much bend in it as it has when the ball is being addressed. The second method of committing the slicing sin is self-explanatory. As for the third, a player falls on the ball, or sways over in the direction of the tee (very slightly, but it is the trifles that matter most) when his weight has not been properly balanced to start with, and when in the course of the swing it has been moved suddenly from one leg to the other instead of quite gradually. But sometimes falling on the ball is caused purely and simply by swaying the body, against which the player has already been warned. When the slicing is bad, the methods of the golfer should be tested for each of these irregularities, and he should remember that an inch difference in any position or movement as he stands upon the tee is a great distance, and that two inches is a vast space, which the mind trained to calculate in small fractions can hardly conceive.

Pulling is not such a common fault, although one which is sometimes very annoying. Generally speaking, a pulled ball is a much better one than one which has been sliced, and there are some young players who are rather inclined to purr with satisfaction when they have pulled, for, though the ball is hopelessly off the line, they have committed an error which is commoner with those whose hair has grown grey on the links than with the beginner whose handicap is reckoned by eighteen or twenty strokes. But after all pulling is not an amusement, and even when it is an accomplishment and not an accident, it should be most carefully regulated. It is the right hand which is usually the offender in this case. The wrist is wrong at the moment of impact, and generally at the finish of the stroke as well,—that is, it is on the top of the club, indicating that the right hand has done most of the work. In a case of this sort the top edge of the face of the club is usually overlapping the bottom edge, so that the face is pointing slightly downwards at the moment of impact; and when this position is brought about with extreme suddenness the ball is frequently foundered. If it escapes this fate, then it is pulled. A second cause of pulling is a sudden relaxation of the grip of the right hand at the time of hitting the ball. When this happens, the left hand, being uncontrolled, turns over the club head in the same manner as in the first case, and the result is the same.

I have found from experience that it is necessary to enjoin even players of some years' standing to make quite certain that they are slicing and pulling, before they complain about their doing so and try to find cures for it. In a great number of cases a player will take his stance in quite the wrong direction, either too much round to the right or too much to the left, and when the ball has flown truly along the line on which it was despatched, the golfer blandly remarks that it was a bad slice or a bad pull, as the case may be. He must bring himself to understand that a ball is neither sliced nor pulled when it continues flying throughout in the direction in which it started from the tee. It is only when it begins performing evolutions in the air some distance away, and taking a half wheel to the right or left, that it has fallen a victim to the slice or pull.

There is one more fault of the drive which must be mentioned. It is one of the commonest mistakes that the young golfer makes, and one which afflicts him most keenly, for when he makes it his drive is not a drive at all; all his power, or most of it, has been expended on the turf some inches behind the ball.   The right shoulder has been dropped too soon or too low.   During the address this shoulder is necessarily a little below the left one, and care must be taken at this stage that it is not allowed to drop more than is necessary.   At the top of the swing the right shoulder is naturally well above the other one, and at the moment of impact with the ball it should just have resumed its original position slightly below the left.   It often happens, however, that even very good golfers, after a period of excellent driving, through sheer over-confidence or carelessness, will fall into the way of dropping the right shoulder too soon, or, when they do drop it, letting it go altogether, so that it fairly sinks away.   The result is exactly what is to be expected.   The head of the club naturally comes down with the shoulder and flops ineffectually upon the turf behind the tee, anything from two to nine inches behind the ball.   Yet, unless the golfer has had various attacks of this sort of thing before, he is often puzzled to account for it.   The remedy is obvious.

I can imagine that many good golfers, now that I near the end of my hints on driving, may feel some sense of disappointment because I have not given them a recipe for putting thirty or forty yards on to their commonplace drives. I can only say that there is no trick or knack in doing it, as is often suspected, such as the suggestion, already alluded to, that the wrists have a little game of their own just when the club head is coming in contact with the ball.   The way to drive far is to comply with the utmost care with every injunction that I have set forth, and then to hit hard but by the proper use of the swing.   To some golfers this may be a dangerous truth, but it must be told: it is accuracy and strength which make the long ball.   But I seem to hear the young player wail, "When I hit hard you say 'Don't press!'" A golfer is not pressing when he swings through as fast as he can with his club, gaining speed steadily, although he is often told that he is.   But it most frequently happens that when he tries to get this extra pace all at once, and not as the result of gradual improvement and perfection of style, that it comes not smoothly but in a great jerk just before the ball is reached. This is certainly the way that it comes when the golfer is off his game, and he tries, often unconsciously, to make up in force what he has temporarily lost in skill. This really is pressing, and it is this against which I must warn every golfer in the same grave manner that he has often been warned before. But to the player who, by skill and dilligence of practice, increases the smooth and even pace of his swing, keeping his legs, body, arms, and head in their proper places all the time, I have nothing to give but encouragement, though long before this he himself will have discovered that he has found out the wonderful, delightful secret of the long ball.

Two chapters of detailed instruction are too much for a player to carry in his mind when he goes out on to the links to practise drives, and for his benefit I will here make the briefest possible summary of what I have already stated. Let him attend, then, to the following chief points:—

Stance.—The player should stand just so far away from the ball, that when the face of the driver is laid against it in position for striking, the other end of the shaft exactly reaches to the left knee when the latter is slightly bent. The right foot may be anything up to seven inches in front of the left, but certainly never behind it. The left toe should be a trifle in advance of the ball. The toes should be turned outwards. Make a low tee.

Grip.—As described. Remember that the palm of the right hand presses hard on the left thumb at all times except when nearing and at the top of the swing. The grip of the thumb and the first two fingers of each hand is constantly firm.

Upward Swing.—The club head must be taken back in a straight line for a few inches, and then brought round gradually—not too straight up (causing slicing) nor too far round in the old-fashioned style. The speed of the swing increases gradually. The elbows are kept fairly well in, the left wrist turning inwards and finishing the upward swing well underneath the shaft. The body must not be allowed to sway. It should pivot easily from the waist. The head must be kept quite still. The weight is gradually thrown entirely on to the right leg, the left knee bends inwards, the left heel rises, and the toe pivots. There must be no jerk at the turn of the swing.

Downward Swing.—There should be a gradual increase of pace, but no jerk anywhere. The arms must be kept well down when the club is descending, the elbows almost grazing the body. The right wrist should not be allowed to get on to the top of the club. The head is still motionless. The left hip is allowed to move forward very slightly while the club is coming down. The weight of the body is gradually transferred from the right leg to the left, the right toe pivoting after the impact, and the left leg stiffening. The right shoulder must be prevented from dropping too much. After the impact the arms should be allowed to follow the ball and the body to go forward, the latter movement being timed very carefully. The head may now be raised. Finish with the arms well up—the right arm above the left.

Slicing.—This may be caused by standing too near to the ball, by pulling in the arms, or by falling on the ball.

Pulling.—Usually caused by the head of the club being turned partly over when the ball is struck, or by relaxing the grip with the right hand.

I can only agree with those who have followed me so patiently through these two chapters, that to drive a golf ball well is a thing not to be learned in a week or a month.

CHAPTER VII

BRASSY AND SPOON

Good strokes with the brassy—Play as with the driver—The points of the brassy
—The stance—Where and how to hit the ball—Playing from cuppy lies—Jab
strokes from badly-cupped lies—A difficult club to master—The man with
the spoon—The lie for the baffy—What it can and cannot do—Character of
the club—The stance—Tee shots with the baffy—Iron clubs are better.

WHEN to your caddie you say " Give me my brassy "
it is a sign that there is serious work to be done—
as serious and anxious as any that has to be accomplished
during the six or seven minutes' journey from the tee to
the hole. Many golfers have a fondness for the brassy
greater even than for the driver, and the brassy shot when
well played certainly affords a greater sense of satisfaction
than the drive—great as is the joy of a good drive—because
one is conscious of having triumphed over difficulties. When
the ball is lying very well when it has to be played through
the green, the driver is naturally taken, but when the lie is
very low, approaching even to a cuppy character, the brassy
is called for so that an effort may be made to pick the ball
up cleanly and despatch it to the full distance. Again, the
stroke with the brassy must always be a first-class one.
One that is a little inferior to the best may place the player
in serious difficulties. On the other hand, the brassy
seldom flatters its user, though in the hands of a master
player it is perhaps the club that will gain a stroke for
him more often than any other, the last bunker being surmounted and the green reached without any need for a short
approach with an iron club. Therefore the golfer must

make up his mind to attain excellence with the brassy, for mediocrity with it will always handicap him severely.

I have already insisted that the method of play, the stance, the swing, and all the rest of it, should be the same with the brassy as with the driver, and that I do not believe in allowing the slightest difference, the only result of which can be to increase the difficulty of the brassy shot. Given a ball through the green lying fairly well, a level piece of earth to stand upon, and a practically unlimited distance to be played, then the brassy stroke is absolutely identical with the drive, and if the ball is sufficiently well teed, or its lie is clean enough, there is no reason whatever why the driver should not be taken for the stroke. Obviously, however, as the lie which you get for your second shot depends on chance, and must be taken as it is found, there are times when a variation from the standard method of driving will be necessary, and it is to the process of play on these occasions that I shall chiefly direct my remarks in this chapter.

First, however, as to the brassy itself. Its shaft should be slightly stiffer than that of the driver, for it has much harder and rougher work to accomplish, for which the whippy stick of a slender driver would be too frail. In a desperate case, when the ball is lying in an apparently impossible place, the brassy is sometimes taken, in the hope that the best may happen and the situation be saved. That is why the brassy has a sole of brass which will cut away obstructions behind the ball as the head of the club is swept on to it. It often happens that you must hit, as it were, an inch or two behind the ball in order to get it up. Therefore let the shaft be strong. It should be exactly the same length as that of the driver, and not a half inch or an inch shorter, as is often recommended. I do not accept any argument in favour of the shorter shaft. The golfer having driven from the tee needs to be persuaded that he has again what is practically a driving shot to make for his second, and thus to be imbued with that feeling of experience and confidence which makes for success. When the clubs are of the same length there is equal familiarity in using them; but if he is given a shorter club to play his brassy shot with, he feels that there is something of a novel nature to be done, and he wonders how. The face of the brassy should be a little shorter than that of the driver, to permit of its being worked into little depressions in which the ball may be lying; but this variation of the construction of the head should not be carried to excess. Obviously there needs to be more loft on the face of the club than on that of the driver.

The stance for the brassy stroke (see Plate VI.) is generally the same as for the drive, and for reasons already stated my recommendation is that, so far as circumstances will permit,—we are not on the teeing ground when we are playing the brassy,—it should always be the same. If the player feels it to be desirable, he may stand an inch or two nearer to the ball, and perhaps as much behind the ball when he wishes to get well underneath so as to lift it up. The swing should be the same, save that more care should be taken to ensure the grip with the hands being quite tight, for as the club head comes into contact with the turf before taking the ball, the club may turn in the hands and cause a slice or pull unless perfect control be kept over it.

A more important question is, where and how to hit the ball. If it is lying fairly well, it is only necessary to skim the top of the turf and take it cleanly. There is no necessity in such a case, as is too often imagined by inexperienced players, to delve down into the turf so that the ball may be lifted up. If the stroke is played naturally, in the way I have indicated, the loft on the face of the brassy is quite sufficient to give the necessary amount of rise to the ball as it leaves the club. But if, as so often happens, the ball is just a trifle cupped, a different attitude must be adopted towards it. It is now desired that the club should come down to the turf about an inch behind the ball, and with this object in view the eyes should be directed to that point, but as in addressing the ball the said point may be covered by the head of the club, the sight should be set, not really on to the top of the club head, but to an imaginary spot just at the side of the ball, so that when the club is drawn back the turf and the point to look at come into full view and retain the attention of the eyes until the stroke has been made. When the club is swung down on to that spot, its head will plough through the turf and be well under the ball by the time it reaches it, and the desired rise will follow. Swing in the same manner as for the drive. The commonest fault in the playing of this stroke comes from the instinct of the player to try to scoop out the ball from its resting-place, and in obedience to this instinct down goes the right shoulder when the club is coming on to the ball. In the theory of the beginner this course of procedure may seem wise and proper, but he will inevitably be disappointed with the result, and in time he will come to realise that all attempts to scoop must fail. What the club cannot do in the ordinary way when pushed through the turf as I have indicated, cannot be done at all, and it is dangerous to the stroke and dangerous to one's game to trifle with the grand principles.

When the ball is really badly cupped, a moment must be given for inspection and consideration, for the situation is an awkward one. At the first glance an iron club is usually suggested, but there are many times when the golfer prefers to take the brassy if there is a reasonable chance of its proving effective. In a case of this sort the ordinary methods of brassy play must necessarily be departed from. What is wanted is a jabbing-out stroke, and to effect it properly the sight must be set (as before) and the club come down on a spot almost two inches behind the ball. There must be no timidity about hitting the ground or anxiety about the follow-through, for in this case the follow-through, as we have understood it so far, is next to an impossibility, and must not be sought for. In the upward swing the club should be taken out straighter than usual, that is to say, the club head should be kept more closely to the A line, and it should not be carried so far back as if an ordinary shot were being played. Obviously the club must be held with an absolutely firm grip, and for the proper execution of a shot like this the shaft should be exceptionally strong and stiff. If there is the least suggestion of whip in it the ball is not extricated in the same way, and moreover there is sometimes a danger of breaking a slender stick. However, if the golfer only carries one brassy in his bag—and the average player will seldom carry two—this stroke might as well be risked, when the necessity for it arises, with the brassy that is carried for all-round work.

Beyond these few observations there is little more to be said about simple brassy play, although it is so difficult to master thoroughly, so supremely important to a good game, and so full of variety and interest. In the use of no club is constant and strenuous practice better rewarded by improvement in play and strokes gained.

The man with the spoon is coming back again to the links, and this seems to be the most convenient opportunity for a few remarks on play with this club—the baffy, as it is frequently called. One rarely mentions the spoon without being reminded of the difficulty as to the nomenclature of golf which beset a certain Frenchman on his first introduction to the game. "They zay to me," he complained, "'Will you take ze tee?' and I answer, 'Ah, oui,' but they give me no tea, but make a leetle hill with the sand. Then they zay, 'Will you take the spoon?' They have give me no tea, but no matter. I answer again, 'Ah, oui, monsieur,' but they give no spoon either. So I give up the thought of the tea, and play with the new club that they do give to me." However, that is neither here nor there. The baffy, or spoon, is a very useful club, which at one time was a great favourite with many fine players, and if it has of late years been largely superseded by the cleek, it is still most valuable to those players who are not so skilful or reliable with this latter instrument as they would like to be. The baffy demands, for the achievement of such success as it can afford, a fairly good lie, and when this is given it is a tolerably easy club to play with. A good lie is essential because of its wooden head and long face, which prevent it from getting down to the ball when the latter is at all cupped, as the cleek would do, or as the brassy may be made to do when the jab shot is played. The baffy with its long face cannot be burrowed into the turf so easily, nor can it nick in between the ball and the side of the cup, but it makes a bridge over it, as it were, and thus takes the ball right on the top and moves it only a few yards. A cleek would take the turf and the ball and make a good hit. Therefore, when the lie is not reasonably perfect, the baffy is of little use, though in favourable circumstances it is a useful stick. The shaft should be slightly longer than that of the cleek, but appreciably shorter than that of the brassy, and it should be fairly stiff. Its face, as already remarked, is much longer than that of the brassy, and it is given several degrees more loft.

The method of play with the spoon is very much the same as with the brassy, with only such modifications as are apparently necessary. For example, the club being shorter, the feet will be placed slightly nearer to the ball; and although the baffy calls for a fairly long swing, the player will find that he is naturally indisposed to take the club head so far round to his back as he was with the other and longer wooden clubs. In other respects, the upward and downward swing, the grip, the follow-through, and everything else are the same. With many players the club is a particular favourite for the tee shot at short holes of, say, 140 to 160 yards length with a tolerably high bunker guarding the green—a type of hole very frequently encountered, and which simply calls for steady, sure play to get the

bogey 3. The baffy does its work very well in circumstances of this kind, and the ball is brought up fairly
quickly upon the green; but the man who is skilled with
his irons will usually prefer one of them for the stroke, and
will get the coveted 2 as often as the man with the spoon.

CHAPTER VIII

SPECIAL STROKES WITH WOODEN CLUBS

WHICH is the master stroke in golf? That is an engaging question. Is it the perfect drive, with every limb, muscle, and organ of the body working in splendid harmony with the result of despatching the ball well beyond two hundred yards in a straight line from the tee? No, it is not that, for there are some thousands of players who can drive what is to all intents and purposes a perfect ball without any unusual effort. Is it the brassy shot which is equal to a splendid drive, and which, delivering the ball in safety over the last hazard, places it nicely upon the green, absolving the golfer from the necessity of playing any other approach? No, though that is a most creditable achievement. Is it the approach over a threatening bunker on to a difficult green where the ball can hardly be persuaded to remain, yet so deftly has the cut been applied, and so finely has the strength been judged, that it stops dead against the hole, and for a certainty a stroke is saved? This is a most satisfying shot which has in its time won innumerable holes, but it is not the master stroke of golf. Then, is it the putt from the corner of the green across many miniature hills and dales with a winding course over which the ball must travel, often far away from the direct line, but which carries it at last delightfully to the opening into which it sinks just as its strength is ebbing away? We all know the thrilling ecstasy that comes from such a stroke as this, but it has always been helped by a little good luck, and I would not call it the master stroke. There are inferior players who are good putters. Which, then, is the master stroke? I say that it is the ball struck by any club to which a big pull or slice is intentionally applied for the accomplishment of a specific purpose which could not be achieved in any other way, and nothing more exemplifies the curious waywardness of this game of ours than the fact that the stroke which is the confounding and torture of the beginner who does it constantly, he knows not how, but always to his detriment, should later on at times be the most coveted shot of all, and should then be the most difficult of accomplishment. I call it the master shot because, to accomplish it with any certainty and perfection, it is so difficult even to the experienced golfer, because it calls for the most absolute command over the club and every nerve and sinew of the body, and the courageous heart of the true sportsman whom no difficulty may daunt, and because, when properly done, it is a splendid thing to see, and for a certainty results in material gain to the man who played it.

I will try, then, to give the golfers who desire them some hints as to how by diligence and practice they may come to accomplish these master strokes; but I would warn them not to enter into these deepest intricacies of the game until they have completely mastered all ordinary strokes with their driver or brassy and can absolutely rely upon them, and even then the intentional pull and slice should only be attempted when there is no way of accomplishing the purpose which is likely to be equally satisfactory. Thus, when a long brassy

PLATE XIV. DRIVER AND BRASSY. STANCE WHEN PLAYING FOR A SLICE

PLATE XV. DRIVER AND BRASSY. TOP OF THE SWING WHEN PLAYING
FOR A SLICE

PLATE XVI. DRIVER AND BRASSY. FINISH WHEN PLAYING FOR A SLICE

shot to the green is wanted, and one is most completely stymied by a formidable tree somewhere in the foreground or middle distance, the only way to get to the hole is by working round the tree, either from the right or from the left, and this can be done respectively by the pull and the slice. Of the two, the sliced shot is the easier, and is to be recommended when the choice is quite open, though it must not be overlooked that the pulled ball is the longer. The slicing action is not quite so quick and sudden, and does not call for such extremely delicate accuracy as the other, and therefore we will deal with it first.

The golfer should now pay very minute attention to the photographs (Nos. XIV., XV., and XVI.) which were specially taken to illustrate these observations. It will be noticed at once that I am standing very much more behind the ball than when making an ordinary straight drive or brassy stroke, and this is indeed the governing feature of the slicing shot as far as the stance and position of the golfer, preparatory to taking it, are concerned. An examination of the position of the feet, both in the photograph (XIV.) and the accompanying diagram, will show that the left toe is now exactly on the B line, that is to say, it is just level with the ball, while the right foot is $25\frac{1}{2}$ inches away from the same mark, whereas in the case of the ordinary drive it was only 19. At the same time the right foot has been moved very much nearer to the A line, more than 10 inches in fact, although the left is only very slightly nearer. Obviously the general effect of this change of stance is to move the body slightly round to the left. There is no mystery as to how the slice is made. It comes simply as the result of the face of the club being drawn across the ball at the time of impact, and it was precisely in this way that it was accidentally accomplished when it was not wanted. In addressing the ball there should be just the smallest trifle of extra weight thrown on the right leg; but care must be taken that this difference is not exaggerated. The golfer should be scarcely conscious of it.

The grip is made in the usual manner, but there is a very material and all-important difference in the upward swing. In its upward movement the club head now takes a line distinctly outside that which is taken in the case of the ordinary drive, that is to say, it comes less round the body and keeps on the straight line longer. When it is half-way up it should be about two or three inches outside the course taken for the full straight drive. The object of this is plain. The inflexible rule that as the club goes up so will it come down, is in operation again. The club takes the same line on the return, and after it has struck the ball it naturally, pursuing its own direction, comes inside the line taken in the case of the ordinary drive. The result is that at the moment of impact, and for that fractional part of a second during which the ball may be supposed to be clinging to the club, the face of the driver or brassy is being, as it were, drawn across the ball as if cutting a slice out of it. There is no means, so far as I know, of gauging how unthinkably short is the time during which this slicing process is going on, but, as we observed, when we were slicing unintentionally and making the ball curl round sometimes to an angle of ninety degrees before the finish of its flight, it is quite long enough to effect the most radical alteration in what happens afterwards. In that short space of time a spinning motion is put upon the ball, and a curious impulse which appears to have something in common with that given to a boomerang is imparted, which sooner or later take effect. In other respects, when a distant slice is wanted, the same principles of striking the ball and finishing the swing as governed the ordinary drive are to be observed. What I mean by a distant slice is one in which the ball is not asked to go round a corner until it is well on its way, the tree, or whatever it is that has to be circumvented, being half-way out or more, as shown in the diagram on opposite page. This is the most difficult kind of slice to perform, inasmuch as the ball must be kept on a straight line until the object is approached, and then made to curl round it as if by instinct. In such a case the club should be drawn very gradually across, and not so much or so suddenly as when the slice is wanted immediately.

When the tree or thicket that stymies you is only twenty or thirty yards away, the short sliced shot is not only the best but perhaps the only one to play, that is to say, if it is first-class golf that is being practised and there is an opponent who is fighting hard. Take a case for exemplification—one which is of the commonest occurrence. There is a long hole to be played, and some thirty yards from the point which will be reached by a good drive, but well away

TRAJECTORY OF BALL WHEN A DISTANT SLICE IS REQUIRED.

to the right there is a spinny of tall trees. The golfer is badly off the line with his drive, with the result that he now has the trees in the direct line between him and the hole which is the best part of a hundred yards from the other edge of the wood, or say a hundred and forty from where the ball is lying. He might by a wonderfully lofted shot play the ball over the obstacle, but he would have to rise at such an angle that any length would be an impossibility, and he would be short of the green. The only alternative to the slice would be to accept the loss of a stroke as inevitable, play away to the right or left, and then get on to the green with the next one. Thus in either case a valuable stroke is lost, and if the enemy is playing the correct game the loss may be most serious. The short or quick slice comes to the rescue admirably. Turn the ball round the spinny, give it as much length as you can in the circumstances, and if the job has been well done you will be on the green after all with the highly comforting sensation that for once you have proved yourself a golfer of the first degree of skill, and have snatched a half when the hole seemed lost. The diagram here presented illustrates the best possibilities of a quick slice. I can explain in a line exactly how this is done, but I cannot guarantee that my readers will therefore be able to do it until they have practised, and practised, and practised yet again. Instead of hitting the ball with the middle of the

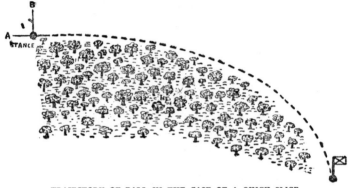

TRAJECTORY OF BALL IN THE CASE OF A QUICK SLICE.

club face as in playing for the distant slice as already explained, hit it slightly nearer the heel of the club. Swing upwards in the same way, and finish in the same way, also. Taking the ball with the heel results in the slice being put on more quickly and in there being more of it, but I need hardly observe that the stroke must be perfectly judged and played, and that there must be no flaw in it anywhere, or disaster must surely follow. As I say, it is not an easy shot to accomplish, but it is a splendid thing to do when wanted, and I strongly recommend the golfer who has gained proficiency in the ordinary way with his wooden clubs, to practise it whenever possible until at length he feels some confidence

PLATE XVII. DRIVER AND BRASSY. PLAYING FOR A PULL. STANCE

PLATE XVIII. DRIVER AND BRASSY. TOP OF THE SWING WHEN PLAYING
FOR A PULL

PLATE XIX. DRIVER AND BRASSY. FINISH WHEN PLAYING FOR A PULL

in playing it. It is one of those strokes which mark the skilled and resourceful man, and which will win for him many a match. Beyond the final admonition to practise, I have only one more piece of advice to give to the golfer who wants to slice when a slice would be useful, and that is in the downward swing he must guard against any inclination to pull in the arms too quickly, the result of his consciousness that the club has to be drawn across the ball. Whatever is necessary in this way comes naturally as the consequence of taking the club head more outwards than usual in the upward swing. Examine the photographs very carefully in conjunction with the study of all the observations that I have made.

Now there is the pulled ball to consider; for there are times when the making of such a shot is eminently desirable. Resort to a slice may be unsatisfactory, or it may be entirely impossible, and one important factor in this question is that the pulled ball is always much longer than the other, in fact it has always so much length in it that many players in driving in the ordinary way from the tee, and desiring only to go straight down the course, systematically play for a pull and make allowances for it in their direction. Now examine Plate XVII. and the accompanying diagram illustrating the stance for the pull, and see how very materially it differs from those which were adopted for the ordinary drive and that in which a slice was asked for. We have moved right round to the front of the ball. The right heel is on the B line and the toe 4 inches away from it, while the left toe is no less than $21\frac{1}{2}$ inches from this line, and therefore so much in front of the ball. At the same time the line of the stance shows that the player is turned slightly away from the direction in which he proposes to play, the left toe being now only $26\frac{1}{2}$ inches away from the A line, while the right toe is 32 inches distant from it. The obvious result of this stance is that the handle of the club is in front of the ball, and this circumstance must be accentuated by the hands being held even slightly more forward than for an ordinary drive. Now they are held forward in front of the head of the club. In the grip there is another point of difference. It is necessary that in the making of this stroke the right hand should do more work than the left, and there- fore the club should be held rather more loosely by the left hand than by its partner. The latter will duly take advantage of this slackness, and will get in just the little extra work that is wanted of it. In the upward swing carry the club head just along the line which it would take for an ordinary drive. The result of all this arrangement, and particularly of the slackness of the left hand and comparative tightness of the right, is that there is a tendency in the downward swing for the face of the club to turn over to some extent, that is, for the top edge of it to be overlapping the bottom edge. This is exactly what is wanted, for, in fact, it is quite necessary that at the moment of impact the right hand should be beginning to turn over in this manner, and if the stroke is to be a success the golfer must see that it does so, but the movement must be made quite smoothly and naturally, for anything in the nature of a jab, such as is common when too desperate efforts are made to turn over an unwilling club, would certainly prove fatal. It follows from what has been happening all the way through, that at the finish of the stroke the right hand, which has matters pretty well its own way, has assumed final ascendancy and is well above the left. Plates XVIII. and XIX. should be carefully examined.

The pulled ball is particularly useful in a cross wind, and this fact leads us naturally to a consideration of the ways and means of playing the long shot with the wooden club to the best advantage when there are winds of various kinds to test the resources of the golfer. Now, however, that this question is raised, I feel it desirable to say without any hesitation that the majority of golfers possess vastly exaggerated notions of the effect of strong cross winds on the flight of their ball. They greatly overestimate the capabilities of a breeze. To judge by their observations on the tee, one concludes that a wind from the left is often sufficient to carry the ball away at an angle of forty-five degrees, and indeed sometimes, when it does take such an exasperating course, and finishes its journey some fifty yards away from the point to which it was desired to despatch it, there is an impatient exclamation from the disappointed golfer, "Confound this wind! Who on earth can play in a hurricane!" or words to that effect. Now I have quite satisfied myself that only a very strong wind indeed will carry a properly driven ball more than a very few yards out of its course, and in proof of this I may say that it is very seldom when I have to deal with a cross wind that I do anything but play straight at the hole without any pulling or slicing or making allowances in any way. If golfers will only bring themselves to ignore the wind, then it in turn will almost entirely ignore their straight ball. When you find your ball at rest the aforementioned forty or fifty yards from the point to which you desired to send it, make up your mind, however unpleasant it may be to do so, that the trouble is due to an unintentional pull or slice, and you may get what consolation you can from the fact that the slightest of these variations from the ordinary drive is seized upon with delight by any wind, and its features exaggerated to an enormous extent. It is quite possible, therefore, that a slice which would have taken the ball only twenty yards from the line when there was no wind, will take it forty yards away with the kind assistance of its friend and ally.

However, I freely admit that there are times when it is advisable to play a fancy shot when there is an excess of wind, and the golfer must judge according to circumstances. Let me give him this piece of advice: very rarely slice as a remedy against a cross wind. Either pull or nothing. If there is a strong wind coming from the right, the immature golfer who has been practising slices argues that this is his chance, and that it is his obvious duty to slice his ball right into the teeth of that wind, so that wind and slice will neutralise each other, and the ball as the result will pursue an even course in the straight line for the flag. A few trials will prove to him that this is a very unsatisfactory business, and after he has convinced himself about it I would recommend him to try pulling the ball and despatching it at once along a line to the right directly against that same wind. When the pull begins to operate, both this and the wind will be working together, and the ball will be carried a much greater length, its straightness depending upon the accuracy of allowance. The diagram explains my meaning.

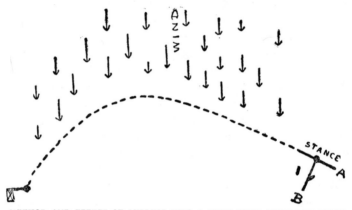

METHOD AND EFFECT OF PULLING INTO A CROSS WIND FROM THE RIGHT.

But I reiterate that the ordinary shots are generally the easiest and best with which to get to the hole. The principle of the golfer should be, and I trust is, that he always wants to reach the hole in the simplest and easiest way, with a minimum of doubt and anxiety about any shot which he is called upon to play, and one usually finds that without these fancy shots one comes to the flag as easily as is possible in all the circumstances. Of course I am writing more particularly with the wind in mind, and am not recommending the ordinary shot when there is a tree or a spinny for a stymie, in contradiction to what I have said earlier in this chapter.

However, there is one kind of wind difficulty which it is certainly necessary to deal with by a departure from the ordinary method of play with the driver or the brassy, and that is when the wind is blowing straight up to the player from the hole, threatening to cut off all his distance. Unless measures are taken to prevent it, a head wind of this description certainly does make play extremely difficult, the comparative shortness of the drive making an unduly long approach shot necessary, or even demanding an extra stroke at long holes in order to reach the green. But, fortunately, we have discovered a means of dealing very satisfactorily with these cases. What we want to do is to keep the ball as low down as possible so as to cheat the wind, for the lower the ball the less opportunity has the breeze of getting to work upon it. A combination of two or three methods is found to be the best for obtaining this low turf-skimming ball, which yet has sufficient driving power in it to keep up until it has achieved a good length. Evidently the first thing to do is to make the tee—if it is a tee shot—rather lower than usual—as low as is consistent with safety and a clean stroke. The player should then stand rather more in front of the ball than if he were playing for an ordinary drive, but this forward position should not by any means be so marked as it was in the stance for the pulled drive. A reference to Plate XX. and the diagram will show that now we have the ball exactly half-way between the toes, each toe being twelve inches to the side of the B line, while both are an inch nearer to the ball than was the case when the ordinary drive was being made. But the most important departure that we make from the usual method of play is in the way we hit the ball. So far we have invariably been keeping our gaze fixed on a point just behind it, desiring that the club shall graze the ground and take the ball rather below the centre. But now it is necessary that the ball shall be struck half-way up and before the club touches the turf. Therefore keep the eye steadily fixed upon that point (see the right-hand ball in the small diagram on page 170) and come down exactly on it. This is not an easy thing to do at first; it requires a vast amount of practice to make sure of hitting the ball exactly at the spot indicated, but the stroke when properly made is an excellent and most satisfying one. After striking the ball in this way, the club head should continue its descent for an instant so that it grazes the turf for the first time two or three inches in front of the spot where the ball was. The passage of the club through the ball, as it were, is the same as in the case of the push shot with the cleek, and therefore reference may usefully be made to the diagram on page 106, which illustrates it. A natural result of the stance and the way the stroke is played is that the arms are more extended than usual after the impact, and in the follow-through the club head keeps nearer to the turf. So excellent are the results obtained when the stroke is properly played, that there are many fine players, having a complete command over it, who systematically play it from the tee whether there is a wind to contend against or not, simply because of the length and accuracy which they secure from it. Braid is one of them. If the teeing ground offers any choice of gradient, a tee with a hanging lie should be selected, and the ball is then kept so low for the first forty or fifty yards that it is practically impossible for the wind to take it off the line, for it must be remembered that even when the wind comes dead from the front, if there is the slightest slice or pull on the ball to start with, it will be increased to a disconcerting extent before the breeze has done with it.

When the wind is at the back of the player blowing hard towards the hole, the situation presents no difficulty and needs very little consideration. The object in this case is to lift the ball well up towards the clouds so that it may get the full benefit of the wind, though care must be taken that plenty of driving length is put into the stroke at the same time. Therefore tee the ball rather higher than usual, and bring your left foot more in a line with it than you would

PLATE XX. DRIVER AND BRASSY. STANCE FOR A LOW BALL AGAINST
THE WIND

PLATE XXI. DRIVER AND BRASSY. STANCE FOR A HIGH BALL WITH
THE WIND

if you were playing in the absence of wind, at the same time moving both feet slightly nearer the ball. Plate XXI. will make the details of this stance quite clear. The ball being teed unusually high, the golfer must be careful not to make any unconscious allowance for the fact in his downward swing, and must see that he wipes the tee from the face of the earth when he makes the stroke.

Though in my explanations of these various strokes I have generally confined myself to observations as to how they may be made from the tee, they are strokes for the driver and the brassy,—for all cases, that is, where the long ball is wanted from the wooden club under unusual circumstances of difficulty. Evidently in many cases they will be more difficult to accomplish satisfactorily from a brassy lie and with the shorter faced club than when the golfer has everything in his favour on the teeing ground, and it must be left to his skill and discretion as to the use he will make of them when playing through the green.

CHAPTER IX

THE CLEEK AND DRIVING MASHIE

A test of the golfer—The versatility of the cleek—Different kinds of cleeks—
Points of the driving mashie — Difficulty of continued success with it —
The cleek is more reliable — Ribbed faces for iron clubs — To prevent
skidding—The stance for an ordinary cleek shot—The swing—Keeping
control over the right shoulder—Advantages of the three-quarter cleek shot
—The push shot—My favourite stroke—The stance and the swing—The
way to hit the ball—Peculiar advantages of flight from the push stroke—
When it should not be attempted—The advantage of short swings as against
full swings with iron clubs—Playing for a low ball against the wind—A
particular stance—Comparisons of the different cleek shots—General observations and recommendations—Mistakes made with the cleek.

I T is high time we came to consider the iron clubs that
are in our bag. His play with the irons is a fine test of
the golfer. It calls for extreme skill and delicacy, and the
man who is surest with these implements is generally surest
of his match. The fathers of golf had no clubs with metal
heads, and for a long time after they came into use there was
a lingering prejudice against them; but in these days there is
no man so bold as to say that any long hole can always be
played so well with wood all through as with a mixture of
wood and iron in the proper proportions. It may be, as we
are often told, that the last improvement in iron clubs has
not yet been made; but I must confess that the tools now at
the disposal of the golfer come as near to my ideal of the
best for their purpose as I can imagine any tools to do, and
no golfer is at liberty to blame the clubmaker for his own
incapacity on the links, though it may frequently happen
that his choice and taste in the matter of his golfing goods

are at fault. There are many varieties of every class of iron clubs, and their gradations of weight, of shape, of loft, and of all their other features, are delicate almost to the point of invisibility ; but the old golfer who has an affection for a favourite club knows when another which he handles differs from it to the extent of a single point in these gradations. Some golfers have spent a lifetime in the search for a complete set of irons, each one of which was exactly its owner's ideal, and have died with their task still unaccomplished. Happy then is the player who in his early days has irons over all of which he has obtained complete mastery, and which he can rely upon to do their duty, and do it well, when the match is keen and their owner is sorely pressed by a relentless opponent.

First of these iron clubs give me the cleek, the most powerful and generally useful of them all, though one which is much abused and often called hard names. If you wish, you may drive a very long ball with a cleek, and if the spirit moves you so to do you may wind up the play at the hole by putting with it too. But these after all are what I may call its unofficial uses, for the club has its own particular duties, and for the performance of them there is no adequate substitute. Therefore, when a golfer says, as misguided golfers sometimes do, that he cannot play with the cleek, that he gets equal or superior results with other clubs, and that therefore he has abandoned it to permanent seclusion in the locker, you may shake your head at him, for he is only deceiving himself. Like the wares of boastful advertisers, there is no other which is "just as good," and if a golfer finds that he can do no business with his cleek, the sooner he learns to do it the better will it be for his game.

And there are many different kinds of cleeks, the choice from which is to a large extent to be regulated by experiment and individual fancy. Some men fancy one type, and some another, and each of them obtains approximately the same result from his own selection, but it is natural that a driving cleek, which is specially designed for obtaining length, having a fairly straight face and plenty of weight, will generally deliver the ball further than those which are more lofted and lighter. Making a broad classification, there are driving cleeks, ordinary cleeks, pitching cleeks, and cleeks with the weight in the centre. For the last-named variety I have little admiration, excellent as many people consider them to be. If the ball is hit with absolute accuracy in the centre of the club's face every time, all is well; but it is not given to many golfers to be so marvellously certain. Let the point of contact be the least degree removed from the centre of the face, where the weight is massed, and the result will usually be disquieting, for, among other things, there is in such cases a great liability for the club to turn in the hands of the player.

As an alternative to the cleek the driving mashie has achieved considerable popularity. It is undoubtedly a most useful club, and is employed for the same class of work as the cleek, and, generally speaking, may take its place. The distinctive features of the driving mashie are that it has a deeper face than that of the cleek, and that this depth increases somewhat more rapidly from the heel to the toe. By reason of this extra depth it is often a somewhat heavier club, and there is rather less loft on it than there is on the average cleek. When you merely look at a driving mashie it certainly seems as if it may be the easier club to use, but long experience will prove that this is not the case. In this respect I think the driving cleek is preferable to either the spoon or the driving mashie, particularly when straightness is an essential, as it usually is when any of these clubs is being handled. It frequently happens that the driving mashie is used to very good effect for a while after it has first been purchased; but I have noticed over and over again that when once you are off your play with it—and that time must come, as with all other clubs—it takes a long time to get back to form with it again,—so long, indeed, that the task is a most painful and depressing one. Five years ago I

myself had my day with the driving mashie, and I played so
well with it that at that time I did not even carry a cleek.
I used to drive such a long ball with this instrument, that
when I took it out of my bag to play with it, my brother
professionals used to say, "There's Harry with his driver
again"; and I remember that when on one occasion Andrew
Kirkaldy was informed that I was playing a driving mashie
shot, he was indignant, and exclaimed, "Mashie! Nay,
man, thon's no mashie. It's jest a driver." Then the day
came when I found to my sorrow that I was off my driving
mashie, and not all the most laborious practice or the fiercest
determination to recover my lost form with it was rewarded
with any appreciable amount of success. After a time I got
back to playing it in some sort of fashion, but I was never
so good with it again as to justify me in sticking to it in
preference to the cleek, so since then I have practically
abandoned it. This, I am led to believe, is a fairly common
experience among golfers, so the moral would seem to be,
that you should make the most of your good days with the
driving mashie, that at the first sign of decaying power with
the club another and most thorough trial should be given to
the deserted cleek, and that at this crisis that club should be
persevered with in preference to the tool which has failed.
The driving mashie usually demands a good lie if it is to be
played with any amount of success. When, in addition to
the lie being cuppy, the turf is at all soft and spongy—and
these two circumstances are frequently combined—the ball
very often skids off the face of the club, chiefly because of
its perpendicularity, instead of rising nicely from the moment
of impact as it would do when carefully played by a suitable
cleek. Of course if the turf is firm there is much greater
chance of success with the driving mashie than if it is loose.
But one finds by long experience that the cleek is the best
and most reliable club for use in all these difficult circumstances. Even the driving cleeks have a certain amount of
loft on their faces which enables them to get nicely under

the ball, so that it rises with just sufficient quickness after being struck. And there is far less skidding with the cleek.

This question of skidding calls to mind another feature of iron clubs generally, and those which are designed for power and length in particular, which has not in the past received all the consideration that it deserves. I am about to speak of the decided advantage which in my opinion accrues from the use of iron clubs with ribbed faces in preference to those which are smooth and plain. Some golfers of the sceptical sort have a notion that the ribs or other marking are merely ornamental, or, at the best, give some satisfaction to the fancy; but these are certainly not their limits. The counteraction to skidding by the ribbed face is undoubtedly very great, and there are certain circumstances in which I consider it to be quite invaluable. Suppose the ball is lying fairly low in grass. It is clear to the player that his iron club, as it approaches it, will be called upon to force its way through some of the grass, and that as it comes into contact with the ball many green blades will inevitably be crushed between the face of the club and the ball, with the result, in the case of the plain-faced club, that further progress in the matter of the follow-through will be to some extent impeded. But when the face of the club is ribbed, at the instant of contact between ball and club the grass that comes between is cut through by the ribs, and thus there is less waste of the power of the swing. The difference may be only small; but whether it is an ounce or two or merely a few pennyweights, it is the trifle of this kind that tells. And, of course, the tendency to skid is greater than ever when the grass through the green, or where the ball has to be played from, is not so short as it ought to be, and the value of the ribbed face is correspondingly increased.

Now we may examine the peculiarities of play with the cleek, the term for the remainder of this chapter being taken to include the driving mashie. It will be found that the

PLATE XXII. FULL SHOT WITH THE CLEEK. STANCE

PLATE XXIII. FULL SHOT WITH THE CLEEK. TOP OF THE SWING

PLATE XXIV. FULL SHOT WITH THE CLEEK. FINISH

PLATE XXV. FULL SHOT WITH THE CLEEK. FINISH

shaft of the cleek is usually some two to four inches shorter than the driver, and this circumstance in itself is sufficient to demand a considerable modification in the stance and method of use.   I now invite the reader to examine the photograph and diagram of the ordinary cleek shot (Plate XXII.), and to compare it when necessary with Plate VI., representing the stance for the drive.   It will be found that the right foot is only 21½ inches from the A line as against 27½ when driving, and the left toe is only 24 inches from it as compared with 34.   From this it appears that the left foot has been brought more forward into line with the right, but it is still behind it, and it is essential that it should be so, in order that the arms may be allowed a free passage through after the stroke.   The feet remain about the same distance apart, but it should be noticed that the whole body has been moved forward some four inches in relation to the ball, the distances of the right and left toes from the B line being respectively 19 and 9½ inches in the case of the drive and 15 and 12 in that of the cleek shot.   The stance in the case of all iron clubs should be studied with great care, for a half inch the wrong way seems to have a much greater power for evil than it does in the case of wooden clubs.

The handle of the cleek is gripped in the same manner as the driver, but perhaps a little more tightly, for, as the club comes severely into contact with the turf, one must guard against the possibility of its turning in the hands. Ground the club behind the ball exactly in the place and in the way that you intend to hit it.   There is a considerable similarity between the swings with the driver and the cleek. Great care must be taken when making the backward swing that the body is not lifted upwards, as there is a tendency for it to be.   When pivoting on the left toe, the body should bend slightly and turn from the waist, the head being kept perfectly still.   Thus it comes about that the golfer's system appears to be working in three independent sections—first from the feet to the hips, next from the hips to the neck, and then the head. The result of this combination of movements is that at the top of the swing, when everything has happened as it should do, the eyes will be looking over the top of the left shoulder—just as when at the top of driving swing. The body should not be an inch higher than when the address was made, and the right leg will now be straight and stiff. When the club is held tightly, there will be practically no danger of overswinging; but, as with the drive, the pressure with the palms of the hands may be a little relaxed at the top. The backward swing must not be so rapid that control of the club is in any degree lost, and once again the player must be warned against allowing any pause at the top. In coming down the cleek should gain its speed gradually, so that at the time of impact it is travelling at its fastest pace, and then, if the toes are right and the shoulders doing their duty, the follow-through will almost certainly be performed properly. The right shoulder must be carefully watched lest it drops too much or too quickly. The club must, as it were, be in front of it all the way. If the shoulder gets in front, a sclaffed ball is almost sure to be the result, the club coming into contact with the turf much too soon. If the stroke is finished correctly, the body will then be facing the flag.

So much, for the time being, for the full shot with the cleek. Personally, however, I do not favour a really full shot either with the cleek or any other iron club. When the limit of capability is demanded with this or most other iron clubs in the bag, it is time to consider whether a wooden instrument should not be employed. Therefore I very seldom play the full cleek shot, but limit myself to one which may be said to be slightly above the three-quarters. This is usually quite sufficient for all purposes of length, and it is easier with this limit of swing to keep the wrists and the club generally more under control. Little more can be said by way of printed instruction regarding the ordinary cleek shot, which is called for when the distance to be played falls short of a full brassy, or, on the other hand, when the lie is of too cuppy a character to render the use of the brassy possible with any amount of safety.

Many players, however, who are young in experience, and some who are older too, seem to imagine that the simplest stroke, as just described, is the limit of the resources of the cleek, and never give it credit for the versatility which it undoubtedly possesses. There is another shot with the cleek which is more difficult than that we have just been discussing, one which it will take many weeks of arduous practice to master, but which, in my opinion, is one of the most valuable and telling shots in golf, and that is the push which is a half shot. Of all the strokes that I like to play, this is my favourite. It is a half shot, but as a matter of fact almost as much length can be obtained with it as in any other way. It is a somewhat peculiar shot, and must be played very exactly. In the first place, either a shorter cleek (about two inches shorter, and preferably with a little more loft than the driving cleek possesses) should be used, or the other one must be gripped lower down the handle. A glance at Plate XXVI. and the diagram in the corner will show that the stance is taken much nearer to the ball than when an ordinary cleek shot was being played, that particularly the right foot is nearer, and that the body and feet have again been moved a trifle to the left. Moreover, it is recommended that in the address the hands should be held a little more forward than usual. In this half shot the club is not swung so far back, nor is the follow-through continued so far at the finish. To make a complete success of this stroke, the ball must be hit in much the same manner as when a low ball was wanted in driving against the wind. In playing an ordinary cleek shot, the turf is grazed before the ball in the usual manner; but to make this half or push shot perfectly, the sight should be directed to the centre of the ball, and the club should be brought directly on to it (exactly on the spot marked on the diagram on

page 170). In this way the turf should be grazed for the
first time an inch or two on the far side of the ball. The
diagram on this page shows the passage of the club through
the ball, as it were, exactly. Then not only is the ball kept
low, but certain peculiarities are imparted to its flight, which
are of the utmost value when a half shot with the cleek
is called for. Not only may the ball be depended upon
never to rise above a certain height, but, having reached its
highest point, it seems to come down very quickly, travelling
but a few yards more, and having very little run on it
when it reaches the turf again. When this shot is once
mastered, it will be found that these are very valuable
peculiarities, for a long approach shot can be gauged with
splendid accuracy. The ball is sent forwards and upwards
until it is almost overhanging the green, and then down it
comes close to the pin. I admit that when the ball is hit
in this way the shot is made rather difficult—though not so

difficult as it looks—and, of
course, it is not absolutely
imperative that this method

THE PUSH SHOT WITH THE CLEEK.   should be followed. Some

good players make the stroke in the same way as the
full shot, so far as hitting the ball is concerned, but in
doing so they certainly lose the advantages I have pointed
out, and stand less chance of scoring through a finely placed
ball. I may remark that personally I play not only my
half cleek stroke but all my cleek strokes in this way, so
much am I devoted to the qualities of flight which are
thereby imparted to the ball, and though I do not insist
that others should do likewise in all cases, I am certainly of
opinion that they are missing something when they do not
learn to play the half shot in this manner. The greatest
danger they have to fear is that in their too conscious
efforts to keep the club clear of the ground until after the
impact, they will overdo it and simply top the ball, when,
of course, there will be no flight at all. I suggest that when

PLATE XXVI.   THE PUSH SHOT WITH THE CLEEK.   STANCE

PLATE XXVII. THE PUSH SHOT WITH THE CLEEK. TOP OF THE SWING

PLATE XXVIII. THE PUSH SHOT WITH THE CLEEK. FINISH

PLATE XXIX. A LOW BALL (AGAINST WIND) WITH THE CLEEK. STANCE

PLATE XXX. A LOW BALL (AGAINST WIND) WITH THE CLEEK.
TOP OF THE SWING

PLATE XXXI. A LOW BALL (AGAINST WIND) WITH THE CLEEK. FINISH.

this stroke is being practised a close watch should be kept over the forearms and wrists, from which most of the work is wanted. The arms should be kept well in, and the wrists should be very tight and firm. It should be pointed out that there are some circumstances in which it is not safe to attempt to play this stroke. When the club comes to the ground after impact with the ball, very little turf should be taken. It is enough if the grass is shaved well down to the roots. But if the turf is soft and yielding, the club head will have an inevitable tendency to burrow, with the result that it would be next to impossible to follow-through properly with the stroke, and that the ball would skid off, generally to the right. The shot is therefore played to greatest advantage on a hard and fairly dry course.

Many people are inclined to ask why, instead of playing a half shot with the cleek, the iron is not taken and a full stroke made with it, which is the way that a large proportion of good golfers would employ for reaching the green from the same distance. For some reason which I cannot explain, there seems to be an enormous number of players who prefer a full shot with any club to a half shot with another, the result being the same or practically so. Why is it that they like to swing so much and waste so much power, unmindful of the fact that the shorter the swing the greater the accuracy? The principle of my own game, and that which I always impress upon others when I have an opportunity, is, "Reach the hole in the easiest way you can." The easier way is generally the surer way. When, therefore, there is a choice between a full shot with one club or a half shot with another, I invariably ask the caddie for the instrument with which to make the half shot. Hence, apart from the advantageous peculiarities of the stroke which I have pointed out, I should always play the half cleek shot in preference to the full iron, because, to my mind, it is easier and safer, and because there is less danger of the ball skidding off the club. In the same way I prefer a half iron shot to a full one with the mashie. If the golfer attains any proficiency with the stroke, he will probably be very much enamoured of it, and will think it well worth the trouble of carrying a club specially for the purpose, at all events on all important occasions.

There is another variety of cleek shot which calls for separate mention. It is played when a low ball is wanted to cut its way through a head wind, and for the proper explanation of this useful stroke I have supplied a special series of photographs from which it may be studied to advantage. As will be seen from them, this stroke is, to all intents and purposes, a modified half or push stroke, the most essential difference being in the stance. The feet are a trifle nearer the ball and considerably more forward, my right heel as a matter of fact being only $2\frac{1}{2}$ inches from the B line. Take a half swing, hit the ball before the turf as in the case of the push, and finish with the shaft of the club almost perpendicular, the arms and wrists being held in severe subjection throughout. The ball skims ahead low down like a swallow, and by the time it begins to rise and the wind to act upon it, it has almost reached its destination, and the wind is now welcome as a brake.

Having thus dealt with these different cleek shots separately, I think some useful instruction may be obtained from a comparison of them, noting the points of difference as they are set forth in the photographs. An examination of the pictures will at once suggest that there is much more in the stance than had been suspected. In the case of the full cleek shot it is noticeable that the stance is opener than in any of the others, and that the body is more erect. The object of this is to allow freedom of the swing without altering the position of the body during the upward movement. I mean particularly that the head is not so likely to get out of its place as it would be if the body had been more bent while the address was being made. It ought not to be, but is the case, that when pivoting on the left foot during the progress of a long upward swing, there is a frequent inclination, as already pointed out, to raise the body, so that the position of the latter at the top of the swing is altogether wrong, and has to be corrected in the downward swing before the ball is reached. When, as often happens, this is done too suddenly, a sclaff is the result. Therefore an obvious recommendation is to stand at the ball with the same amount of erectness as there will be at the top of the swing. And remember that when you pivot on the left toe, the lift that there is here should not spread along to the head and shoulders, but should be absorbed, as it were, at the waist, which should bend inwards and turn round on the hips. Once the head has taken its position, it should never move again until the ball has been struck. Mind that you do not fall away from the ball when the club is about to come into contact with it. I have observed a considerable tendency in that direction on the part of many young players. I have pressed several of these points home in other places, but the success of the stroke is so bound up with a proper observation of them that I think they cannot be too frequently or too strongly insisted upon.

If we take one more glance at all the different cleek stroke photographs, we shall see that in each case the toes are turned well outwards. I find that unless they take this position the player has not the same freedom for turning upon them. In the case of full shots the weight is more evenly divided upon both feet than in the case of others. Thus, when the stance for a half or three-quarter cleek shot is taken, the weight of the body falls more on the right leg than on the left. As you have not to swing so far back, you are able to maintain this position. You could not do so if a full stroke were being taken; hence you would not then adopt it. Again, one allows the wrists and muscles less play in the case of half shots than in full ones. There is more stiffness all round. This, however, must not be taken to suggest that even in the case of the full shot there is any looseness at the wrists. If there were, it would be most in evidence just when it would be most fatal, that is to say, at the moment of impact. The wrists must always be kept severely under control. It will also be noticed from the photographs, that at the top of the swings for both the full shot and the half shot the body is in much the same position, but when the low shot against the wind is being played it is pushed a little forward. I mention these details by way of suggesting how much can be discovered from a close and attentive study of these photographs only. Little things like these, when not noticed and attended to, may bother a player for many weeks; while, on the other hand, he may frequently find out from a scrutiny of the pictures and diagrams the faults which have baffled him on the links. In this connection the "How not to do it" photographs should be of particular value to the player who is in trouble with his cleek. Look at the faulty stance and address in Plate XXXII. At the first glance you can see that this is not a natural stance; the player is cramped and uncomfortable. The grip is altogether wrong. The hands are too far apart, and the right hand is too much under the shaft. The body would not hold its position during the swing, and in any case a correct swing would be impossible. Yet this photograph does not exaggerate the bad methods of some players. In Plate XXXIII. we have the player in a stance which is nearly as bad as before; but it is evident that in this case the body has been lifted during the upward swing, and the left hand is rather too much on the top of the shaft.

Evidently it will take some time to bring the cleek completely into subjection. There is, of course, no such thing as an all-round club in golf, but the nearest to it is this one, and the man who is master of it is rarely in a serious difficulty. He can even play a respectable round with a cleek alone, and there is no form of practice less

PLATE XXXII. FAULTY PLAY WITH THE CLEEK

The stance in this case is very bad. The whole of the weight is on the left leg instead of being evenly divided. The hands are too far apart, and the right hand is far too much underneath the shaft. Moreover the player is bending too far towards his ball. He must stand up to his work. The almost certain consequence of this attitude is a foozle.

PLATE XXXIII. FAULTY PLAY WITH THE CLEEK

Some very common and very fatal defects in the swing are illustrated here. It is evident that both the body and the head have been lifted as the club has been swung up, and the whole arrangement is thus thrown out of gear. Both hands are in wrong positions (compare with XXIII) with the result that the toe of the club is pointing sideways instead of to the ground. Result—the player is likely to strike anything except the ball.

PLATE XXXIV. FAULTY PLAY WITH THE CLEEK

Here at the finish of the stroke the position of the arms is exceedingly bad. They are bent and huddled up towards the body, plainly indicating that they did not go through with the ball. There was no power in this stroke, nothing to send the ball along. Therefore length was impossible, and a foozle was quite likely. Compare with XXIV.

PLATE XXXV. FAULTY PLAY WITH THE CLEEK

The mistakes here are numerous, but less pronounced than before. The stance is not accurate, but it is not bad enough to be fatal in itself. The player is very uncomfortable with his left arm, which is in a badly cramped position. The hands are too far apart and the left wrist is too high. The result is rather doubtful. Quite possibly the ball will be pulled. Anyhow a good shot is out of the question.

PLATE XXXVI. FAULTY PLAY WITH THE CLEEK

In the case of this finish the player has fallen away from the ball instead of go'ng forward with it as in XXIV. It is evident that the club has been drawn across the ball. Result—a slice.

wearisome, more diverting, or more eminently valuable and instructive, than that which is to be obtained on a fine afternoon by taking out the cleek and doing a round of the course with it from the tee to the hole in every case, and making use of all the different strokes that I have described in the course of this chapter.

CHAPTER X

PLAY WITH THE IRON

The average player's favourite club—Fine work for the iron—Its points—The right and the wrong time for play with it—Stance measurements—A warning concerning the address—The cause of much bad play with the iron—The swing—Half shots with the iron—The regulation of power—Features of erratic play—Forced and checked swings—Common causes of duffed strokes—Swings that are worthless.

WHEN I mention that useful iron-headed club that goes by the simple name of iron, I am conscious that I bring forward a subject that is dear to the hearts of many golfers who have not yet come to play with certainty with all their instruments. For the iron is often the golfer's favourite club, and it has won this place of affection in his mind because it has been found in the course of long experience that it plays him fewer tricks than any of the others—that it is more dependable. This may be to some extent because with the average golfer such fine work is seldom required from the simple iron as is wanted from other clubs from time to time. The distance to be covered is always well within the capabilities of the club, or it would not be employed, and the average golfer of whom we speak, who has still a handicap of several strokes, is usually tolerably well satisfied if with it he places the ball anywhere on the green, from which point he will be enabled to hole out in the additional regulation two strokes. And the green is often enough a large place, so the iron is fortunate in its task. But it goes without saying that by those who have the skill for it, and sufficiently realise the possibilities of all their tools, some of the finest work in golf may be done with the iron. When it is called for the player is within easy reach of the hole. The really long work has been accomplished, and the prime consideration now is that of accuracy. Therefore the man who feels himself able to play for the pin and not merely for the green, is he who is in the confidence of his iron and knows that there are great things to be done with it.

The fault I have to find with the iron play of most golfers is that it comes at the wrong time. I find them lunging out with all their power at full shots with their irons when they might be far better employed in effecting one of those pretty low shots made with the cleek at the half swing. It is not in the nature of things that the full iron should be as true as the half cleek, where there is such a reserve of strength, and the body, being less in a state of strain, the mind can be more concentrated on straightness and the accurate determination of length. I suspect that this full shot is so often played and the preference for the iron is established, not merely because it nearly always does its work tolerably satisfactorily, but because in the simple matter of looks there is something inviting about the iron. It has a fair amount of loft, and it is deeper in the face than the cleek, and at a casual inspection of its points it seems an easy club to play with. On the other hand, being a little nearer to the hole, the average player deserts his iron for the mashie much sooner than I care to do. Your 10-handicap man never gives a second thought as to the tool he shall use when he has arrived within a hundred yards of the hole. Is he not then approaching in deadly earnest, and has he not grown up in golf with a definite understanding that there is one thing, and one only, with which to give the true artistic finish to the play through the green? Therefore out of his bag comes the mashie, which, if it could speak, would surely protest that it is a delicate club with some fine breeding in it, and that it was never meant to do this slogging with long swings that comes properly in the departments of its iron friends. I seldom use a mashie until I am within eighty yards of the hole. Up to that point I keep my iron in action. Much better, I say, is a flick with the iron than a thump with the mashie.

The iron that I most commonly use is nearly two inches shorter than my cleek. It follows that the stance is taken slightly nearer to the ball; but reason for moving closer to our A line is to be found in what I might describe as the more upright lie of an iron as compared with a cleek. When the lower edge of the club is laid evenly upon the level turf, the stick will usually be found to be a trifle more vertical than in the case of the cleek, and therefore for the proper preservation of the natural lie of the club the golfer must come forward to it. Consequently I find that when I have taken my stance for an iron shot (Plate XXXVII.), my right foot has come forward no less than $8\frac{1}{2}$ inches from the point at which it rested when I was taking a tolerably full shot with the cleek. The left foot is $3\frac{1}{2}$ inches nearer. Thus the body has been very slightly turned in the direction of the hole, and while the feet are a trifle closer together, the ball is rather nearer to the right toe than it was when being addressed by the cleek. Those are the only features of the stance, and the only one I really insist upon is the nearness to the ball. The commonest defect to be found with iron play is the failure to address the ball and play the stroke through with the sole of the club laid evenly upon the ground from toe to heel. When the man is too far from the ball, it commonly follows that the blade of the club comes down on to the turf heel first. Then something that was not bargained for happens. It may be that the ball was taken by the centre of the iron's face, and that the upward and downward swings and the follow-through were all perfection, and yet it has shot away to one side or the other with very little flight in it. And perhaps for a week or two, while this is constantly happening, the man is wondering why. When, happily, the

PLATE XXXVII. FULL IRON SHOT. STANCE

PLATE XXXVIII. FULL IRON SHOT. TOP OF THE SWING

PLATE XXXIX. FULL IRON SHOT. FINISH

PLATE XL. PLAY WITH THE IRON FOR A LOW BALL (AGAINST WIND).
STANCE

PLATE XLI. PLAY WITH THE IRON FOR A LOW BALL (AGAINST WIND).
TOP OF THE SWING

PLATE XLII. PLAY WITH THE IRON FOR A LOW BALL (AGAINST WIND).
FINISH

reason is at last made apparent, the man goes forward to its correction with that workmanlike thoroughness which characterises him always and everywhere, and lo! the erring ball still pursues a line which does not lead to the green. At the same time it may very likely be noticed that the slight sense of twisting which was experienced by the hands on the earlier occasion is here again.   The truth is that the first fault was over-corrected, and the toe of the club, instead of the heel, has this time had the turf to itself while the ball was being removed. Obviously, when either of these faults is committed, the club head is twisted, and nothing is more impossible than to get in a perfect iron shot when these things are done.   I am making much ado about what may seem after all to be an elementary fault, but a long experience of the wayward golfer has made it clear to me that it is not only a common fault, which is accountable for much defective play with the iron, but that it is often unsuspected, and lurks undiscovered and doing its daily damage for weeks or even months. The sole of the iron must pass over the turf exactly parallel with it.

There is nothing new to say about the swing of the iron. It is the same as the swing of the cleek.   For a full iron the swing is as long as for the full cleek, and for the half iron it is as long as for the half cleek, and both are made in the same way.   The arms and wrists are managed similarly, and I would only offer the special advice that the player should make sure that he finishes with his hands well up, showing that the ball has been taken easily and properly, as he may see them in the photograph (Plate XXXIX.), which in itself tells a very good story of comfortable and free play with the club, which is at the same time held in full command.   The whole of the series of photographs of iron shots brings out very exactly the points that I desire to illustrate, and I cannot do better than refer my readers to them.

When it is desired to play a half iron shot that will give a low ball for travelling against the wind, the same methods may be pursued as when playing the corresponding shot with the cleek.

When one comes to play with the iron, and is within, say, 130 yards of the hole, the regulation of the precise amount of power to be applied to the ball becomes a matter of the first importance, and one that causes unceasing anxiety. I feel, then, that it devolves upon me to convey a solemn warning to all players of moderate experience, that the distance the ball will be despatched is governed entirely by the extent of the backward swing of the club. When a few extra yards are wanted, put an additional inch or two on to the backward swing, and so on; but never, however you may satisfy yourself with excuses that you are doing a wise and proper thing, attempt to force the pace at which the club is travelling in the downward swing, or, on the other hand, attempt to check it. I believe in the club being brought down fairly quickly in the case of all iron shots; but it should be the natural speed that comes as the result of the speed and length of the upward swing, and the gain in it should be even and continuous throughout. Try, therefore, always to swing back at the same rate, and to come on to the ball naturally and easily afterwards. Of course, in accordance with the simple laws of gravity and applied force, the farther back you swing the faster will your club be travelling when it reaches the ball, and the harder will be the hit. Therefore, if the golfer will learn by experience exactly how far back he should swing with a certain club in order to get a certain distance, and will teach himself to swing to just the right length and with always the same amount of force applied, the rest is in the hands of Nature, and can be depended upon with far more certainty than anything which the wayward hands and head of the golfer can accomplish. This is a very simple and obvious truth, but it is one of the main principles of golf, and one that is far too often neglected. How frequently do you see a player take a full swing when a half shot is all that is wanted, and even when his instinct tells him that the half shot is the game.   What happens?   The instinct assumes the upper hand at the top of the swing, and the man with the guilty conscience deliberately puts a brake on to his club as it is coming down. He knows that he has gone too far back, and he is anxious then to reduce the speed of the club by unnatural means. But the principles of golf are not to be so lightly tampered with in this manner, and it affords the conscientious player some secret satisfaction to observe that very rarely indeed is anything of a success made of shots of this sort.   A duffed stroke is the common result.   In such cases the swing is of no more value than if it had not taken place at all.

CHAPTER XI

APPROACHING WITH THE MASHIE

The great advantage of good approach play—A fascinating club—Characteristics of a good mashie—Different kinds of strokes with it—No purely wrist shot —Stance and grip—Position of the body—No pivoting on the left toe— The limit of distance—Avoid a full swing—The half iron as against the full mashie—The swing—How not to loft—On scooping the ball—Taking a divot—The running-up approach—A very valuable stroke—The club to use —A tight grip with the right hand—Peculiarities of the swing—The calculation of pitch and run—The application of cut and spin—A stroke that is sometimes necessary—Standing for a cut—Method of swinging and hitting the ball—The chip on to the green—Points of the jigger.

THERE is an old saying that golf matches are won on the putting greens, and it has often been established that this one, like many other old sayings, contains an element of truth, but is not entirely to be relied upon. In playing a hole, what is one's constant desire and anxiety from the tee shot to the last putt? It is to effect, somehow or other, that happy combination of excellent skill with a little luck as will result practically in the saving of a whole stroke, which will often mean the winning of the hole. The prospect of being able to exercise this useful economy is greatest when the mashie is taken in hand. The difference between a good drive and a poor one is not very often to be represented by anything like half a stroke. But the difference between a really good mashie approach stroke and a bad one is frequently at least a stroke, and I have known it to be more. Between the brilliant and the average it is one full stroke. Of course a stroke is saved and a hole very often won when a long putt is holed, but in cases of this kind the proportion of luck to skill is much too great to give perfect satisfaction to the conscientious golfer, however delightful the momentary sensation may be. When a man is playing his mashie well, he is leaving himself very little to do on the putting green, so that, if occasionally he does miss a putt, he can afford to do so, having constantly been getting so near to the flag that one putt has sufficed. When the work with the mashie is indifferent or poor, the player is frequently left with long putts to negotiate, and is in a fever of anxiety until the last stroke has been made on the green. It often happens at these times that the putting also is poor, and when this is the case a sad mess is made of the score. Therefore, while I say that he is a happy and lucky man who is able constantly to save his game on the putting greens, happier by far is he who is not called upon to do so. In this way the skilled golfer generally finds the mashie the most fascinating club to play with, and there are few pleasures in the game which can equal that of laying the ball well up to the pin from a distance of many yards. One expects to get much nearer to it with this last of the irons than with the cleek or the simple iron, and the more nearly the flag is approached the greater the skill and experience of the player. Here, indeed, is a field for lifelong practice, with a telling advantage accruing from each slight improvement in play.

First a word as to the club, for there is scarcely an article in the golfer's kit which presents more scope for variety of taste and style. Drivers and brassies vary a little, cleeks and irons differ much, but mashies are more unlike each other than any of them. So much depends upon this part of the game, and so much upon the preferences and peculiarities of the player, that it is unlikely that the first mashie in which he invests will go alone with him through his experience as a golfer. To his stock there will be added other mashies, and it is probable that only after years of experiment will he come to a final determination as to which is the best for him to use. In this question of the choice of mashie it is necessary that taste and style should be allowed to have their own way. However, to the hesitating golfer, or to him whose mashie play so far has been somewhat disappointing, I give with confidence the advice to use a mashie which is very fairly lofted and which is deep in the blade. I can see no use in the mashie with the narrow blade which, when (as so often happens when near the green) the ball is lying in grass which is not as short as it might be, often passes right under the ball—a loss of a stroke at the most critical moment, which is the most exasperating thing I know. Again, for a last hint I suggest that he should see that his shaft is both stiff and strong. This instrument being used generally for lighter work than the other iron clubs, and the delicacy and exactness of it being, as a rule, the chief considerations, there is a natural tendency on the part of the golfer sometimes to favour a thinner stick than usual. But it should be borne in mind that there should be no trace of " give " in the shaft, for such would be all against the accuracy that is wanted, and a man when he is playing the short approach shot wants to feel that he has a club in his hand that can be relied upon in its every fibre. Moreover, gentle as is much of its work, even the mashie at times has some very rough jobs to accomplish. So let the stick be fairly stiff.

Of mashie shots there is an infinite variety. In this stroke not only are the lie of the ball and the distance it has to be sent controlling factors in the way it has to be played, but now the nature and qualities of the green which is being approached constitute another, and one which occasions more thought and anxiety than any. Generally all mashie shots may be separated into three groups. There is what we may call the ordinary mashie shot to begin with—meaning thereby a simple lofted stroke,—there is the running-up mashie shot, and there is the special stroke which applies extra spin and cut to the ball. There are very pronounced differences between these strokes and the ways of playing them.   One is often told that "all mashies should be played with the wrist." I beg to differ. As I have said before, I contend that there is no such thing as a purely wrist shot in golf—except on the putting green. If anybody really made up his mind to play his mashie with his wrist and his wrist alone, he would find the blade of his club in uncomfortable proximity to his face at the finish of the stroke, and I should not like to hazard a guess as to where the ball might be. The fact of the matter is, that those who so often say that the mashie must be played with the wrist never attempt to play it in this way themselves. They are merely misled by the fact that for the majority of mashie strokes a shorter swing and less freedom of the arms are desirable than when other iron clubs are being employed. An attempt has been made to play a pure wrist shot in the "How not to do it" photograph, No. XLVIII., and I am sure nobody ever made a success of a stroke like that.

The stance for the mashie differs from that taken when an iron shot is being played, in that the feet are placed nearer to each other and nearer to the ball. Comparison between the photographs and diagrams will make the extent of these differences and the peculiarities of the stance for the mashie quite clear. The right toe is advanced until it is within 11 inches of the A line, the ball is opposite the left heel, the left foot is turned slightly more outwardly than usual. As for the grip, the only observation that it is necessary to make is, that if a very short shot is being played it is sometimes best to grasp the club low down at the bottom of the handle, but in no circumstances do I approve of the hands leaving the leather and getting on to the wood as players sometimes permit them to do. When the player is so desperately anxious to get so near to the blade with his hands, he should use a shorter club. It should also be noticed that the body is more relaxed than formerly, that there is more bend at the elbows, that the arms are not so stiff, and that there is the least suspicion, moreover, of slackness at the knees. The whole attitude is arranged for ease, delicacy of touch, and extreme accuracy, whereas formerly simple straightness and power were the governing considerations.   To the eye of the uninitiated, many of these photographs may seem very much alike; but a little attentive study of those showing the stances for the iron and mashie will make the essential differences very apparent.   In the address the right knee is perceptibly bent, and all the weight of the body is thrown on to it.   In the backward swing the right knee stiffens and the left bends in, the left foot leaning slightly over to facilitate its doing so.   There is a great tendency on the part of inexperienced or uncertain players to pivot on the left toe in the most exaggerated manner even when playing a very short mashie stroke.   Unless a full shot is being taken, there should not only be no pivoting with the mashie, but the left heel, throughout the stroke, should be kept either touching the ground or raised only the least distance above it.   In the backward swing the right knee is stiffened and the left knee bends in towards the ball, simply in order to let the club go back properly, which it could hardly do if the original pose were retained.   It is particularly requisite that, though there is so much ease elsewhere, the club in the case of these mashie shots should be held quite tightly.   They are not played with the wrists alone, but with the wrists and the forearms, and a firm grip is an essential to success.

When considering the nature of the backward swing, the question arises as to how far it should be prolonged, and I have already declared myself against making long shots with the mashie.   It is my strong conviction that a man is playing the best and safest golf when he attempts nothing beyond eighty yards with his mashie, using an iron or a cleek for anything longer.   It is very seldom that I play my mashie at a distance of over eighty yards, and the limit of the swing that I ever give to it is a three-quarter, which is what I call an ordinary mashie stroke, and should be sufficient to do anything ever to be attempted with this

PLATE XLIII. MASHIE APPROACH (PITCH AND RUN). STANCE
(Distance 70 to 80 yards from the hole.)

PLATE XLIV. MASHIE APPROACH (PITCH AND RUN). TOP OF THE SWING
(Distance 70 to 80 yards from the hole.)

PLATE XLV. MASHIE APPROACH (PITCH AND RUN). FINISH
(Distance 70 to 80 yards from the hole.)

PLATE XLVI. MISTAKES WITH THE MASHIE

The hands are too far apart. Whatever method of grip is favoured at least the right thumb should be down the shaft to guide it in the case of this delicate shot. The face of the club is turned in slightly from the toe, and the face also is too straight up and is not allowed its natural angle. The toe of the club is likely to come on to the ball first, and that will cause a pull. In any case the club cannot be guided properly, and there can be no accuracy.

PLATE XLVII. MISTAKES WITH THE MASHIE

Here in this upward swing the body is being held too stiffly. It is not pivoting from the waist as it ought to do. Besides the hands being too far apart, the left one is spoiling everything. It is out of control and is trying to get above the shaft, instead of being underneath it at this stage. The result will either be a foozle or a pulled ball. The face of the mashie will not be straight at the moment of impact.

PLATE XLVIII.   MISTAKES WITH THE MASHIE

This is merely a " wrist shot," such as is often recommended, and which I say cannot possibly give a good result.   There is no mere wrist shot.   The result of an attempt of this kind is always very doubtful.   In any case, even when the ball is fairly hit, there can be no length from the stroke.

PLATE XLIX. RUNNING UP APPROACH WITH MASHIE OR IRON.
FINISH, WITH STANCE ALSO INDICATED

PLATE L. A CUT APPROACH WITH THE MASHIE. STANCE

PLATE LI. A CUT APPROACH WITH THE MASHIE. TOP OF THE SWING

PLATE LII. A CUT APPROACH WITH THE MASHIE. FINISH

club. But some golfers like taking the fullest mashie stroke that they can, and, when hesitating between the use of an iron or the lofting club, they usually decide in favour of the latter. " I think I can reach it with my mashie," they always say, and so they whirl away and commit the most frightful abuse on a splendid club, which was never intended to have its capabilities strained in order to reach anything. Instead of saying that "they think they can reach it with their mashie," these golfers should try to decide that " a half iron will not carry them too far." It is easier and safer. Whenever a ball has a distance to go, I believe in keeping it fairly low down, as low as the hazards will permit, believing that in this way by constant practice it is possible to ensure much greater accuracy than in any other way. No golfer has much control over a ball that is sent up towards the sky. The mashie is meant to loft, and it is practically impossible to play a long shot with it without lofting the ball very much and exposing it to all the wind that there is about. As very little driving power has been imparted to the ball, what wind there may be has considerably more effect upon it than upon the flight of other balls played with other iron clubs.

The line of the backward swing should be much the same as that for the half shot with the cleek, but the body should be held a little more rigidly, and not be allowed to pivot quite so much from the waist as when playing with any of the other clubs which have been described. The downward swing is the same as before, and in the case of the ordinary stroke which we are speaking of, the turf should be hit immediately behind the ball. As soon as the impact has been effected, the body should be allowed to go forward with the club, care being taken that it does not start too soon and is in front.

The great anxiety of the immature player when making this stroke is to get the ball properly lofted, and in some obstinate cases it seems to take several seasons of experience to convince him completely that the club has been specially made for the purpose, and, if fairly used, is quite adequate. This man cannot get rid of the idea that the player lofts the ball, or at least gives material assistance to the club in doing it. What happens? Observe this gentleman when he and his ball are on the wrong side of a hazard which is guarding the green, and notice the very deliberate way in which he goes about doing the one thing that he has been told hundreds of times by the most experienced players can only be attended by the most disastrous and costly failure. He has made up his mind that he will scoop the ball over the bunker. He will not trust to his club to do this important piece of business. So down goes the right shoulder and into the bunker goes the ball, and one more good hole has been lost. He doesn't know how it happened; he thinks the mashie must be the most difficult club in the world to play with, and he complains of his terrible luck; but by the time the approach shot to the next hole comes to be played he is at it again. There is nobody so persistent as the scooper, and the failure that attends his efforts is a fair revenge by the club for the slight that is cast upon its capabilities, for the chances are that if the stroke had been played in just the ordinary manner without any thought whatever of the bunker, and if the ground had been hit just a trifle behind the ball, the latter would have been dropped easily and comfortably upon the green. Some golfers also seem to imagine that they have done all that they could reasonably be expected to do when they have taken a divot, and even if the shot has proved a failure they derive some comfort from the divot they have taken, the said divot usually being a huge slab of turf, the removal of which makes a gaping wound in the links. But there is nothing to be proud of in this achievement, for it does not by any means imply that the stroke has been properly made. To hit the ball correctly when making an approach with the mashie, it is necessary to take a little —just a very little—turf. This is so, because the ball will not fly and rise properly as the club desires to make it do, unless it is taken in the exact middle of the club, which has a deeper face than others. I mean middle, not only as regards the distance from heel to toe, but between the top edge of the blade and the sole. A moment's consideration will make it clear that if the stroke were to be made quite cleanly, that is to say, if the club merely grazed the ground without going into it, the ball would inevitably be taken by the lower part of the blade near to the sole and much below the centre where the impact ought to be. Therefore it is apparent that, in order to take it from the centre, the blade must be forced underneath, and if the swing is made in the manner directed and the turf is taken just the least distance behind the ball—which, of course, means keeping the eye just so much more to the right than usual—all that is necessary will be easily accomplished. Apart from the loft, I think a little more accuracy is ensured by the removal of that inch or two of turf.

Now there is that most valuable stroke, the running-up approach, to consider. When skilfully performed, it is often most wonderfully and delightfully effective. It is used chiefly for short approaches when the ground outside the putting green is fairly good and there is either no hazard at all to be surmounted, or one that is so very low or sunken as not to cause any serious inconvenience. When the running-up shot is played in these circumstances by the man who knows how to play it, he can generally depend on getting much nearer to the hole than if he were obliged to play with a pitch alone. It is properly classified as a mashie shot, but there are golfers who do it with an iron. Others like a straight-faced mashie for the purpose; and a third section have a preference for the ordinary mashie, and play for a pitch and run. These are details of fancy in which I cannot properly interfere. The stance for the stroke differs from that for an ordinary mashie shot in that the feet and body are further in front, the right toe, for instance, being fully six inches nearer to the B line (see Plate XLIX.). The club may be gripped lower down the handle. Moreover, it should be held forward, slightly in front of the head. The swing back should be very straight, and should not be carried nearly so far as in playing an ordinary mashie stroke, for in this case the ball requires very little propulsion. This is one of the few shots in golf in which the right hand is called upon to do most of the work, and that it may be encouraged to do so the hold with the left hand should be slightly relaxed. With the right hand then fastening tightly to the handle, it comes about that the toe of the club at the time of the impact is slightly in front of the heel, and this combination of causes tends to give the necessary run to the ball when it takes the ground. The work of the right hand in the case of this stroke is delicate and exact, and it must be very carefully timed, for if it is done too suddenly or too soon the result is likely to be a foundered ball. The club having been taken so straight out in the backward swing, the natural tendency will be to draw it very slightly across the ball when contact is made, and the blade, then progressing towards the left foot, should to finish be taken a few inches further round towards the back than in the case of an ordinary mashie shot. One cannot very well compare the two in words, however, for the finishes are altogether different, as an examination of the illustration of the finish of the running-up stroke will show. In this case the swing stops when the shaft of the club is pointing a little to the left of the direction of the ball that is speeding onwards, the blade being on a level with the hands. It will be observed that at the finish the right hand is well over on the handle. This is the kind of stroke that the practised and skilful golfer loves most, for few others afford him such a test of calculation and judgment. It will not do to make the stroke haphazard. Before the blade of the club is moved for the upward swing, a very clear understanding should have been formed as to the amount of pitch that is to be given to the ball and the amount of run. They must be in exactly the proper proportion to suit the circumstances, which will vary almost every time the stroke is made. Nearly everything depends on the state of the land that is to be traversed. The fact of the matter is, that this shot is really a combination of lofting and putting with many more uncertain quantities to be dealt with than when one is really putting on the green. When one has decided where the pitch must be, the utmost pains should be taken to pitch there exactly, which, as the distance will usually be trifling, ought not to be a difficult matter. An error of even a foot in a shot of this kind is sometimes a serious matter. When properly done it is an exceedingly pretty shot, and one which brings great peace to the soul of the man who has done it.

And now we come to that exquisite stroke, the approach, to which much cut and spin have been applied for a specific purpose. It is a shot which should only be played when circumstances render it absolutely necessary. There are times when it is the only one which will afford the golfer a good chance of coming well through a trying ordeal. When we play it we want the ball to stop dead almost as soon as it reaches the turf at the end of the pitch. If there is a tolerably high bunker guarding the green, and the flag is most awkwardly situated just at the other side, it is the only shot that can be played. A stroke that would loft the ball over the bunker in the ordinary manner would carry it far beyond the hole—too far to make the subsequent putting anything but a most difficult matter. Or, on the other hand, leaving out of the question the hole which is hiding just on the other side of the hazard protecting the green, it often happens in the summer-time, when greens are hard and fiery, that it is absolutely impossible to make a ball which has been pitched on to them in the ordinary manner stay there. Away it goes bouncing far off on to the other side, and another approach shot has to be played, often by reason of a hazard having been found, more difficult than the first. If there must be a pitch, then the thing to do is to try to apply a

brake to the ball when it comes down, and we can only do
this by cutting it. There are greens which at most seasons
of the year demand that the ball reaching them shall be cut
for a dead drop, such as the green laid at a steep angle
when the golfer has to approach it from the elevated side. A
little cut is a comparatively easy thing to accomplish, but
when the brake is really wanted it is usually a most pronounced cut, that will bring the ball up dead or nearly so,
that is called for, and this is a most difficult stroke. I regard
the ordinary mashie as the best club with which to make it,
but there are some good golfers who like the niblick for
this task, and it is undoubtedly productive of good results.
However, I will suppose that it is to be attempted with the
mashie.

The stance is quite different from that which was adopted
when the running-up shot was being played. Now the man
comes more behind the ball, and the right foot goes forward
until the toe is within 8 inches of the A line, while the instep
of the left foot is right across B. The feet also are rather
closer together. An examination of Plate L. will give an
exact idea of the peculiarities of the stance for this stroke.
Grip the club very low down on the handle, but see that the
right hand does not get off the leather. This time, in the
upward swing let the blade of the mashie go well outside the
natural line for an ordinary swing, that is to say, as far away
from the body in the direction of the A line as is felt to be
comfortable and convenient. While this is being done, the
left elbow should be held more stiffly and kept more severely
under control than the right. At the top of the swing—
which, as will be seen from the picture of it (Plate LI.), is only
a short half swing, and considerably shorter than that for an
ordinary mashie shot—neither arm is at full length, the right
being well bent and the left slightly. When this upward swing
has been made correctly, the blade of the mashie naturally
comes across the ball at the time of impact, and in this way
a certain amount of cut is applied. But this is not the limit

of the possibilities of cutting, as many golfers seem to imagine, nor is it sufficient to meet some of the extreme cases which occasionally present themselves.   To do our utmost in this direction we must decide that extremely little turf must be taken, for it is obvious that unless the bare blade gets to work on the ball it cannot do all that it is capable of doing. The metal must go right underneath the ball, just skimming the grass in the process, and scarcely removing any of the turf.   It is also most important that at the instant when ball and club come into contact the blade should be drawn quickly towards the left foot.   To do this properly requires not only much dexterity but most accurate timing, and first attempts are likely to be very clumsy and disappointing.   But many of the difficulties will disappear with practice, and when at last some kind of proficiency has been obtained, it will be found that the ball answers in the most obedient manner to the call that is made upon it.   It will come down so dead upon the green that it may be pitched up into the air until it is almost directly over the spot at which it is desired to place it.   In playing this stroke a great deal depends on the mastery which the golfer obtains over his forearms and wrists. At the moment of impact the arms should be nearly full length and stiff, and the wrists as stiff as it is possible to make them.   I said that the drawing of the blade towards the left foot would have to be done quickly, because obviously there is very little time to lose; but it must be done smoothly and evenly, without a jerk, which would upset the whole swing, and if it is begun the smallest fraction of a second too soon the ball will be taken by the toe of the club, and the consequences will not be satisfactory.   I have returned to make this the last word about the cut because it is the essence of the stroke, and it calls for what a young player may well regard as an almost hopeless nicety of perfection.

There is another little approach shot which is usually called the chip on to the green, but which is really nothing but the pitch and run on a very small scale.   It is used when the ball has only just failed to reach the green, or has gone beyond it, and is lying in the rougher grass only a very few yards from the edge of it. It often happens in cases of this sort that the putter may be ventured upon, but when that is too risky a little pitch is given to the ball and it is allowed to run the last three or four yards to the hole. An ordinary iron will often be found the most useful club for the purpose.

Latterly a new kind of club has become fashionable in some quarters for approaching. They call it the jigger, and, having a longer blade than the ordinary mashie, its users argue that it is easier to play with. That may be true to a certain extent when the ball is lying nicely, but we are not always favoured with this good fortune, and I have no hesitation in saying that for inferior or cuppy lies the jigger is a very ineffectual instrument. The long head cannot get into the cups, and the accuracy that is always called for in approaching is made impossible. If a jigger must be carried in the bag, it should be merely as an auxiliary to the ordinary mashie.

Such are the shots with the mashie, and glad is the man who has mastered all of them, for he is then a golfer of great pretensions, who is to be feared by any opponent at any time or place.

CHAPTER XII

ON BEING BUNKERED

The philosopher in a bunker—On making certain of getting out—The folly of trying for length—When to play back—The qualities of the niblick—Stance and swing—How much sand to take—The time to press—No follow-through in a bunker—Desperate cases—The brassy in a bunker—Difficulties through prohibited grounding—Play straight when length is imperative—Cutting with the niblick.

THIS is a hateful subject, but one which demands the most careful and unprejudiced consideration, for are not even the best of us bunkered almost daily? There is nothing like the bunkers on a golf links for separating the philosophic from the unphilosophic among a golfing crowd, and when a representative of each section is in a bunker at the same time it is heavy odds on the philosopher winning the hole. There are two respects in which he differs from his opponent at this crisis in his golfing affairs. He does not become flurried, excited, and despondent, and give the hole up for lost with a feeling of disgust that he had committed the most unpardonable sin. He remembers that there are still various strokes to be played before the hole is reached, and that it is quite possible that in the meantime his friend may somewhere lose one and enable him to get on level terms again. When two players with plus handicaps are engaged in a match, a bunkered ball will generally mean a lost hole, but others who have not climbed to this pinnacle of excellence are far too pessimistic if they assume that this rule operates in their case also. The second matter in which the philosophic golfer rises superior to his less favoured brother when there is a bunker stroke to be played, is that he fully realises that the bunker was placed there for the particular purpose of catching certain defective shots, and that the definite idea of its constructors was that the man who played such a shot should lose a stroke as penalty for doing so—every time.   It is legitimate for us occasionally to put it to ourselves that those constructors did not know the long limits of our resource nor the craftiness we are able to display when in a very tight corner, and that therefore, if we find a favourable opportunity, we may cheat the bunker out of the stroke that it threatens to take from us.   But this does not happen often.   When the golfer has brought himself to realise that, having played into a bunker, he has lost a stroke or the best part of one, and accepts the position without any further ado, he has gone a long way in the cultivation of the most desirable proporties of mind and temperament with which any player of the game can be endowed.   This man, recognising that his stroke is lost, when he goes up to his ball and studies the many difficulties of its situation, plays for the mere purpose of getting out again, and probably putting himself on the other side in that one stroke which was lost.   It does not matter to him if he only gets two yards beyond the bunker—just far enough to enable him to take his stance and swing properly for the next shot.   Distance is positively no object whatever, and in this way he insures himself against further loss, and goes the right way to make up for his misfortune.

Now, what does the other man do in like circumstances? Unreasonably and foolishly he refuses to accept the inevitable, and declines to give up the idea of getting to a point a hundred yards or more in front with his next shot, which he would have reached if he had not been in the bunker. He seems to think that the men who made the bunkers did not know their business. Having been bunkered, he says to himself that it is his duty to himself and to the game to make up for the stroke which was lost by supremely brilliant

recovery under the most disheartening circumstances. He
insists that the recovery must be made here in the bunker,
and thereafter he will progress as usual. It never occurs to
him that it would be wiser and safer to content himself
with just getting out the hazard, and then, playing under
comparatively easy and comfortable conditions, to make his
grand attempt at recovering the lost stroke. He would be
much more likely to succeed. A stroke lost or gained is of
equal value at any point on the route from the tee to the
hole, and it is a simple fact, too often never realised, that a
long putt makes up for a short drive, and a mashie shot laid
dead for a previous stroke from which the ball was trapped in
the bunker. But the unphilosophic gentleman, who is ignorant
of, or tries to resist, these truths, feels that his bunkered
stroke must be compensated for by the next one or never.
What is the result? Recklessly, unscientifically, even ludi-
crously, he fires away at the ball in the bunker with a
cleek or an iron or a mashie, striving his utmost to get
length, when, with the frowning cliff of the bunker high in
front of him and possibly even overhanging him, no length
is possible. At the first attempt he fails to get out. His
second stroke in the hazard shares the same fate. With a
third or a fourth his ball by some extraordinary and lucky
chance may just creep over the top of the ridge. How it
came to do so when played in this manner nobody knows.
The fact can only be explained by the argument that if you
keep on doing the same thing something is sure to happen
in the end, and it is a sufficient warning to these bunkered
golfers that the gods of golf have so large a sense of justice
and of right and wrong that by this time the hole has for
a certainty been lost. The slashing player who wants to
drive his long ball out of the bunker very rarely indeed gets
even this little creep over the crest until he has played two
or three more, and is in a desperate state of lost temper.
An alternative result to his efforts comes about when he has
played these three or four more, and his ball is, if anything,

more hopelessly bunkered than ever.   All sense of what is due to the game and to his own dignity is then suddenly lost, and a strange sight is often seen.   Five, six, and seven more follow in quick succession, the man's arms working like the piston of a locomotive, and his eyes by this time being quite blinded to the ball, the sand, the bunker, and everything else.   As an interesting feature of what we might call golfing physiology, I seriously suggest that players of these habits and temperament, when they begin to work like a steam-engine in the bunker, do not see the ball at all for the last few strokes.   The next time they indulge in their peculiar performance, let them ask themselves immediately afterwards whether they did see it or not, and in the majority of cases they will have to answer in the negative.   When it is over, a few impious words are uttered, the ball is picked up, and there is a slow and gloomy march to the next tee, from which it is unlikely that a good drive will be made.   The nervous system of the misguided golfer has been so completely upset by the recent occurrences, that he may not recover his equanimity until several more strokes have been played, or perhaps until the round is over and the distressing incidents have at last passed from his mind.

This has been a long story about a thing that happens on most links every day, but the moral of it could hardly have been emphasised properly or adequately if it had been told in fewer words, or if the naked truth had been wrapped up in any more agreeable terms.   The moral obviously is, that the golfer on being bunkered must concentrate his whole mind, capabilities, and energies on getting out in one stroke, and must resolutely refrain from attempting length at the same time, for, in nine cases out of ten, length is impossible.   There are indeed occasions when so light a sentence has been passed by the bunker on the erring ball that a long shot is practicable, but they are very rare, and come in an entirely different category from the average bunkered ball, and we will consider them in due course

On the other hand, there are times when it is manifestly impossible even to get to the other side of the bunker in a single stroke, as when the ball is tucked up at the foot of a steep and perhaps overhanging cliff. Still the man must keep before himself the fact that his main object is to get out in the fewest strokes possible, and in a case of this sort he may be wise to play back, particularly if it is a medal round that he is engaged upon. If he plays back he is still in the running for his prize if his golf has been satisfactory up to this point, for an addition of two strokes to his score through such an accident, though a serious handicap, is seldom a hopeless one. If he does not play back his chance of victory may disappear entirely at this bunker. His instinct tells him that it probably will do so. Which then is the wiser and better course to take?

Now, then, let us consider the ways and means of getting out of bunkers, and take in our hands the most unpopular club that our bags contain. We never look upon the niblick with any of that lingering affection which is constantly bestowed on all the other instruments that we possess, as we reflect upon the splendid deeds that they have performed for us on many memorable occasions. The niblick revives only unpleasant memories, but less than justice is done to this unfortunate club, for, given fair treatment, it will accomplish most excellent and remunerative work in rescuing its owner from the predicaments in which his carelessness or bad luck in handling the others has placed him. There is little variety in niblicks, and therefore no necessity to discourse upon their points, for no professional is ever likely to stock a niblick for sale that is unequal to the performance of its peculiar duties. It has rougher and heavier work to do than any other club, and more brute force is requisitioned in employing it than at any other time. Therefore the shaft should be as strong as it is possible for it to be, and it should be so stiff that it will not bend under the most severe pressure. The head should be rather small and round, with plenty of loft upon it, and very heavy. A light niblick is useless.

It is difficult to advise as to the stance that should be taken for a niblick shot in a bunker, inasmuch as it so frequently happens that this is governed by circumstances which are quite beyond the golfer's control. He must learn to adapt himself in the best possible manner to the conditions in which he finds himself, and it will often happen that he is cramped for space, he may be unable to get a proper or comfortable place for one or both of his feet, or he may be obliged to stand with one foot—generally the left one—considerably above the other. But when there are none of these difficulties besetting him, it may be said that generally the stance most suited to a stroke with the niblick is similar to that which would be taken for a long shot with an iron, except perhaps that the player should stand a little nearer to the ball, so that he may be well over it while making his swing. The most important respect in which the swing differs from that of the iron is that the club is brought up much straighter. By this I mean that the head of the club should not be allowed to come round quite so much, but throughout its course should be kept as nearly as possible overhanging what we have been calling the A line. The swing, indeed, is much more of what I call an upright character than that of any other stroke in the game, and at the top of it, the blade having passed over the right shoulder and the golfer's head, the shaft should be nearly horizontal and right over the back of the head, an example of which may be seen in Plate LIII., where I have a fairly good lie, but am rather badly bunkered for all that, being only a couple of feet from the base of a high and tolerably steep bank.

If there is such a thing as an average bunker shot, this is the one, and I am now describing the method of dealing with cases of this and similar character. There must be no thought of hitting the ball cleanly with the club in a case of

PLATE LIII. THE NIBLICK IN A BUNKER. TOP OF AN ORDINARY STROKE
WHEN IT IS INTENDED TO TAKE MUCH SAND

PLATE LIV. "WELL OUT!" FINISH OF AN ORDINARY STROKE IN A BUNKER WHEN MUCH SAND IS TAKEN. THE BALL MAY BE SEEN RISING ABOVE THE BUNKER

PLATE LV. ANOTHER BUNKER STROKE. TOP OF THE SWING WHEN
INTENDING TO TAKE THE BALL CLEANLY AND WITH A LITTLE CUT

PLATE LVI. FINISH AFTER TAKING THE BALL CLEANLY FROM A BUNKER

this kind, or in any other than the most exceptional situations or emergencies when bunkered. The club must hit the sand, and the sand must move the ball, but the iron blade of the niblick must hardly ever come into contact with the ball. To prevent its doing so, and to ensure the blade getting underneath sufficiently to lift the ball up at the very sharp angle that is necessary if it is to surmount the obstruction in front of it, the sand should be struck at a point fully two inches behind the ball. If the sand is exceedingly light and dry, so that it offers very little resistance to the passage of the club, this distance may be slightly increased, or it may be diminished if the lie in the bunker is very heavy, consisting of gravel or clay. It is on this point, so far behind the ball, that the eye must, of course, be sternly and rigidly fixed, and it is a duty which the beginner frequently finds most difficult to fulfil. In the downward swing the club should be brought on to the spot indicated with all the speed and force of which the golfer is capable. At other times he may have had a yearning to press, which he has with difficulty stifled. He may make up for all these ungratified desires by pressing now with all the strength in his body, and the harder the better so long as he keeps his eye steadily fixed on that point behind the ball and is sure that his muscular efforts will not interfere with his accuracy. After all, the latter need not be quite so fine in this case as in the many others that we have already discussed, for an eighth of an inch one way or the other does not much matter in the case of a niblick shot where there are two inches of sand to plough through. Swing harder than ever on to the sand, with the knowledge that the swing will end there, for a follow-through is not desired and would in many cases be impossible. When the heavy blade goes crash into the sand and blows it, and the ball with it, up into the air as if the electric touch had been given to an explosive mine, the club has finished its work, and when the golfer is at rest again and is surveying the results of his labours—with his eyes, let

us hope, directed to the further side of the hazard—the blade
will still remain in the cavity that it has made in the floor
of the bunker.   If any attempt were made to follow through,
it is highly probable that sufficient sand would not be taken
to make the ball rise up soon enough.

However, the more one reflects upon bunkers and niblicks, the more does one feel that the circumstances must
govern the method of playing each of these strokes, and
there is no finer field for the display of the golfer's judgment
and resource than this.   The next best accomplishment to
the negative one of avoiding bunkers is that of getting out
again with the least waste of strokes and distance; and,
indeed, I should say that the man who is somewhat addicted
to being bunkered but invariably makes a good recovery, is
at least on level terms with another who is in trouble not
quite so frequently but who suffers terribly when he is.   The
golden rule—I say it once again—is to make certain of
getting out; but now that I have sufficiently emphasised this
point, I am ready to consider those few occasions when it
appears a little weak and unsatisfactory.   Certainly there
are times, as we all know, when the enemy, having had
matters his own way at a hole, it will not be of the slightest
use merely to scramble out of a bunker in one stroke.   The
case is so desperate that a stroke that will carry the ball for
perhaps 100 or 120 yards is called for.   Such a necessity does
not affect my rule as to making certain of getting out, for
in practical golf one cannot take any serious account of
emergencies of this kind.   But there are times when every
player must either attempt the shot that most frequently
baffles his superiors, or forthwith give up the hole, and it is
not in human nature to cave in while the faintest spark of
hope remains.   In thus attempting the impossible, or the
only dimly possible, we are sometimes led even to take the
brassy in a bunker.   In a case of this sort, of course, everything depends on the lie of the ball and its distance from
the face of the bunker.   When it is a shallow pot bunker,

the shot is often practicable, and sometimes when one is bunkered on a seaside course the hazard is so wide that there is time for the ball to rise sufficiently to clear the obstruction.   But the average bunker on an inland course, say four feet high with only six feet of sand before it, presents few such loopholes for escape.   The difficulty of playing a shot from a bunker when any club other than the niblick, such as the brassy, is chosen with the object of obtaining length by hitting the ball clean, is obviously increased by the rule which prohibits the grounding of the club in addressing.   To be on the safe side, the sole of the club is often kept fully an inch and a half above the sand when the address is being made, and this inch and a half has to be corrected down to an eighth in the forward swing, for of all shots that must be taken accurately this one so full of difficulty must be.   In making his correction the man is very likely to overdo it and strike the sand before the ball, causing a sclaff, or, on the other hand, not to correct sufficiently when the only possible result would be a topped ball and probably a hopeless position in the hazard.   It is indeed a rashly speculative shot, and one of the most difficult imaginable.   It comes off sometimes, but it is a pure matter of chance when it does, and the lucky player is hardly entitled to that award of merit which he may fancy he deserves.

When the situation of the bunkered ball is unusually hopeful, and there does really seem to be a very fair prospect of making a good long shot, I think it generally pays best to play straight at the hazard, putting just a little cut on the ball to help it to rise, and employing any club that suggests itself for the purpose.   I think, in such circumstances, that it pays best to go straight for the hazard, because, if length is urgently demanded, what is the use of playing at an angle?   Again, though there is undoubtedly an advantage gained by taking a bunker crossways, and thus giving the ball more time to rise, the advantage is often greatly exaggerated in the golfer's mind.   When a ball is bunkered right on the edge of the green, it is sometimes best to try to pick it up not quite but almost cleanly with the niblick or mashie, in the hope that one more stroke afterwards will be sufficient either to win or halve the hole, whereas an ordinary shot with the niblick would not be likely to succeed so well. If, after due contemplation of all the heavy risks, it is decided to make such an attempt, the stroke should be played very much after the fashion of the mashie approach with cut. I need hardly say that such a shot is one of the most difficult the golfer will ever have occasion to attempt. The ordinary cut mashie stroke is hard to accomplish, but the cut niblick is harder still. I have already given directions for the playing of such shots, and the rest must be left to the golfer's daring and his judgment.

CHAPTER XIII

SIMPLE PUTTING

PUTTING in golf is a game within another game. While I am not prepared to endorse the opinion that is commonly expressed, that a golfer is born and not made, I am convinced that no amount of teaching will make a golfer hole out long putts with any frequency, nor will it even make him at all certain of getting the short ones down. But it will certainly put him in the right way of hitting the ball, which after all will be a considerable gain. Experience counts for very much, and it will convert a man who was originally a bad putter into one who will generally hold his own on the greens, or even be superior to the majority of his fellows. Even experience, however, counts for less in putting than in any other department of the game, and there are many days in every player's life when he realises only too sadly that it seems to count for nothing at all. Do we not from time to time see beginners who have been on the links but a single month, or even less than that, laying their long putts as dead as anybody could wish almost every time, and getting an amazing percentage of them into the tin itself? Often enough they seem to do these things simply because, as we should say, they know nothing at all about putting, which is perhaps another way of saying that their minds are never embarrassed by an oppressive knowledge of all the difficulties which the ball will meet with in its passage from the club to the hole, and of the necessity of taking steps to counteract them all. They are not afraid of the hole. The fact is that putting is to a far greater extent than most of us suspect purely a matter of confidence. When a man feels that he can putt he putts, and when he has a doubt about it he almost invariably makes a poor show upon the greens. Do I not know to my cost what it is to feel that I cannot putt, and on those occasions to miss the most absurdly little ones that ever wait to be popped into the hole without a moment's thought or hesitation? It is surely the strangest of the many strange things in golf, that the old player, hero of many senior medal days, victor in matches over a hundred links, will at times, when the fortunes of an important game depend upon his action, miss a little putt that his ten-year-old daughter would get down nine times out of ten. She, dear little thing, does not yet know the terrors of the short putt. Sometimes it is the most nerve-breaking thing to be found on the hundred acres of a golf course. The heart that does not quail when a yawning bunker lies far ahead of the tee just at the distance of a good drive, beats in trouble when there are but thirty inches of smooth even turf to be run over before the play of the hole is ended. I am reminded of a story of Andrew Kirkaldy, who in his young days once carried for a young student of divinity who was most painfully nervous on the putting greens, and repeatedly lost holes in consequence. When Andrew could stand this reckless waste of opportunities no longer, he exclaimed to his employer, " Man, this is awfu' wark. Ye're dreivin' like a roarin' lion and puttin' like a puir kittlin'." But the men whose occupations are of the philosophical and peaceful kind are not the only ones who may be fairly likened to Andrew's " puir kittlin' " when there are short putts to be holed. Is there not the famous case of the Anglo-Indian sportsman, one of the mightiest of hunters, who feared nothing like the hole when it lay so near to him that his tears of agony might almost have fallen into it? It was this man who declared, " I have encountered all the manifold perils of the jungle, I have tracked the huge elephant to his destruction, and I have stood eye to eye with the man-eating tiger. And never once have I trembled until I came to a short putt." Yet with such facts as these before us, some people still wonder wherein lies the fascination of golf. How often does it happen that an inch on the putting green is worth more than a hundred yards in the drive, and that the best of players are confounded by this circumstance? It is very nearly true, as Willie Park has so often said, that the man who can putt need fear nobody. Certainly a player can never be really great until he is nearly always certain to hole out in two putts on the green, and to get down a few in one. The approach stroke has been well played when the ball comes to rest within four or five feet of the pin, but what is the use of that unless the ball is to be putted out more often than not in one more stroke?

For the proper playing of the other strokes in golf, I have told my readers to the best of my ability how they should stand and where they should put their feet. But except for the playing of particular strokes, which come within the category of those called "fancy," I have no similar instruction to offer in the matter of putting. There is no rule, and there is no best way. Sometimes you see a player bend down and hold the putter right out in front of him with both wrists behind the shaft. This is an eccentricity, but if the player in question believes that he can putt better in this way than in any other, he is quite justified in adopting it, and I would be the last to tell him that he is wrong. The fact is that there is more individuality in putting than in any other department of golf, and it is absolutely imperative that this individuality should be allowed to have its way. I believe seriously that every man has had a particular kind of putting method awarded to him by Nature, and when he putts exactly in this way he will do well, and when he departs from his natural system he will miss the long ones and the short ones too. First of all, he has to find out this particular method which Nature has assigned for his use. There ought not to be much difficulty about this, for it will come unconsciously to his aid when he is not thinking of anybody's advice or of anything that he has ever read in any book on golf. That day the hole will seem as big as the mouth of a coal mine, and putting the easiest thing in the world. When he stands to his ball and makes his little swing, he feels as easy and comfortable and confident as any man can ever do. Yet it is probable that, so far as he knows, he is not doing anything special. It may happen that the very next day, when he thinks he is standing and holding his club and hitting the ball in exactly the same way, he nevertheless feels distinctly uncomfortable and full of nervous hesitation as he makes his stroke, and then the long putts are all either too short, or too long, or wide, and the little ones are missed.

I don't think that the liver or a passing variation in temperament is altogether the cause of this. I believe it is because the man has departed even by a trifle from his own natural stance. A change of the position of the feet by even a couple of inches one way or the other may alter the stance altogether, and knock the player clean off his putting. In this new position he will wriggle about and feel uncomfortable. Everything is wrong. His coat is in the way, his pockets seem too full of old balls, the feel of his stockings on his legs irritates him, and he is conscious that there is a nail coming up on the inside of the sole of his boot. It is all because he is just that inch or two removed from the stance which Nature allotted to him for putting purposes, but he does not know that, and consequently everything in the world except the true cause is blamed for the extraordinary things he does. A fair sample of many others was the clergyman who, having missed a short putt when playing in a match over a Glasgow links, espied in the distance on an eminence fully a quarter of a mile away from the green, an innocent tourist, who was apparently doing nothing more injurious to golf than serenely admiring the view. But the clerical golfer, being a man of quick temper, poured forth a torrent of abuse, exclaiming, "How could I hole the ball with that blockhead over there working his umbrella as if it were the pendulum of an eight-day clock!" When this is the kind of thing that is happening, I advise the golfer to try variations in his stance for putting, effecting the least possible amount of change at a time. There is a chance that at last he will drop into his natural stance, or something very near it, and even if he does not there is some likelihood that he will gain a trifle in confidence by the change, and that will count for much. And anyhow there is ample justification for any amount of manœuvring of the body and the feet when one is off one's putting, for at the best, to make use of something like an Irishism, the state of things is then hopelessly bad, and every future tendency must be in the way of improvement. There is one other suggestion to make to those golfers who believe what I say about the natural stance, and by this time it will have become more or less obvious to them. It is that when they are fairly on their putting, and are apparently doing all that Nature intended them to do, and are feeling contented in body and mind accordingly, they should take a sly but very careful look at their feet and body and everything else just after they have made a successful long putt, having felt certain all the time that they would make it. This examination ought not to be premeditated, because that would probably spoil the whole thing; and it usually happens that when one of these long ones has been successfully negotiated, the golfer is too much carried away by his emotions of delight to bring himself immediately to a sober and acute analysis of how it was done. But sometime he may remember to look into the matter, and then he should note the position of everything down to the smallest detail and the fraction of an inch, and make a most careful note of them for future reference. It will be invaluable. So, as I hold that putting is a matter of Nature and instinct, I make an exception this time to my rule in the matter of illustrations, and offer to my readers no diagram with stance measurements. From the two photographs of myself putting in what I had every reason to believe at the time was my own perfectly natural stance, they may take any hints that they may discover.

In the matter of putters, of which there is an infinite variety and a new one invented almost every month, I believe in a man playing with just that kind that he has most confidence in and which he fancies suits him best. Whether it is a plain gun-metal instrument, a crooked-necked affair, a putting cleek, an ordinary aluminium, a wooden putter, or the latest American invention, it is all the same; and if it suits the man who uses it, then it is the best putter in the world for him, and the one with which he will hole out most frequently. In no other sense is there such a thing as a best putter. The only semblance of a suggestion that I will presume to offer in this connection is, that for very long putts there is something to be said in favour of the wooden and aluminium putters, which seem to require less exertion than others, and to enable the player to regulate the strength of the stroke more exactly. For the shorter ones, I like the putting cleek best. But even these are matters of fancy, and what a great deal even the vaguest, most unreasoning belief in a putter has to do with the success with which it is manipulated I have as good a reason as anyone to understand, since I owe my first Championship largely to the help of a putter which I had never used before, and which was really not a putter at all, but, as I have explained elsewhere, simply a little cleek which I picked up accidentally in a professional's shop on the eve of the struggle, and in which

PLATE LVII. PUTTING

PLATE LVIII. PUTTING

I had a new shaft fixed to my own liking. On that occasion I putted with this instrument as the winner of a championship ought to putt, but I have never been able to do any good with it since, and in these days it is resting idly in my shop, useless but quite unpurchasable for any money. I do believe that it is a good thing to be the possessor of two putters, with both of which you have at one time or another done well, and in which you have unlimited confidence. Don't carry them both in the bag at the same time, but keep one safe in the locker, and when the day comes, as it surely will, when you are off your putting, take it out on to the links for the next round and see what you can do with it. Your weakness on the green may no more have been the fault of the other putter than the tourist was the cause of the clergyman missing the little one at Glasgow, but very much will be gained if you can persuade yourself that it was.

It is to a certain extent possible to be definite in remarking upon the grip. Some good golfers clasp their putters tightly with both hands; others keep the left hand loose and the right hand firm; and a third selection do the reverse, each method being justified on its day. But in this part of the game it is quite clear that the right hand has more work to do than the left. It is the right hand that makes the stroke, and therefore I consider that it should be allowed plenty of play, and that the left wrist should be held more loosely than the right. For my part I use the same overlapping grip in putting as in all the other strokes, making just this one small variation, that instead of allowing the right thumb to fall over the shaft, as when driving or playing through the green, I place it on the top of the shaft and pointing down it. This seems to me to make for accuracy.

In playing what we may call an ordinary putt, that is to say, one presenting no difficulties in the way of stymies, slopes of the green, or anything of that kind, I think it pays best in the long run to make a point of always hitting the ball with the middle of the face of the club, although, I believe, Willie Park, one of the greatest of putters, always hits the ball off the toe of the club and comes in to the hole from the right-hand side of it. Other players consistently and by design half top the ball when they are putting. There should be no sharp hit and no jerk in the swing, which should have the even gentle motion of a pendulum. In the backward swing, the length of which, as in all other strokes in golf, is regulated by the distance it is desired to make the ball travel, the head of the putter should be kept exactly in the line of the putt. Accuracy will be impossible if it is brought round at all. There should be a short follow-through after impact, varying, of course, according to the length of the putt. In the case of a long one, the club will go through much further, and then the arms would naturally be more extended. In the follow-through the putter should be kept well down, the bottom edge scraping the top of the grass for some inches. It is easy to understand how much more this course of procedure will tend towards the accuracy and delicacy of the stroke than the reverse method, in which the blade of the putter would be cocked up as soon as the ball had left it.

Before I close my remarks on the simple putt, I feel that it is a duty to repeat once more those wise maxims relating to putting that have been uttered some tens of thousands of times already. " Never up, never in." There is nothing so true, and the number of matches and medals that have been lost through the reckless and foolish disregard of this rule must be enormous. The hole will never come to you; therefore make up your mind that you will always go to the hole, and let it be an invariable practice to play for the back of the tin so that you will always have just a little in hand. The most deadly accuracy and the nicest calculations are all wasted if the ball is just half a turn short of the opening, and there is nothing in the whole of the play between one tee and the next more exasperating than the long putt which hesitates and stops on the very lip of the hole. There is another very good reason for always playing very well up to the hole, which may not have occurred to all golfers who read these lines. Suppose that in the exercise of this rule about always being up at any cost, too much has been put into the ball, and, refusing to die when it ought to do, it skips over the hole and comes to a standstill several inches beyond. "That's the result of being up!" exclaims the irritated golfer. But he feels at any rate that he has given the hole the chance for which it asked, and has a far greater sense of satisfaction and of duty done than if the ball had stopped a foot or more short of the place that was made for it. This may be the reason why an eighteen-inch or two-feet putt back to the hole from the far side always seems easier and is less frequently missed than a putt of the same distance from the original side, which is merely making up for the shortage in the first putt. Whether that is the reason or not, there is the fact, and though they may not have considered the matter hitherto, I feel confident that on reflection, or when they take note of future experiences, most of my readers will admit that this is so. It is a final argument for playing to the back of the hole and never being short. One of the greatest worries of the glorious life of old Tom Morris was that for a long time when in the middle of his career he was nearly always short with his long putts, and his son, young Tom, used wickedly to say that his father would be a great putter if the hole were always a yard nearer. Tom, I believe, was always conscious of his failing, and made the most strenuous efforts to correct it, and this only shows what a terrible and incurable habit this one of being short can become, and what necessity there is for the golfer to exercise his strength of mind to get rid of it in his early days, and establish the practice of being up every time. Often enough he will run over, but sometimes the kind hole will gobble the ball, and on the average he will gain substantially over the nervous, hesitating player who is always short.

CHAPTER XIV

COMPLICATED PUTTS

Problems on undulating greens—The value of practice—Difficulties of calculation —The cut stroke with the putter—How to make it—When it is useful— Putting against a sideways slope—A straighter line for the hole—Putting down a hill—Applying drag to the ball—The use of the mashie on the putting green—Stymies—When they are negotiable and when not—The wisdom of playing for a half—Lofting over the stymie—Running through the stymie—How to play the stroke, and its advantages—Fast greens for fancy strokes—On gauging the speed of a green.

NOW we will consider those putts in which it is not all plain sailing from the place where the ball lies to the hole. The line of the putt may be uphill or it may be downhill, or the green may slope all the way from one side to the other, or first from one and then the other. There is no end to the tricks and difficulties of a good sporting green, and the more of them the merrier. The golfer's powers of calculation are now in great demand.

Take, to begin with, one of the most difficult of all putts —that in which there is a more or less pronounced slope from one side or the other, or a mixture of the two. In this case it would obviously be fatal to putt straight at the hole. Allowances must be made on one side or the other, and sometimes they are very great allowances too. I have found that most beginners err in being afraid of allowing sufficiently for the slope. They may convince themselves that in order to get near the hole their ball should be a yard or so off the straight line when it is half-way along its course, and yet, at the last instant, when they make the stroke their nerve and resolution seem to fail them, and they point the

ball but a few inches up the slope, with the result that before
it reaches the hole it goes running away on the other side
and comes to a standstill anything but dead. Putting practice on undulating greens is very valuable, not so much
because it teaches the golfer exactly what allowance he
should make in various cases, but because it helps by
experience to give him the courage of his convictions. It is
impossible to give any directions as to the precise allowance
that should be made, for the simple reason that this varies in
every case. The length of the putt, the degree of slope, and
the speed of the green, are all controlling factors. The
amount of borrow, as we term it, that must be taken from
the side of any particular slope is entirely a matter of
mathematical calculation, and the problem will be solved to
satisfaction most frequently by the man who trains himself
to make an accurate and speedy analysis of the controlling
factors in the limited amount of time available for the purpose. The putt is difficult enough when there is a pronounced slope all the way from one particular side, but the
question is much more puzzling when it is first one and then
the other and then perhaps a repetition of one or both. To
begin with, there may be a slope of fifteen degrees from the
right, so the ball must go away to the right. But a couple
of yards further on this slope may be transformed into one
of thirty degrees the other way, and after a short piece of
level running the original slope, but now at twenty degrees,
is reverted to. What in the name of golf is the line that
must be taken in a tantalising case of this kind? It is plain
that the second slope if it lasts as long as the first one more
than neutralises it, being steeper, so that instead of borrowing
from the first one we must start running down it in order to
tackle the second one in good time. But the third slope
again, to some extent, though not entirely, neutralises the
second, and this entirely upsets the calculation which only
included the first two. It is evident that the first and third
hold the advantage between them, and that in such a case as

this we should send the ball on its journey with a slight borrow from the first incline with which it had to contend. As I have just said, in these complicated cases it is a question of reckoning pure and simple, and then putting the ball in a straightforward manner along the line which you have decided is the correct one.

But there are times when a little artifice may be resorted to, particularly in the matter of applying a little cut to the ball. There is a good deal of billiards in putting, and the cut stroke on the green is essentially one which the billiard player will delight to practise. But I warn all those who are not already expert at cutting with the putter, to make themselves masters of the stroke in private practice before they attempt it in a match, because it is by no means easy to acquire. The chief difficulty that the golf student will encounter in attempting it will be to put the cut on as he desires, and at the same time to play the ball with the proper strength and keep on the proper line. It is easy enough to cut the ball, but it is most difficult, at first at all events, to cut it and putt it properly at the same time. For the application of cut, turn the toe of the putter slightly outwards and away from the hole, and see that the face of the club is kept to this angle all the way through the stroke. Swing just a trifle away from the straight line outwards, and the moment you come back on to the ball draw the club sharply across it. It is evident that this movement, when properly executed, will give to the ball a rotary motion, which on a perfectly level green would tend to make it run slightly off to the right of the straight line along which it was aimed. Here, then, the golfer may arm himself with an accomplishment which may frequently prove of valuable service. He may dodge a stymie or circumvent an inconvenient piece of the green over which, without the cut, the ball would have to travel. But most frequently will the accomplished putter find the cut of use to him when there is a pronounced slope of the green from the right-hand side of

the line of the putt.   In applying cut to the ball in a case of
this kind, we are complicating the problem by the introduction of a fourth factor to the other three I have named,
but at the same time we are diminishing the weight of these
others, since we shall enable ourselves to putt more directly
at the hole.   Suppose it is a steep but even slope all the
way from the ball to the hole.   Now, if we are going to putt
this ball in the ordinary manner without any spin on it, we
must borrow a lot from the hill, and, as we shall at once
convince ourselves, the ball must be at its highest point
when it is just half-way to the hole.   But we may borrow
from the slope in another way than by running straight up
it and straight down again.   If we put cut on the ball, it will
of itself be fighting against the hill the whole way, and
though if the angle is at all pronounced it may not be able
to contend against it without any extra borrow, much less
will be required than in the case of the simple putt up the
hill and down again.   Now it must be borne in mind that
it is a purely artificial force, as it were, that keeps the ball
from running down the slope, and as soon as the run on the
ball is being exhausted and the spin at the same time,
the tendency will be not for the ball to run gradually down
the slope—as it did in the case of the simple putt without
cut—but to surrender to it completely and run almost
straight down.   Our plan of campaign is now indicated.
Instead of going a long way up the hill out of our straight
line, and having but a very vague idea of what is going to
be the end of it all, we will neutralise the effect of the slope
as far as possible by using the cut and aim to a point much
lower down the hill—how much lower can only be determined with knowledge of the particular circumstances, and
after the golfer has thoroughly practised the stroke and
knows what he can do with it.   And instead of settling
upon a point half-way along the line of the putt as the
highest that the ball shall reach, this summit of the ascent
will now be very much nearer to the hole, quite close to it in

fact. We putt up to this point with all the spin we can get on the ball, and when it reaches it the forward motion and the rotation die away at the same time, and the ball drops away down the hill, and, as we hope, into the hole that is waiting for it close by. Now, after all this explanation, it may really seem that by using the cut in a case of this kind we are going about the job in the most difficult manner, but when once the golfer has made himself master of this cut stroke, and has practised this manner of attacking slopes, he will speedily convince himself that it is the easier and more reliable method—certainly more reliable. It seems to be a great advantage to be able to keep closer to the straight line, and the strength can be more accurately gauged. The diagram which I have drawn on this page

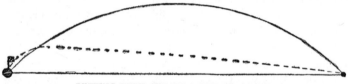

PUTTING WITH CUT ON A SLOPING GREEN.

shows relatively the courses taken by balls played in the two different styles, and will help to explain my meaning. The slope is supposed to be coming from the top of the page, as it were, and the plain curved line is the course taken by the ball which has had no cut given to it, while that which is dotted is the line of the cut ball. I am giving them both credit for having been played with the utmost precision, so that they would find their way to the tin. I submit all these remarks as an idea, to be followed up and elaborated in much practice, rather than as a definite piece of instruction, for the variety of circumstances is so bewildering that a fixed rule is impossible.

One of the putting problems which strike most fear into the heart of the golfer is when his line from the ball to the hole runs straight down a steep slope, and there is some considerable distance for the ball to travel along a fast green. The difficulty in such a case is to preserve any control over the ball after it has left the club, and to make it stop anywhere near the hole if the green is really so fast and steep as almost to impart motion of itself. In a case of this sort I think it generally pays best to hit the ball very nearly upon the toe of the putter, at the same time making a short quick twitch or draw of the club across the ball towards the feet. Little forward motion will be imparted in this manner, but there will be a tendency to half lift the ball from the green at the beginning of its journey, and it will continue its way to the hole with a lot of drag upon it. It is obvious that this stroke, to be played properly, will need much practice in the first place and judgment afterwards, and I can do little more than state the principle upon which it should be made. But oftentimes, when the slope of the green is really considerable, and one experiences a sense of great risk and danger in using the putter at all, I strongly advise the use of the iron or mashie; indeed, I think most golfers chain themselves down too much to the idea that the putter, being the proper thing to putt with, no other club should be used on the green. There is no law to enforce the use of the putter, but even when the idea sometimes occurs to a player that it would be best to use his mashie on the green in particular circumstances, he usually rejects it as improper. On a steep incline it pays very well to use a mashie, for length in these circumstances can often be judged very accurately, and, the ball having been given its little pitch to begin with, does not then begin to roll along nearly so quickly as if the putter had been acting upon it. There are times, even when the hole is only a yard away, when it might pay best to ask for the mashie instead of the instrument which the caddie will offer.

Upon the very difficult and annoying question of stymies there are few hints that I can offer which will not suggest themselves to the player of a very little experience. The fact which must be driven home is that some stymies are negotiable and others are not—not by any player or by any method. When the ball that stymies you dead is lying on the lip of the hole and half covering it, and your own is some distance away, the case is, to all intents and purposes, hopeless, but if you have only got this one stroke left for the half, you feel that an effort of some kind must be made, however hopeless it may be. The one chance—and even that is not always given—is to pass the other ball so very closely that yours will touch the rim of the hole and then, perhaps, if it is travelling slowly enough, be influenced sufficiently to tumble in. Luck must necessarily have a lot to do with the success of a stroke of this kind, and the one consolation is that, if it fails, or if you knock the other ball in—which is quite likely—things will be no worse than they appeared before you took the stroke. If, in the case of a dead and hopeless stymie of this kind, you had two strokes for the half and one for the hole, I should strongly advise you to give up all thoughts of holing out, and make quite certain of being dead the first time and getting the half. Many golfers are so carried away by their desire to snatch the hole from a desperate position of this sort, that they throw all prudence to the winds, attempt the impossible, and probably lose the hole at the finish instead of halving it. They may leave themselves another stymie, they may knock the other ball in, or they may be anything but dead after their first stroke,—indeed, it is when defying their fate in this manner that everything is likely to happen for the worst.

The common method of playing a stymie is by pitching your ball over that of your opponent, but this is not always possible. All depends on how near the other ball is to the hole, and how far the balls are apart. If the ball that stymies you is on the lip and your own is three yards away, it is obvious that you cannot pitch over it. From such a distance your own ball could not be made to clear the other one and drop again in time to fall into the tin. But, when an examination of the situation makes it clear that there is really space enough to pitch over and get into the hole, take the most lofted club in your bag—either a highly lofted mashie or even a niblick—and when making the little pitch shot that is demanded, apply cut to the ball in the way I have already directed, and aim to the left-hand side of the tin. The stroke should be very short and quick, the blade of the club not passing through a space of more than nine inches or a foot. The cut will make the ball lift quickly, and, with the spin upon it, it is evident that the left-hand side of the hole is the proper one to play to. Everything depends upon the measurements of the situation as to whether you ought to pitch right into the hole or to pitch short and run in, but in any case you should pitch close up, and in a general way four or five inches would be a fair distance to ask the ball to run. When your own ball is many yards away from the hole, and the one that makes the stymie is also far from it as well as far from yours, a pitch shot seems very often to be either inadequate or impossible. Usually it will be better to aim at going very near to the stymie with the object of getting up dead, making quite certain at the same time that you do not bungle the whole thing by hitting the other ball, or else to play to the left with much cut, so that with a little luck you may circle into the hole. Evidently the latter would be a somewhat hazardous stroke to make.

There is one other way of attacking a stymie, and that is by the application of the run-through method, when the ball in front of you is on the edge of the hole and your own is very close to it—only just outside the six inches limit that makes the stymie. If the balls are much more than a foot apart, the "follow-through method" of playing stymies is almost certain to fail. This system is nothing more than the follow-through shot at billiards, and the principles upon which the strokes in the two games are made are much the same. Hit your own ball very high up,—that is to say, put all the top and run on it that you can, and strike the other ball fairly in the centre and fairly hard. The object is to knock the stymie right away over the hole, and to follow through with your own and drop in. If you don't hit hard enough you will only succeed in holing your opponent's ball and earning his sarcastic thanks. And if you don't get top enough on your own ball you will not follow through, however hard you bang up against the other. This is a very useful stroke to practise, for the particular kind of stymie to which it applies occurs very frequently, and is one of the most exasperating of all.

Most of these fancy putting strokes stand a very poor chance of success on a very slow green. Cut and top and all these other niceties will not work on a dull one. It is the sharp, fiery green that comes to the rescue of the resourceful golfer in circumstances such as we have been discussing. It seems to me that golfers in considering their putts very often take too little pains to come to an accurate determination of the speed of the greens. There are a score of changing circumstances which affect that speed, but it frequently happens that only a casual glance is given to the state of the turf, and the rest of the time is spent in considering the distance and the inclines that have to be contended against. The golfer should accustom himself to making a minute survey of the condition of things. Thus, to how many players does it occur that the direction in which the mowing machine has been passed over it makes an enormous difference to the speed of the particular piece of the green that has to be putted over? All the blades of grass are bent down in the direction that the machine has taken, and their points all face that way. Therefore the ball that is being putted in the opposite direction encounters all the resistance of these points, and in the aggregate this resistance is very considerable. On the other hand, the ball that has to be putted in the same direction that the machine went has an unusually smooth and slippery surface to glide over. It is very easy to see which way the machine has gone. On a newly-cut green there are stripes of different shades of green. The points of the grass give the deeper tints, and therefore the machine has been coming towards you on the dark stripes, and along them you must putt harder than on the others.

The variety of the circumstances to be taken into consideration render putting on undulating greens very attractive to the man who makes a proper and careful study of this part of the game, as every player ought to do.

CHAPTER XV

SOME GENERAL HINTS

Too much golf—Analysis of good strokes—One's attitude towards one's opponent—Inaccurate counting of strokes—Tactics in match play—Slow couples on the course—Asking for halves—On not holing out when the half is given—Golfing attire—Braces better than belts—Shoes better than boots—How the soles should be nailed—On counting your strokes—Insisting on the rules—Play in frosty weather—Chalked faces for wet days—Against gloves—Concerning clubs—When confidence in a club is lost—Make up your mind about your shot—The golfer's lunch—Keeping the eye on the ball—The life of a rubber-core—A clean ball—The caddie's advice—Forebodings of failure—Experiments at the wrong time—One kind of golf at a time—Bogey beaten, but how?—Tips for tee shots—As to pressing—The short approach and the wayward eye—Swinging too much—For those with defective sight—Your opponent's caddie—Making holes in the bunkers—The golfer's first duty—Swinging on the putting greens—Practise difficult shots and not easy ones, etc.

THE following are detached suggestions, each of which, I think, is of value and importance. In most cases they are such as I have not had an opportunity of making in any other chapter; but in a few others they are repetitions of former injunctions, for the sake of further emphasis:—

Don't play too much golf if you want to get on in the game. Three rounds a day are too much for any man, and if he makes a practice of playing them whenever he has the opportunity, his game is sure to suffer. He often says that his third round is the best of the day. But what about the first next morning? Two rounds a day are enough, and these two rounds on three days of the week are as much golf as is good for any player who does not want to become careless and stale.

Remember that the player who first settles down to the serious business of a hard match has the advantage. In a majority of cases concentrated purpose is the secret of victory.

You must be thoughtful if you want to get on in golf. Most players when they make an exceptionally good stroke gaze delightedly at the result, and then begin to talk about it to their opponent and the caddie. They rarely give a thought as to exactly how they did it, though it must be obvious that for that good result to have been obtained the stroke must have been played in a particularly correct and able manner. Unless by pure accident, no good ever comes of a bad stroke. When you have made a really wonderfully good shot—for you—bring yourself up sharply to find out exactly how you did it. Notice your stance, your grip, and try to remember the exact character of the swing that you made and precisely how you followed through. Then you will be able to do the same thing next time with great confidence. Usually when a player makes a really bad stroke you see him trying the swing over again—without the ball—wondering what went wrong. It would pay him much better to do the good strokes over again in the same way every time he makes them, so as to impress the method of execution firmly upon his mind.

Don't praise your own good shots. Leave that function to your partner, who, if a good sort, will not be slow in performing it. His praise will be more discriminating and worth more than yours. And don't say spiteful and unkind things about his good shots, or be continually talking about his luck. If you do he will hate you before the game is over.

When a hole is being keenly contested, and you look as though you are having the worst of it, try not to appear pleased when your opponent makes a bad stroke or gets into serious trouble, however relieved or even delighted you may feel. It is human nature to feel the better for your opponent's mistake in a crisis of this kind, but it is not good manners to show that you feel it. And, however well you may know your friend, it is not half so funny as you think it is to laugh at such a time or shout out that you rejoice. It is simply bad taste, for your opponent at that time is suffering from a sense of keen disappointment, and is temporarily quite unable to appreciate jokes of this kind. He is inclined to think he has been mistaken in you all along, and that you are much less of a gentleman and a sportsman than he had imagined.

If he is playing several more in a vain endeavour to extricate himself from a bunker, do not stand near him and audibly count his strokes. It would be justifiable homicide if he wound up his pitiable exhibition by applying his niblick to your head. It is better to pretend that you do not notice these things. On the other hand, do not go out of your way to say that you are sorry when these misfortunes happen. Such expressions imply a kind of patronage for which your opponent will not thank you, and he knows all the time that you do not really mean it, and therefore infers that you are a hypocrite. The best golf is that which is played in comparative silence.

At the beginning of a match do not worry yourself with the idea that the result is likely to be against you. By reflecting thus upon the possibilities of defeat one often becomes too anxious and loses one's freedom of style.

Take more risks when you are down to your opponent than when you are up on him. If you play a difficult shot successfully, the circumstance will probably have some effect upon the other man.

It is a mistake continually to exercise extreme caution. One's play is severely cramped by an excess of care.

Try, whenever possible, to make matches with opponents who are at least as good, if not better than yourself. This will do your game more good than playing with an inferior player against whom you will always be liable to play in a careless manner.

Always make an effort to improve your game, and do not content yourself with the idea that you go out on the links for the exercise only. It is no more difficult or less pleasant trying to play better than it is to go on continually in the same old way.

When making a match, do not try to get a greater allowance of strokes than that to which you are entitled on your handicap, alleging to your opponent that the said handicap is an unfair one. Your opponent may think you are a little too " keen "; and if he grants your improper request, and you should then win the match, he may think some other things besides.

Remember that more matches are lost through carelessness at the beginning than through any other cause. Always make a point of trying to play the first hole as well as you have ever played a hole in your life. The favourite saying of some players, " I never try to win the first hole," is the most foolish thing ever said in connection with the game of golf. Win as many holes as you can in the early part of the game. They may be useful for you to fall back upon later on.

Try to avoid an unnecessary expenditure of nerve force by treating your adversary—with all due respect to him— as a nonentity. Whatever brilliant achievements he may accomplish, go on quietly playing your own game.   There is always the probability that sooner or later he will make enough mistakes to bring him back to you.   It is the steadier player who plays his own game from the first tee to the last green, and who never allows himself to be upset by anything that happens, who wins the match.

Never hurry when playing a match or a medal round, or indeed any kind of golf.   Haste will affect your nerves and spoil your play.   The record for playing a round in the shortest possible space of time is not worth the holding.   Take time enough, but don't be unnecessarily slow.

If from any cause whatever you are playing a very slow game, don't miss an opportunity of inviting the couple behind you to pass.   It will please them, and will be far more comfortable for you.   But if your match is behind a slow one, do not be offensive in pressing upon the match in front by making rude remarks and occasionally playing when they are within range.   You do not know what troubles they are enduring.   Remember the story of the old player, who, on a ball being driven past him by the couple behind, sent his caddie with his card to the offender, and with it the message, " Mr. Blank presents his compliments, and begs to say that though he may be playing slowly he can play a devil of a lot more slowly if he likes ! "

Be careful that you always stand on the proper side of the tee when your opponent is preparing to drive.   At this most anxious moment for your friend do not be practising your own swing or move about or talk.   You would be intensely annoyed with him if he did these things when you were driving.   If he lost the match through a foozled drive, he would be justified in saying that you did not play the game.

In playing through the green, avoid as far as possible getting in your opponent's line of sight when he is making his stroke. Also do not stand so near to him that he can see you through the corner of his eye when he is taking his swing.

Do not get into the habit of asking for a half on the putting green when in your own opinion you are lying dead and have one stroke left for the half. You may not be as dead as you think, and your opponent may not consider you are dead at all. He naturally wonders why you ask for the half when it would be so easy to putt the ball. It would be excusable if he were to offer to make you a present of the ball you have on the match. These propositions about the giving of halves should invariably come from the other side. Besides, when you have asked for a half and your opponent says "No; putt it out," you not only look foolish, but you are so irritated that you may very likely miss the putt Then you will look more foolish than ever, and the next thing you will lose is the match.

But when your opponent of his own free will says, " I will give you that," meaning the little putt for the half, show your appreciation of his confidence in your putting by picking up the ball and saying no more about it. Don't insist on putting the ball into the hole either with one hand or in any other way. You are sure to be playing carelessly ; and suppose you fail to hole? Your opponent said he gave you the half, and yet you failed afterwards to get it when you insisted on playing. Of course you have a right to the half that he gave you, but you will have an uneasy conscience, and your friend will be sorry that he was so generous. Also, when you have carelessly missed a six-inch putt for the half, do not remark to your opponent, as some players do, "Of course, if you insist upon it, I will give you the hole." It is no question of insistence; it is the rule of the game. I say, stick to the rules of the game.

Never use long headed clubs. The shorter headed clubs are easier to play with and are more accurate.

Do not wear too tightly fitting clothes. Particularly be careful to see that there is plenty of spare cloth under the arms. Tightness here, where there should be the utmost freedom, means the wholesale ruination of what would otherwise have been good strokes.

Always use braces in preference to a belt round the waist. I never play with a belt. Braces seem to hold the shoulders together just as they ought to be. When a man plays in a belt he has an unaccustomed sense of looseness, and his shoulders are too much beyond control. It is a mistake to imagine you can swing better with a belt than with braces. For the same reason I do not advise a golfer to play without his coat, even on the warmest day, if he wants to play his best game.

Whenever possible, use shoes for golfing instead of boots. They allow more freedom to the ankles, and make it much easier to pivot on the toes. Keep the leather of your boots and shoes soft and pliable. Apply dubbin to them in the winter.

Take care that there are plenty of nails on the soles of your boots and shoes, and that they are in good condition and the heads not worn away. Nails in this state are almost useless, and create a great tendency towards slipping. Aluminium nails, though very light, wear away too quickly, and have a tendency to drop out. I do not like big nails of any description, nor do I favour small ones arranged in clusters. Those that I prefer have round heads about the

size of a small pea, and are fluted down the sides. I have
the soles and heels of my boots freely studded with these,
and always according to the same system.
There are twenty-five nails on the sole of
each boot and fourteen on each heel, and
they are arranged as in the accompanying
diagram. It will be observed that there are
plenty of nails in the fore part of the sole
on which the pivoting is done, and where
there is the greatest tendency to slip.

Do not get into the habit of counting
your strokes from the beginning of the round
in every match that you play, in the hope
that each time you may be able to beat your
own record for the course. If you do so, and
play one or two bad holes to begin with, you
will suffer from a sense of disappointment which may
have a bad effect upon your play for the remainder of the
game.

NAILS IN
GOLFING BOOTS
AND SHOES.

Obtain a thorough knowledge of the rules of the game,
always play strictly according to them, and adhere rigidly to
the etiquette of golf. When you insist upon the rules being
applied to yourself, even to your own disadvantage, you are
in a stronger position for demanding that your opponent
shall also have the same respect for them. When play is
always according to the rules, with no favour shown on
either side, the players know exactly where they are. When
the rules are occasionally overthrown, difficulties and dissatisfaction constantly ensue.

When playing in frosty weather, do not take it for
granted that because the greens are hard they are also fast.
Unless the greens were exceedingly smooth when the frost
began, they will be covered with an abundance of little

frozen knobs and pimples which greatly retard the progress of the ball.

In wet weather it is a good thing to carry a piece of chalk in your pocket, and to rub the face of the driver and brassy with it each time before making a stroke. It prevents the ball from skidding.

Unless you have a very good and special reason for doing so, do not play in gloves. The grip is seldom so secure and exact as when it is effected with the bare hands.

Always use the club that takes the least out of you. Play with an iron instead of forcing your shot with a mashie. Never say, "Oh, I think I can reach it with such and such a club." There ought never to be any question of your reaching it, so use the next more powerful club in order that you will have a little in hand. It will be easier, and the result will be much better, or at least it ought to be.

Never use thick handle grips. They place weight at the wrong end of the club. I like the thinnest I can get. I do not advise playing with rubber grips if they can be avoided. On a wet day they might be the cause of a lost match.

Always use spliced in preference to socketed clubs. They are better in every way.

Do not be tempted to invest in a sample of each new golfing invention as soon as it makes its appearance. If you do you will only complicate and spoil your game and encumber your locker with much useless rubbish. Of course some new inventions are good, but it is usually best to wait a little while to see whether any considerable section of the golfing public approves of them before rushing to a shop to order one.

If you have completely lost confidence for the time being in any particular club, even though it may be one with which you have performed brilliantly in days gone by, leave it out of your bag altogether for a short season and try to forget all about it. The day will come before very long when you will feel that it is once more the very club you are wanting to make your game perfect, and you will rejoice to renew its acquaintance when you take it out of your locker. We can see too much of even our best friends.

Always make up your mind definitely and finally before taking up your stance what club you are going to use and exactly the kind of shot that you want to play with it. When you have taken up your position but still ponder in a state of uncertainty, it is very probable that your mind will be affected by your hesitation, and then your swing and the result thereof will be bad.

There are fewer certainties in golf than in any other game, and dogged pluck is rarely so well rewarded as on the links.

If you are playing golf in the afternoon, do not lunch any more heavily that you feel to be necessary. A heavy lunch tends to take the keenness out of a golfer, and at the same time it has—what very few people suspect—a very serious effect upon the eye and its capacity for work. The golfer's eyes often give way to the strain that is put upon them long before his limbs.

When we talk about keeping the eye on the ball, we do not mean the top of the ball. Your object is not to hit the top of the ball with the bottom of your club. For an ordinary stroke keep your attention fixed on the grass immediately behind the ball. This should result in the sole of your club sweeping evenly along the turf and taking the ball just as it ought to be taken. But there are special occasions, as when a low shot against the wind is wanted (fully explained in previous chapters), when it is desirable to hit the ball rather higher up. The eye should then be fixed on the edge of the ball just half-way up from the bottom to the top. The accompanying diagram shows exactly the points to be looked at when playing the different strokes. You may get in good strokes when looking at the top of the ball, but it is only because you have accustomed yourself by long experience to make a small allowance for so doing. The practice is theoretically bad, and it is mainly the reason why beginners top their balls so frequently. Of course when you look down the side of it in the manner indicated, you have the ball always in view.

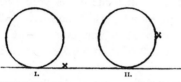

POINTS TO LOOK AT WHEN ADDRESSING THE BALL — (I.) FOR AN ORDINARY STROKE; (II.) FOR A PUSH SHOT.

The life of a rubber-cored ball does not always last as long as its shell, and its best driving capacity has often disappeared when there is scarcely a scratch upon it. Therefore, if you are playing in an important match with a ball that has already been used at a large number of holes, it may be advisable to put down a new one when long work with the driver and brassy is a vital necessity. A close watch for loss of shape should also be kept on these rubber-cored balls. They vary very much in this respect, and not only is it impossible to putt well with a ball that is not perfectly round, but it never flies so well as one which is quite true.

Always use a clean ball, and carry a sponge to keep it clean with. It detracts from the pleasure of a game more than you may imagine if your ball is always dirty and cannot be seen from a distance. Besides, the eye is less strained when a clean white ball is played with, and there is less likelihood of foozled strokes. Moreover, your dirty ball is a constant irritation to your opponent.

Don't act upon the advice of your caddie when you are convinced in your own mind that he is wrong. If you do so, you will very likely play the stroke hesitatingly and without confidence, and the result in these circumstances is seldom satisfactory. It is not impossible that the caddie knows less about the game than yourself, and, on the other hand, his views as to the best thing to do in a particular situation are often regulated by what he has seen the scratch men do at such times. You may not be a scratch man.

When playing in a foursome, never forget that you have a partner. If you are the inferior player, make a rule, when in any doubt, of asking him what he would prefer you to do.

When you are addressing the ball, and a conviction forces itself on your mind just before making the stroke that your stance or something else is radically wrong, do not be persuaded that it is best to get the stroke done with notwithstanding. In such circumstances it is almost certain to be a failure, and you will wish then that you had taken a fresh stance, as you knew you ought to have done, and made a proper job of it, even at the risk of annoying your partner by fiddling about on the tee.

At a crisis in a match, some golfers, fighting desperately for victory or a half, give themselves up when on the tee to hideous thoughts of all the worst ways in which they have ever made that particular drive and of the terrible consequences that ensued. This is fatal. A golfer must never be morbid. If he cannot school himself to think that he is going to make the best drive of his life, just when it is most wanted, he should try not to think of anything at all.

Don't try experimental shots on a new system when your opponent is dormy. It may be quite true that those you make on the old system are very bad, but you had better stick to them until the end of this match at any rate.

Do not attempt to play two kinds of golf at the same time; that is to say, if you are playing for a medal, do not keep up a hole-to-hole match with your partner. You will become confused, with no clear idea of what you are trying to do, and you will probably win neither the medal nor the match. If you feel that you must match yourself in some manner with the man who is going round with you, back your net return against his.

Because you do a hole in bogey, or even sometimes in one stroke less, do not always take it for granted that you have therefore played perfect golf. Some bogeys are very easy, and some shots are very fluky. A man may miss his drive, run a bunker, and hole out with his mashie, beating bogey by a stroke. But he would be well advised not to say anything about it afterwards, lest he should be asked for details. Not the smallest credit attaches to him for this remarkable performance.

Always play from a low tee, except when the wind is behind you.

See that your head remains rigid, from the moment when you have finally taken up your position and are ready for your swing, until you have struck the ball.

In addressing, always oppose to the ball that part of the face of the club with which you want to hit it.

Go slowly back, but be quick on the ball. But do not swing back too slowly or you will lose control over your club. Gain speed gradually.

At the finish of the swing for a full shot, the right heel should be well up and the toe pointed downwards. The chest should then be facing the hole. But these and all similar movements should be quite natural. If they are forced they are useless and dangerous, and only indicate that your methods and your swing are altogether wrong. In such a dilemma study the photographs in this volume, particularly those that show you how you ought *not* to do the various strokes. If these do not provide you with a cure, consult the professional at your club.

Don't press, but note the definition of pressing in Chapter VI. You can hit hard without pressing, which really means jumping at the ball. When your swing is working to perfection and you are full of confidence, you may let yourself go as much as you please. It is not true, as some golfers say, that a gently hit ball will travel as far as one which has been hit with much more force, but otherwise in precisely the same manner.

You must be particularly on your guard against pressing —real pressing—when you are two or three holes down, and are becoming anxious about the match. Perfect confidence and a calm mind are necessary for the success of every stroke.

Keep your eye on the side of the ball, particularly when you are near the hole and perhaps playing a little chip shot on to the green. There is a tendency at such a time, so great is the anxiety of the golfer to know whether he is laying himself dead or not, to take the eye from the ball and direct its attention to the pin before the downward swing is complete and the stroke has been made. But I do not approve of keeping the eye fixed upon the place where the ball lay, so that the grass is seen after the ball has departed. Keep your eye on the ball until you have hit it, but no longer. You cannot follow through properly with a long shot if your eye remains fastened on the ground. Hit the ball, and then let your eye pick it up in its flight as quickly as possible. Of course this needs skilful timing and management, but precision will soon become habitual.

When you hit the small of your back with the head of your club in the upward swing, it is not so much a sign that you are swinging too far back as that your wrists are enjoying too much play, that you are not holding your club with sufficient firmness, and that your arms are thrown too much upwards. Try a tighter grip. Remember that the grip with *both* hands should be firm. That with the right hand should not be slack, as one is so often told.

If your eyesight is not good and you are obliged to resort to artificial aids when playing the game, wear spectacles rather than eye-glasses, and specially made sporting spectacles in preference to any others. It is of the utmost importance that the glasses should not only be perfectly steady at all times, but that the rims should not be so near to the centre of vision as to interfere with it under any circumstances. The sporting spectacles which I recommend are similar to those used for billiards and shooting. The rims and the glasses are circular and not oval in shape, and they are unusually large—about $1\frac{1}{2}$ inches in diameter. By the use of them the player is afforded a field of vision as wide as with the naked eye, so that practically he is not conscious that he is wearing glasses at all. The eye is a factor of such immense importance in the proper playing of golf, that this is a matter to be strongly insisted upon. My own eyesight is perfect, and I have never had occasion to resort to artificial assistance of it, but I adopt these suggestions from players of experience who have worn these glasses ana upon whose judgment I can rely.

If you have no caddie, do not order your opponent's caddie about as if you were paying for his services. Any assistance that he may give you is an act of courtesy extended to you by your opponent.

Always fill in afterwards every hole that you make in a bunker. If all players do that, both you and the others will benefit constantly.

Make a point of seeing that your caddie always replaces your divots, or replace them yourself if you have no caddie. This, as we all know, is a golfer's first duty. If your ball, at any time came to rest in a hole where a divot had not been replaced, you would be extremely annoyed, would say hard things about the other players on the links, and would declare that the course was badly kept.

Never practise swinging on the putting green. It is not good for the green, and the greenkeeper who takes a pride in the results of his work is not usually in the best of tempers when he sees you at this little game.

When carrying your own clubs, do not throw the bag down on the greens. If you do so the toes of the iron clubs are certain to make marks, which neither improve the greens nor the game of the players who follow you.

Never try your shots over again when there are other players behind you. It makes your partner uncomfortable, and he feels that he ought to apologise on your behalf to those who are kept waiting.

When practising, use the club that gives you the most trouble, and do not waste your time in knocking a ball about with the tool that gives you the most satisfaction and with which you rarely make a bad stroke.

CHAPTER XVI

COMPETITION PLAY

IT is the same game whether it is match or medal play, and the same whether you are merely engaged in friendly rivalry with an old friend, with half a crown or nothing at all but the good game itself at stake, or testing your skill and giving rein to your ambition in a club or open tournament with gold medals and much distinction for the final victors. But, same game as it is, how convinced have we all been at times that it is a very hard thing to play it always in the same way. How regularly does an evil fate seem to pursue us on those days when we are most desirous of doing ourselves full justice. Five times in a week will a golfer go round the course and beat bogey, reckoning after each performance that he has only to repeat it on Saturday to win the prize which he covets, with several strokes to spare. Then Saturday comes, and a sad falling off is there. By the time the sixth or seventh hole is reached, the all-important card has perhaps been torn up into little pieces and flung contemptuously into a convenient ditch.

Of course much of this sort of thing is due to nervousness, and there is no game in which full control of the nerves and extreme coolness are more necessary than in golf. Let the player be as keen as he likes—the keener the better —but if he is apt to become too anxious at the critical stage of a round or match, he is not the man who will ever win prizes in great competitions. He who is the most composed when in difficulties and when the game is going against him, and who treats each fresh trouble as it comes along as a part of the ordinary day's work to be surmounted in the best manner possible, is the player who will most frequently come out the conqueror. In many cases the tendency to fall into a highly nervous state at the smallest provocation will disappear with time and lengthening experience. Each year of golf should bring increasing steadiness, and the steadier a golfer becomes the more frequently will he do his best scores when they are most wanted. And so I must leave it to time and practice and the proper cultivation of the best methods to bring the ambitious beginner along into the front rank of his contemporaries. But still there are some useful hints which I may offer him and which may facilitate his progress towards the acquisition of medals and cups.

To begin with, there is a little sermon to be preached on that torn card. "Nil desperandum" should always be the motto of the competition player, and it is a motto that will probably pay better in golf than in any other game. I think it is very likely that some scores of monthly medals have been lost through a too precipitate destruction of the scoring card when everything seemed to be going the wrong way. Every player should remember that it is indeed a perfect card that is without a blemish, and that on the other hand there are few rounds played by a man who knows anything about the game that are bad all through. But some men, because they have the misfortune to be debited with a couple of 8's in the first four or five holes, forthwith give up the ghost and rend their cards into small pieces with many and varied

expressions of disgust.   Thereafter they play well, and at the
conclusion of the match are inclined to think that they were
rather in too much of a hurry to be out of the competition in
its early stages.   If they had made a fine card for fourteen or
fifteen holes from the beginning, they might have taken two
8's towards the end much less seriously to heart.   They would
have said to themselves that at all events there were many
very fine holes, and the misfortunes which came later were
not sufficient to spoil their chances of success.   Well, then,
when these annoyances happen near the beginning, why not
take a philosophical view of them and say that as they had
to come it was best that they should come quickly and be
done with, and then go on playing hole after hole coolly and
properly until at the end it is found that the early misfortunes have been amply retrieved?   I am aware that this
is very simple advice, and that it appears like a string of
platitudes, but it is extremely sound and yet it is ignored
on every medal day.   Never, never tear up your card, for
golf is indeed a funny game, and no man knows what is
going to happen when it is being played.   There are
numberless historic instances to support this counsel, but I
will quote only one which came under my personal observation recently, and which to my mind is one of the most remarkable of all.   It occurred at a London club.   Six players
were left in the final round for a cup competition, and the
conditions of playing in this final were that a medal round
should be played on two different Saturdays.   On the first
Saturday three of the players tore up their cards, and so
only three remained to fight out the issue on the second
Saturday.   On this occasion one of the remaining three tore
up his card very early, and soon afterwards a second did so
each being unaware of the other's action, the third player
being likewise ignorant of the fact that his rivals had disappeared from the contest, and that now, being the only
man left in, he could make any return he liked and become
the possessor of the cup.   Presently he also fell into grievous

difficulties, and was on the point of tearing up his card like the others, when the player who was marking for him stayed his hand. He had some idea of what had happened, and, bad score as his man's was, he insisted on its being completed, with the result of course that he was hailed as the winner of the tournament. He at all events would for the rest of his golfing days respect the moral which I have here endeavoured to convey; and what must have been the reflections of the other competitors who threw up the sponge, when they discovered afterwards that if they had kept plodding along they would still have had an excellent chance!

Similarly in match-play competitions, do not get into the way of thinking that your chance is hopeless just because your opponent becomes two or three up on you, or even more than that, early in the game; and, above all, do not alter your style of play in consequence. Nothing pays like your own best and steadiest game and a stolid indifference to all the brilliant things that your opponent is doing. It is unlikely that he will keep on doing them all through the game, and when the reaction comes you will speedily make up the leeway. There are many ups and downs in a game of golf; and when the players are at all evenly matched, and neither has lost his head, early differences have a way of regulating themselves before the game is very far advanced. No doubt it is disconcerting to be three down after only three have been played; but are there not fifteen still to come? But it often appears that an even greater danger awaits the inexperienced golfer than that of funk when things are going against him, in that he is too frequently apt to become careless when he has obtained a trifling advantage. Never slacken your efforts when you are two or three holes up, but continue to play with all your might and with an extreme of cautiousness until at last you are one more up than there are holes still to play, for not until then are you sure of victory. When a man has once held a good lead, but by playing carelessly has allowed his opponent to get on level terms with him again, the moral effect upon him is usually extremely bad. When this has happened he is inclined to regard himself not as still on equal terms with his opponent, but as having suffered a great loss and being in grave danger of defeat. And this feeling is the prelude to actual defeat and the bitter self-accusations that must inevitably follow. I may have seemed to labour these simple points, but every old golfer will bear me out in saying that a proper regard for the essence of this advice is the first necessity for the man who covets honours in the golfing world.

I say that all golf is the same, and no matter whether it is match or medal play, the simple object is to hole out each time in the fewest number of strokes; but the fact that a single bad hole counts far more heavily against you in a medal round, where all the strokes are added together at the finish, than in match play, where the bad hole is simply one of eighteen, and in which there is only one man to be beaten, of whose performances you are a spectator, instead of an invisible field—this difference generally calls for a change in tactics, particularly on the part of the player who knows to a nicety his own capabilities and limitations. Score play is not, of course, so generally interesting as match play, and for this reason will never be so popular; but from my point of view it is the best golf and the best test of golf; indeed, in these respects I think there is really no comparison between the two systems. Score play tests the qualities of both the golfer and the sportsman. If he makes a bad hole and drops two or three to bogey, he must not lose his temper, which proceeding is both useless and fatal, but must screw up his determination, and realise that if he can snatch a stroke from bogey at the next two or three holes, all will be just as well as ever. He must always be hopeful. If we never made a bad hole, were never set any difficult task, always did just what we tried to do—well, what then would be the use of playing golf? We should very soon ask ourselves this question, and as there would be no satisfactory answer to it, we should cease to play. The difficulties and the annoyances of golf are after all the things that make the game so attractive and render it so subtly fascinating.

But all the same, when you are playing a medal round in a competition, give due consideration beforehand to this overwhelming fact, that bad holes do tell more heavily against you than in match play, and that when they are made they are not over and done with, but are on permanent record as faults to be atoned for before the round is completed. When the score player sends his ball into a bunker, takes two to escape, and holes out in eight strokes instead of in five, his punishment is not completed at this stage, as in match play. The case is held over in view of what his future conduct may be. He is, in fact, ordered to come up for judgment if called upon. Now, to avoid the pain and anxiety of all this, I suggest to the player who takes out a card in a score competition, that he should make up his mind at the beginning of the round that from the first hole to the finish he will be more than usually cautious. By this I do not mean to say that he should always play the strict safety game, for the man who invariably plays for safety and nothing else will soon find his card running up very high. Certain risks must be taken; but do not accept the very doubtful risks. In match play, I say always play the bold game. Go for everything that you can. If there is a bunker somewhere about the limit of your best possible carry, go for it. If you have a long putt for the hole, give the hole a chance, and either be in or beyond. But I do not suggest that these things should also be done in score-play competitions. If the hole is guarded by a bunker, and you have reason to fear that you cannot carry that bunker, it is in these circumstances a thousand times better to play short than to take the risk of putting your ball into it and making a serious blot upon your card.   Similarly, when on the putting green, and there is a long distance between your ball and the hole, bring your mind to realise that it is really of less importance that you should hole out in one stroke than that you should do so in not more than two, and therefore concentrate your whole energies on placing yourself dead for the second putt.   Therefore I say, accept a risk now and then when there is a fairly good prospect of success, and when the reward for it will be commensurate with the danger that was incurred.

The last-named is an important clause.   The course should be studied hole by hole for medal play, and the competitor should come to an exact understanding with himself as to the things that must be done and what things need not be done.   Thus it frequently happens that a player, seeing a bunker some distance in front of him but yet not quite out of his range, goes for it as a matter of course. Obviously he must incur a certain amount of risk, and it may happen that even if he carries it in safety he may not be better off at all than if he were ten or fifteen yards on the playing side.   In either case it may be an easy shot to the green, and it may even happen that of the two the longer one would be the easier for this particular golfer.   But it is quite likely that he never took any account of that when taking the risk of the bunker.   Now this man is to be remonstrated with, for, with the best intentions, he has displayed not courage but folly.   He must realise that all bunkers are not of necessity to be carried with long shots. If all golfers played the same game, and always their best game, and, moreover, if all bunkers were placed in the proper places for bunkers, then it would be their duty to go for them every time.   But either through the very good or the very bad shots that have gone before, we find that these carries vary very much, and, besides, the bunkers on all courses are certainly not placed exactly where they ought to be, and so for reckoning up the proper mode of play in order that the hole may be captured in the fewest possible number of strokes, they can sometimes for all practical purposes be disregarded.

A golfer is often in an anxious state of mind when the day of a competition in which he wishes to do well arrives, and he is painfully conscious that he is completely off his play with one or other of his clubs, and has an abiding fear that it will bring him to grief. When he feels like this about the club, it will probably do so. Now the question is, whether at this crisis he shall take out a new one with which he is entirely unfamiliar and trust to luck with it, or put his faith once more in the instrument which of late has repeatedly spoilt his game. He is usually advised that in such circumstances he should not indulge in any risky experiments, and that it is madness to take a new and untried club out with him when it is more or less imperative that he should play one of his best rounds. But I am not by any means sure that this advice is well founded. No golfer plays well with a club in which he has completely lost confidence. It may not be the fault of the club at all; but there is the fact. On the other hand, the player is always possessed of a certain amount of hope when he takes a new implement in his hands. He has convinced himself beforehand, or at least ought to have done, that its points are just what he most admires, and that he is likely to do well with it. And so he probably will, even if it is only for a round or two. It is the confidence trick again. What I suggest, therefore, is that when this grave uncertainty exists about the kind of performance that will probably be made with one of the articles in the bag, and there is a new and good substitute ready at hand, the latter should not be disregarded because of a kind of instinct that in a big fight it is best to stick to the old weapons. Take the new one out with you, but do not call it into service for the first hole or two. During this preliminary stage give the old but disappointing favourite another chance to show that it will not desert you in the hour of need; but if it fails to rise to the occasion and you blunder with it during the play at the first and second holes, pass sentence upon it forthwith and relegate it finally to your bag. Then at the third hole let the new one have its trial. Over and over again have I found this method succeed most wonderfully, and I am a particular believer in it in connection with putters. A golfer may have been putting badly for a long time, but directly he takes a new putter in his hand he feels that a great change for the better has been effected, and forthwith he begins to astonish himself by holing out from almost anywhere, or at least always getting his ball dead the first time. There is no accounting for these things. They seem very absurd. But there they are, and no doubt it will be agreed that a medal or a cup is worth a new putter any time.

I do not believe in any sort of training for important golf matches. It is not necessary, and it generally upsets the man and throws him off his game. If he is a smoker let him smoke all the time, and if he likes an occasional glass of wine let him take it as usual. A sudden stoppage of these luxuries causes a feeling of irritation, and that is not good for golf. The game does not seem the same to you as it was before. For my part I am neither a non-smoker nor an abstainer, and I never feel so much at ease on the links and so fully capable of doing justice to myself as when smoking. But at the same time I believe in the most complete moderation. Only by the constant exercise of such moderation can that sureness of hand and eye be guaranteed which are absolutely necessary to the playing of good golf. On one occasion when I had a championship in view I stopped the tobacco for a short period beforehand, and I am bound to confess that the results seemed excellent, and perhaps some day I may repeat the experiment. But there was nothing sudden about the abstinence in this case, and by the time the big days came round I had become thoroughly accustomed to the new order of things, and the irritation had passed away. However, these are matters which every man may be left to decide for himself according to his own good common sense, and the only object I had in introducing them was to counsel the avoidance of sudden whims and freaks, which are never good for golf.

Another question is how much or how little golf should be played beforehand when a man desires to give himself the best chance of playing his best game on a certain specified day. That depends largely upon how much golf he is in the habit of playing in the ordinary course. If he is a man who plays regularly, almost every day when it is fine, I think he will generally do far better for himself by abstaining altogether for a day or two before the competition. Then, when he goes out to play in it, he will experience a zest and keenness which will be very much in his favour. There is no danger that in this brief period of rest he will have forgotten anything that he knew before, but, on the other hand, he will have a greatly improved capacity for taking pains, and every stroke will be easy to him. His confidence will be refreshed. If he continues to play his round or two rounds every day right up to the date of the competition, he will undoubtedly be "over-golfed," will have a great tendency to fall into errors, and will be generally careless. But if the would-be prize-winner is a man who has usually to content himself with week-end golf, it would be all in his favour if he could put in a day or two of practice before taking part in the big event. There will be no possibility of his becoming stale by so doing.

When a competitor has the choice of playing his round either in the morning or the afternoon, I strongly advise him to select the former and get the thing over as soon as possible. I am positive that his chances of success are usually greater when he does so, especially if, in case of his electing to play in the afternoon, he has nothing particularly to occupy his mind and attention in the interval except his prospects in the forthcoming contest. Golfers are freshest and keenest in the morning, their bodies and limbs are most vigorous and anxious for work, and—a very important consideration—their eyes are most to be depended upon. And it is not an unimportant consideration that there is no indigestible lunch to interfere with the perfect ease of mind and body which are necessary to the making of a good card.

But often, particularly in the case of important open competitions, the times of starting are decided by lot, and the competitor, on arriving at the course, finds that he has to accept the disadvantages of a late draw, and must endure a period of waiting for his turn to tee up. It is best to dispose of these wearisome periods not in hanging about the tee or in the vicinity of the club-house, but by going out with one of the early couples, watching their methods, and making note of the exact manner in which their best holes are played. If the course is a strange one, the information which the watcher thus derives will be invaluable to him when he comes to play his own round, for he will now be possessed of the most excellent hints as to difficulties which demand special efforts to avoid, and of particular strokes which it is in the highest degree necessary to play well. Not until he has watched the play of others in this manner will the enormous significance of the position of a particular bunker be made clear to him; he will discover the great danger of being short with certain strokes, and of overrunning the green at various holes. By thus watching other competitors' play he will probably learn more about the nature and peculiarities of the course and the way it is playing on this particular occasion, than if he were doing a round with his own clubs. Therefore, if there is time to be killed, this is most decidedly the way in which to kill it, and I may add that it is the method which I myself adopt on every possible occasion. I know that in championships and tournaments I have reaped great advantage in watching closely the play of my fellow-competitors, their triumphs and their failures, while waiting for my own turn to begin.

CHAPTER XVII

ON FOURSOMES

I THINK it is to be regretted that the old-fashioned foursome, in which the respective partners play together with the same ball, has so completely lost favour of late, and that it has been superseded to a large extent by the four‑ball foursome. To my mind the old foursome provided a much more interesting and enjoyable game than its successor, and tended much more to the cultivation of good qualities in a golfer. It seems to me that this new four-ball game is a kind of mongrel mixture. It is played, I presume, because men feel that they would like to have a game of partners and yet are unwilling to sacrifice half the strokes of a round, as they do in the old game, and also because the man who is on his game desires all his power and brilliancy to count, and that they may not be interfered with by the possibly erratic procedure of his partner. But this is a selfish spirit, and quite opposed to that which should properly animate the men who play in combination. When a golfer is thus anxious for the display of his skill surely an ordinary single-ball match is the proper thing for

him. The four-ball foursome, I admit, has much to recommend it when the partners are equally matched, when both
are really good players—more likely to do a hole in bogey
than not—and when the course is clear and there is no
prospect of their protracted game interfering with other
players who may be coming up behind. When a short-
handicap man is mated with a long one, the place of the
latter in a foursome of the new kind is to my thinking not
worth having. Is it calculated to improve his golf, or to
afford him satisfaction of any kind whatever, if he plays
his ball round in what is for him very good form, and yet
only contributes the halving of a single hole as his share of
the victory of the combination? Very likely after such a
game he will feel that he must fall back once more on that
old excuse of the golfer for a disappointing day, that at all
events he has had the fresh air and the exercise. The tast-
ing of the pure atmosphere and the working of limb and
muscle are splendid things, enough to justify any day and
any game, but no golfer is heard to put them in the forefront
of the advantages he has derived from his day's participation
in the game unless the golf he has played has been miserably
disappointing. This new foursome is also a selfish game,
because it is generally played with too little regard for the
convenience and feelings of other golfers on the links. It
is very slow, and couples coming up behind, who do not
always care to ask to be allowed to go through, are often
irritated beyond measure as they wait while four balls are
played through the green in front of them, and eight putts
are taken on the putting green. The constant waiting puts
them off their game and spoils their day.

Another objection that I urge against this kind of game
is, that even when there is nobody pressing behind and
there is no particular reason for hurry, there is a natural
tendency on the part of each player to make haste so that
he shall not delay the other three. This is the case all the
way through the green, and particularly when the hole is

reached and the putters are taken out. Then everybody's ball seems to be in the way of the others, there is continual lifting and replacing, more hurrying, and then, to make matters worse, there is a doubt as to what a man should do in order to help his side—whether he should hole out in one or two, or whether there is any use in holing out at all. Consequently his mind is in a confused state of reckoning and doubt when he makes his putt, and poor putt it is likely to be in such circumstances. Frequently, when a blind hole is being played, it needs a few minutes' close examination to decide which ball is which after the drive, unless each has been carefully marked to distinguish it from the others. As a final indictment against this species of golf, I would say that even when the partners are equally matched and both good players, there is still a tendency for their individual play to be spoiled, inasmuch as there is the feeling constantly present in the mind of each, that even if he does happen to do a bad hole it will not matter very much after all, as the other man is sure to come to the rescue. When it happens that just the same thought enters the brain of that other man, a lost hole is likely to be the result. Decidedly this is not the sort of game to improve the golfer's play.

The four-ball foursome is so very like two single matches that there is little special advice to offer concerning the playing of it. One of the few special points to be observed by the player who is taking part in such a match is that, without being unduly selfish and grasping, he should as frequently as possible avoid being the last man of the four to make his drive from the tee. The man who drives last is at a very obvious disadvantage. In the first place, if he has seen the other three make really good drives, he is too much tempted to try to beat them all, and the usual result of such temptation is a bad stroke. On the other hand, if he has seen two or three foozles, it is quite possible that he will follow the bad example that has been set him.

Thus, whatever has happened before, the last man has no
real encouragement offered to him.   In addition to these
objections, when three men have driven from the tee they
are somewhat impatient to be moving on and playing their
second shots, and in this mood they have little care for what
happens to the last drive.   They have already had quite
enough of driving.   The fourth man is quite conscious of
this impatience on their part, even though it may not be
openly expressed by the smallest sign.   So he is in a hurry
to oblige, and his effort is then disappointing.   I seldom hit
my best ball when I am driving fourth in a four-ball foursome.   Of course somebody must drive last, but not necessarily the same man every time.   All that I wish to suggest
is, that a player should not be too self-sacrificing, and should
not, with too much modesty about his own prowess on the
tee, always volunteer to drive after his partner.

The old-fashioned or two-ball foursome makes a really
fine and enjoyable game.   It brings golfers together on
even more intimate and friendly relations than usual.
Partners in a foursome see very deep down into the human
nature of each other.   They are overwhelmingly conscious
of each other's faults and weaknesses.   They are enormously
dependent upon each other.   At the same time I do not
think that even this kind of foursome is the best thing in
the world for the improvement of a man's game, and I advise the young player to resist the temptation to take part
in too many foursomes, to the neglect of ordinary match
play in singles.   For one thing, the partners, of course, only
get half as much golf as they would if they were playing a
round in a single match, and for another, they are too constantly anxious to play their best game.   The sense of
responsibility is frequently a little too much for their nerves,
and you often see a man, a most dogged and persistent
player in an ordinary match, who is a consistent failure in
foursomes, and who in this style of game ought to be rated
at six strokes higher handicap than his allowance for ordi-

nary purposes. One feels in a foursome that one must be so very careful, and take so much extra pains, and when that feeling is uppermost in the mind while the stroke is being made, the result is often disastrous.

It is unwise to interfere unduly with a partner's system of play while a match is in progress. He may be missing his drive because his stance is wrong or his swing is faulty, but the state of affairs would probably be worse than ever if an attempt were made to put him right while the game is going on. The hint will be more useful when the match is over. And if he has a particular fancy for playing his brassy, when experience tells you that an iron club should be taken, it will not generally pay to make the suggestion at the time. The man naturally takes the club with which he has most confidence and with which he believes he can make the shot that is wanted. It is fatal to interfere with confidence of this kind, and to substitute for it the hesitation and doubt which inevitably take possession of the man when he takes in his hands a weapon with which he rarely does well, and which, whatever you may tell him, he is convinced is utterly inadequate for the purposes of the situation. Let each man play the various strokes that have to be made in a foursome in his own way without interference, for nothing but chaos and a lost match can follow upon the enforcement upon each other of individual ideas and methods.

This, of course, is not saying that each man should not play his game so that it may fit as well as possible into that of his partner. He may play with the club he particularly fancies, and play it in his own way, but there should be some sort of a general understanding about what he is going to do and the exact effect which his performance is likely to have upon the way the hole is played if everything happens according to programme. This makes it very desirable that the partners in a foursome match to which any importance is attached, should have more than a passing knowledge of each other's play, and of individual weaknesses and excellences. One partner may be particularly good at making a fairly full iron shot, but shaky indeed when it comes to a little pitch with the mashie over the bunker that guards the green. It is clear, on reflection, that the chief part in this playing up to each other's game should be taken by the man who has the longer handicap, and is therefore the weaker all-round player. The scratch man, being a wise and experienced golfer, will naturally place his nervous 18-handicap friend in as few difficulties as he can, and will constantly exert himself to leave him a comparatively simple shot which he may be depended upon with some certainty to accomplish in a workmanlike fashion. But the junior player must remember that it behoves him to be the most careful and considerate in matters of this kind, for in an emergency it is generally the senior who must be depended upon to win the hole or pull the match out of the fire. Let him, therefore, impose upon himself a considerable measure of self-sacrifice, playing up to his partner for all he is worth, contented in the knowledge that he is doing the proper thing, and that, though he is sinking his own individuality and doing much of what can only be described as donkey work, he is being considerably honoured by being invited to play in such superior company. It is not always the place of the junior partner to take risks; that is the prerogative of the senior. There may be a particular carry on the course which the young player is always doubtful about, but which when playing alone he constantly makes an attempt to accomplish, and very properly so. But if his effort is as often as not a failure—with the result that he is badly bunkered and the hole is lost—it would be madness for him to attempt the carry when he is playing in a foursome with a far better man than himself as his partner. He must depart from his usual custom, and play short for safety. It will be a great relief to his partner. Not lately, but in the early years of my experience, I have seen this principle carried to a curious excess. When there was a difficult carry from the tee, and an inferior player and short driver had the turn to make the stroke, I have seen his partner instruct him to miss the ball altogether—not tap it off the tee, but miss it. Thus the other man, presumably a good driver, had the ball left teed for him. These men reckoned between them that on an average it would prove of more advantage to be well over the far hazard in two strokes, than to take the risk of being short with the tee shot and possibly not getting over with the second or even the third. However, there is no doubt that performances of this kind were a violation of the spirit of golf. It is the game to hit the ball, and it is unsportsmanlike to try to miss it. Nowadays the golfing world quite realises that this is the case.

In the same way, in playing through the green and in putting, it must be the constant object of the junior to play the safety game and to feed his skilful partner with as many as possible of those strokes at which he is best. Do not let him try for a desperately long second, emulating the example which his partner set him on the tee, in the hope that he may land the ball on the green. He is not expected to do anything of the kind. If he should happen to be successful, his partner would know that it was not his usual custom, that he had played beyond himself, and that therefore there was something of the fluke in the stroke after all. He would be much more likely to fail and foozle, and then what a miserable golfer would he be! His obvious duty is to play a simple, easy stroke which will be practically certain of placing the ball in such a position that his partner will have no difficulty in getting on the green with his third. And on the putting green, when anything over ten feet distance intervenes between the ball and the hole, while always giving the latter a chance, he should remember that his first duty is to lay the ball dead. If he holes out, well and good, but his partner insists first of all that the ball should be laid dead. At this crisis, also, he should be particularly careful that he never commits the unpardonable sin of laying himself, or rather his partner, a stymie. Of all the stymies in the world, that which has been laid you by your own partner in a foursome is the most exasperating.

Of course, for the proper blending of each partner's game with that of the other, it is advisable, or rather necessary, that before the first stroke in the match is taken there should be some kind of general understanding about the policy that is to be pursued. First consideration is given to the turn in which the tee shots are to be taken, and the drives are so arranged that the better player takes them at a majority of the tees where good drives are most wanted. But it seems to me that very often an arrangement of this sort is arrived at without sufficient consideration. For example, it frequently happens that a long-handicap man is a very good driver indeed, better in fact than the man who is his partner and has a handicap of many strokes less. And in the same way it commonly occurs that a short-handicap man may be decidedly weak with his short approaches. On the average of the play from the tee to the hole the senior player may be fully so much better than the other as the difference in their handicaps suggests, but it by no means follows that in particular features of the game there is the same difference. Therefore the wise partners will adapt themselves to each other, so that they will get all the good out of themselves and leave untouched that which is bad. And when this compact is completed and honourably adhered to, there are at hand the makings of a victory.

When four players have decided among themselves to play a foursome, and there are wide differences in their respective handicaps, there is often considerable difficulty in arranging the best partnerships. It is good to be guided by mutual preferences, for preference means confidence, and that is everything in foursome play. But at the same time it is always advisable to sort out the players in such a manner that there is as little as possible of giving and receiving strokes. For example, where there is a scratch man, two 9's (or a 6 and a 10), and an 18, the best and most enjoyable match is always likely to result from a combination of the scratch man with the 18 against the two players of medium handicaps, although the scratch man, if a selfish player, may not be disposed to saddle himself with the unreliable person at the other end of the scale. It is a point to be borne in mind that the 18 man, if, despite his handicap, he is a real and conscientious golfer, is more likely to play above his handicap than the scratch man. It is much easier for an 18-handicap player to perform like a 12 than it is for a scratch man to play like a plus 3. In my opinion the arranging of strokes to be given and received in foursome play is far too delicate and complicated. In ordinary single-match play handicapping does not always work out very well, and it is often made to look foolish in a foursome. Far better is it than adding up and dividing by clumsy fractions, and then finding that one party gets five strokes or eight, that the players should take a broad view of their respective merits, and then decide that they will either play on level terms or that a third or a half shall be given and received. The best foursome of all is one played on level terms, and an effort should always be made, and even a point strained here and there, to effect such partnerships as will make this arrangement feasible.

A really good foursome, when the partners play harmoniously and the holes are well fought out, is a splendid diversion from the ordinary game of golf. The interest and excitement of each member of the party often seems to affect the others, and to lead up to an intense mutual keenness which is often superior even to that experienced in single play. There is a wholesome satisfaction in the community of interests. The winning of a hole is coveted as it was never coveted before. Have you heard what should be a classical story about the foursome? The match was all square on the sixteenth green, and one excited Scot stood by while his partner made a drive upon which the fortunes of a hard-fought game might rest. The caddies had been sent forward. The tee shot was pulled, and the ball went twisting round in the direction of the driver's boy. It struck him and he fell flat upon the ground. The driving partner dropped his club, and, with his face turned pale, muttered hoarsely to his friend, " Tonalt, I've kilt the caddie!" But Donald's mind was fixed upon other matters than the mere question of life and death, and with many excited gestures and a shriek of despair he exclaimed, " Then, tamn it all, we've lost the hole," as under Rule 25 they had.

At the end of this chapter I will make the simple remark, that you can pay a golfer no higher compliment than to say that he is a good foursome player, for such a one must not only be a good golfer and a steady one, but a man of the serenest and even most delightful temperament. You must always feel that you could not play in the company of such a man too often, either with him or against him.

CHAPTER XVIII

GOLF FOR LADIES

SOME people say that golf is not a ladies' game, and from time to time one hears of something in the nature of dissensions within the family circle when there are wives and sisters anxious to take up the sport which palpably affords their male relatives one of the greatest enjoyments of life, and when there are husbands and brothers who, it is said, advance arguments which for number and ingenuity would do credit to a King's Counsel, designed to show the absurdity and the futility of the desire expressed. It is a question upon which it would be out of place for me here to take any side, though it seems to me that there is something to be said for the complete separation of the men's golf from the ladies' golf, particularly in the case of large clubs and crowded courses. Golf is essentially a sport of freedom. Restraint of even the most trivial and conventional character in regard to manners and customs is irksome when there are holes to be played and tight matches to be pulled out of the fire. I like to see a lady go out on the golf links in whatever costume she thinks fit to wear for her own comfort and good play, and generally to do as she likes, as if there were nothing but

Nature and a little white ball and the hole with the flag in
it in all the world.   I have a great admiration for the
American lady golfer, whom I have several times had the
opportunity of studying on her native tees, and the other
day I read the perfectly true story of an American clergyman making a scathing attack from the pulpit one Sunday
upon lady golfers, of whom he numbered many in his congregation.   The reverend gentleman exclaimed that some
of the lady members of his congregation attended divine
service in the customary manner on the Sabbath, and then
" swore like troopers " on the golf links on the Monday.
The conduct of these ladies was no doubt exaggerated; but
it appears as if it may have been reprehensible.   However,
it shows the keenness and the enthusiasm of the American
lady golfer; and I am not at all sure that the answer of the
English lady player, when she was asked if those bad words
were ever uttered in this country, that the Englishwoman
made fewer bad shots and had no occasion for an extended
vocabulary, was entirely convincing.   One hears that the
ladies have coined new words for the expression of their
disgust at the results of their strokes, and, on the other hand,
that the limits of expletive which they permit themselves
when bunkered consist of the chiding utterance, " Oh, you
naughty, naughty little ball!"   However this may be, I
know not, and I would only remark, without presumption,
to the ladies, as I have done in another place to their husbands and brothers, that golf is a game for thought and
silence.

Now, I am glad to see so many ladies taking up the
game year by year, and thus giving the best possible answer
to the question whether it is a real ladies' game or not.
And furthermore, I am pleased to bear witness that the
standard of ladies' golf in this country is improving every
season, so that now it needs a fine man golfer to give a third
to the best of the gentler sex.   These good lady players, or
some of them, are attiring themselves in these days as I like

to see lady golfers attired, that is to say, there is evidence that they think a trifle less of fashion and dainty appearance than they do of security, comfort, and freedom of limb and muscle. But the majority of lady players do not attach the proper amount of importance to these considerations, and that is why one is sometimes a little doubtful as to the prospects of ladies' golf generally in this country in comparison with those of American ladies' golf. The American girls are adopting the game more whole-heartedly and thoroughly than their English sisters, and their devotion to it will tell. The lady of the States who is a golfer dresses for golf and for golf only. Very seldom do you see in America a lady golfer wearing a hat, or head covering of any description. When she has one, it is almost invariably a light tam o' shanter, or something very small and soft, which clings closely to the hair and does not get in the way of the swing of the club. She tucks up her sleeves like a man, and in the soles of her shoes she has plenty of goodly sized nails. And she does not look a tittle the worse for any of these things; indeed, the picture of the determined, strenuous, and yet charming lady golfer was one of the most attractive that I saw when in America. The average English girl does not appear willing to make so many sacrifices for golf as the American. She seems too often to say to herself that it is only a little game after all, and there is an end of it; and yet she is always desirous of getting on and reducing her handicap. I need hardly say that this is not the proper spirit in which to achieve success at golf. We see too many ladies on our links with big hats and no nails in their shoes. I have no faith whatever in their future as golfers. It is impossible to play good golf if one is not fitted out properly for the game, whether the player be lady or man. Few players of our sex would dream of going on to the links in a tightly fitting coat and smooth-soled shoes. But the ladies are more venturesome.

After this brief lecture on attire, let me at once declare

that there are many points about our English lady golfer
that I greatly admire. It has been my privilege to teach
the first principles of the game to many of them, and I am
bound to say that for the most part I have found them
excellent pupils—better generally than the men learners.
They seem to take closer and deeper notice of the hints you
give them, and to retain the points of the lesson longer in
their memories. They are painstaking; and if she begins
to play early enough in her life, adopts sensible methods,
and is possessed of an average amount of athleticism, I can
see no reason why any lady should not become a very fair
golfer. Many somewhat spoil their prospects by concluding
too hastily that they must play an altogether different game
from that of their men friends, that they must have special
clubs, special methods, and so forth. This is not the case.
No doubt it is well for ladies to admit at once that they
cannot drive as far as the men. But otherwise the man's
game and the lady's game are the same in principle and in
practice. As for the manner in which to play, I have not a
single special piece of instruction to offer, and can only refer
the lady neophyte to the previous pages, in which I have set
forth as well as I am able the precise method in which each
of the many strokes in golf should be played. I have
merely to insist that they shall not deviate from these
methods in one or two special matters in which they are
advised or inclined to do.

Ladies are frequently advised that they ought never to
take a full swing. Of course in the foregoing pages I have
frequently insisted that a golfer should avoid the absolutely
full swing with all iron clubs, believing that he gets for the
most part at least as good results with a good three-quarter
swing. But those people who warn the ladies against the
full swing, not only with their irons but with their wooden
clubs also, advise the half swing because they say it is better
for them for physical reasons, and that their results will be
practically as good as if they had taken the three-quarter

or the full. Now I am convinced that this is altogether wrong, and, without encouraging any of my lady readers to the development of a big swing and a slashing style, I do say that they will do well for themselves and for their golf if they will train themselves to the making of at least a full three-quarter. I believe that the half swing entails a severer strain upon the body when made under these circumstances than the full three-quarter, and that the body does altogether more work than is good for it, while the delusion is entertained by those who recommend the short swing that the opposite is the case. In this half swing the body seems to get too much in front of the club and to labour heavily, while in the three-quarter the arms do most of the work, as they ought to do, and the body comes in at the proper time for the remainder. Though in previous chapters I have strongly advised golfers to play a half shot with one club in preference to a full shot with one less powerful, I only do so obviously when the distance is fixed and the half shot will reach it. In playing from the tee it is an altogether different matter. In this case the distance is not fixed. The object is usually to drive as far as possible, so no half shots are wanted here.

As a general rule, ladies make use of clubs that are far too light for them. Frequently they do so by advice, and then their own instinct suggests to them that they should employ weapons less weighty than those of their male relations. This would be very sensible and proper if the clubs which men make use of were the heaviest that they could swing with effect. But a man only uses a club of a certain weight, because experience has proved that it is the best and most effectual for its purpose, and usually he has a very great reserve of strength which could be employed with heavier clubs if necessary. There is no reason at all why ladies should not employ clubs of good average weight instead of featherweights. By so doing they would spare themselves a great amount of exertion, and they would certainly get better results, for it is always much more difficult to get good results with a light club than with one of medium weight. With the featherweight the swing is very liable to get out of gear. It is cut short, and is apt to wander out of its proper direction. There is, in fact, no such control over the club as there is when one can feel the weight of the head at the end of the shaft. A lady may require clubs a trifle shorter in the shaft, but this is the only difference which need exist, and it is not of itself sufficient to make any perceptible difference in the weight.

So far as I have discovered, ladies have no special faults or weaknesses of their own, as distinct from other players, but I have found them more than usually addicted to inaccuracy in the backward swing, causing the toe of the club to be pointing upwards instead of downwards at the turning-point. This is the result of wrong action and loss of control over the wrists, and a study of my remarks on driving, where this matter is specially dealt with, should do much to obviate it. It is possible, however, that the lady's inferior strength of wrist, as compared with a man's, may have much to do with the fault, but even in that case it only needs caution and care to bring about a cure. I should say that fully three ladies out of every five whose play I have watched make this mistake, and it is a fault which has very serious consequences. I should advise all of them to make a periodical examination of the position of the club head at the top of the swing, as I indicated when discussing the drive, and if they find the toe is upwards they must make up their minds to get rid of this bad habit at any cost. If it has already become a part of the player's system, it will not be abolished without considerable difficulty. To begin with, she should try swinging back more slowly, as a too rapid backward swing has often much to do with it.

Finally, I would suggest that any lady who aspires to be a really good golfer should take numerous lessons from those players superior to herself who are qualified to give them. I have already said that I have found ladies exceedingly good pupils, and when they set about learning the game in the right way, they often make really astonishing progress. But it must be confessed that in too many cases they do not treat the difficulties of the game with sufficient seriousness, and are inclined to think that they can get on best in their own way and by the adoption of their own methods. When once a lady has been given a couple of lessons in the swing for the drive, she often insists on finding out the rest for herself, and then a bad result is inevitable. All the practice and patience in the world will not make a good lady golfer if she does not learn the game in the right way. The simple fact is that, when a man sets about the game he admits its difficulties from the beginning, and goes about surmounting them in the right manner if he is really ambitious and covetous of a short handicap. But it often seems that ladies will not admit these difficulties, and persist in their attempt to make golfers of themselves unaided. Perhaps that is one reason why ladies do not always continue with the game with that increasing eagerness and enthusiasm which is an almost invariable characteristic of the man golfer. Learn properly, and practise much; and—well, yes, do the rest like a man, and not as if there were a special woman's way. That is the essence of my counsel to the lady aspirant on the links,

THE CONSTRUCTION OF COURSES

MANY as are the golf courses with which the coast, the country, and the suburbs of the towns and cities of Great Britain are studded, they will no doubt be still more numerous as time goes on, and it is earnestly to be desired that in the laying out of links in the future, more thought and ingenuity may be exercised than has been the case in far too many instances during the past few years, when clubs have been formed and links have been made in a hurry. Certainly some are excellent, and I cast not the least disparagement upon them. I enjoy them. Frequently the hand of the master architect of golf is visible where one observes how shrewdly and exactly the hazards have been placed, and the peculiarities of the conformation of the country turned to the utmost account when useful, or cunningly dodged when it has been considered that they could be no good to the golfer. Without a doubt, generally speaking, those courses are the best which have been designed by good players, because none know better than they what makes the best golf. A man whose handicap is some distance removed from scratch, but who has played golf for many years, and thinks with good reason that he knows a fine course when he sees one, would nevertheless, in designing a new one, be led unconsciously to make holes which would be more or less suited to his own style of play. He might, indeed, in a most heroic spirit, place a bunker at a point which he knew would be more than usually dangerous for him, and he would feel a better and a braver man for this act; but a hundred of its kind would not prevent the course from being the ideal of the long-handicap man and not the ideal of the fine player. If plans were prepared for a new links over a particular piece of territory by a 12-handicap man and a scratch player, it is highly probable that in the most material matters they would differ greatly, and it is fairly certain that a committee of the oldest and most experienced golfers would unanimously pick out the scratch player's plans from all the others as being the best and soundest, and that without knowing who had prepared them. Time and the aggregate of pleasure given to golfers of all degrees would justify the selection.

Therefore, when a new club is established and a new course is to be laid out, I suggest that it is the wiser and the better plan to take time over it and to secure the best advice. A good links is not made in a day or a week. Perhaps the cleverest and most ingenious constructor could not in a whole year make one which was in all respects the best that the land could give. Almost every time that the course was played over during the first hundred rounds, a new thought for its improvement in some small detail would occur. The moving of a tee twenty yards to the right, the addition of a couple of yards to the end of one of the bunkers, the placing of a shallow pot bunker some eight or ten yards across at some particular point—all these and many other matters of equal significance will constantly suggest themselves. My experience tells me that the perfection of a good course is slowly attained. Like wine, it takes time for the richness of its qualities to mature. Therefore, when the committee of a new club in the country sits in conference with a plan of its newly-acquired land laid on the table, and decides unanimously that a tee shall be placed at a point marked A, a bunker along the line B, another bunker at C, and the hole at D, and so forth, I protest that they are doing poor justice either to themselves or to the game. But on many links made during the past few years—made in a hurry—the results of such mechanical methods are only too apparent. I hope that the few hints that I offer in this chapter may be of service to old clubs with improvable courses and new ones with none as yet, and to those fortunate individuals who contemplate laying out a course in their private grounds for the use of themselves and their friends. Private courses are increasing in number; and for my part, though I must obviously be guilty of prejudice, I can conceive of no more enjoyable acquisition to a country house than a nine-hole course, and assuredly the possessor of it will be envied and his invitations to week-ends much coveted.

The question of the amount of land that shall be called into service for the fulfilment of a scheme for a new links is one that is usually outside the control of those who project it. They have to cut according to their cloth. I need only say here, therefore, that in a general way some thirty or forty acres of land are necessary to make such a nine-hole course as shall possess a satisfactory amount of variety, and not less than seventy acres for a full-sized eighteen-hole course, this as a matter of fact being the acreage of the South Herts Club's course at Totteridge, with which I am at present associated. By great economy of space and the exercise of unlimited ingenuity, courses might be made from a trifle less land, but they are better when they are made from more. Two or three hundred acres are sometimes utilised for a good links. Where land is very scarce, and there is no possibility of obtaining more of it, I earnestly advise private owners and committees to content themselves with a nine-hole course which will have plenty of length and good sporting quality about it, rather than sacrifice the good golf that is thus within their reach in a desire to possess a regulation eighteen-hole links that could only give complete satisfaction to ladies and children. Too many courses, with scarcely a brassy shot upon them, have been ruined by this greed for holes.

When the land has been allotted to the purpose, a very thorough and careful survey should be made of all its features. This is not to be done in one morning. The land, no doubt, is very rough, and at the first glance it looks ill-adapted to the golfer's purpose. Many times I have had the task of making a course from materials which at first seemed so unpromising as to be hopeless. There should be no hurry at this time. Let those who are designing the links walk slowly and meditatively over nearly every square yard of the land at least two or three times before coming to any final decision as to where to place a single tee, bunker, or hole. An open mind is the best to begin with. After one or two of these preliminary surveys, some general idea of the possible formation of the links will begin to shape itself in the mind, and this having been done, it will be practically impossible for an intelligent person to make additional journeys over the land without being struck with an idea for a great improvement at one or other of the holes which he has fashioned in his mind. If it is possible, take two or three weeks over this slow process of creation of the links. They may be altered afterwards to some extent, but for good or ill their main features will probably remain as at the beginning, and may endure for centuries. Having secured to the mind this general and somewhat vague idea of the plan of the links, it is a good thing to plant a stake at each spot where it is proposed to make a hole; and when the land is all staked out in this manner, there is, as it were, a solid foundation upon which to build up the links. The location of the stakes can be inspected from a distance and from different points of view, and it will constantly happen on these occasions that for the improvement of one or other of the holes its removal to a different place will be suggested.   Continue your walks, examining the stakes from north, south, east, and west, and moving them here and there until you begin to feel a trifle weary of the business, and confident that you have planned the best possible holes out of the country that you have to deal with.   Then you may proceed with perhaps the more interesting but certainly the harder part of your task.

It is useless to think about fashioning the links from the plan which will now have been formed, until those natural disadvantages of the land, which cannot be allowed to remain, have been removed.   Gorse and rocks may have to be cleared, and it is essential that at this stage an effort should be made to rid the course of rabbits and other undesirable vermin if any should infest it.   Rabbits help to keep the grass nice and short; but they make too many holes in the course, and there is no alternative but to regard them as the enemies of golf, and to make out the death warrants of them all accordingly. The quickest and surest way of getting rid of them is to search for every hole, apply the ferrets, stop up the holes afterwards, and to keep a watch for any that return.   If only one or two are left here and there, they will play much havoc with the course in the future.   From this point the way in which the work is proceeded with will naturally depend to a large extent on the length of the schemers' purse, and on their optimism or otherwise as to their future prospects; but I am sure that it is best to employ as many men as can be afforded at the outset, and so grapple with the execution of the plans in a thorough and determined manner.   In the making of a golf course it is very easy to be " penny wise and pound foolish."

The situation of the greens having been decided upon,

the question as to the length of the holes, as to which some general impression will already have been formed, comes up for decision. A proposed teeing ground should be selected for each hole, the lengths of the holes then examined and compared, and the tees moved nearer or further back as seems desirable for the improvement of individual holes or the increase of variety. If at this stage there is any chance of finding a ball afterwards, it is a good thing to drive a few from each tee and play them with the brassy, cleek, irons, or mashie up to the green. If you drive half a dozen from each tee and play them through the green to the place where the holes will be, there will surely be one or two that have turned out excellently if you are a player of any skill whatever, and a study of the strokes which have been applied to these one or two, the point of pitching, and the final lie, will reveal the entire character of the hole you are making, and tell you plainly how it must be bunkered. In a nine-hole course I think there should be seven medium or long holes, and two short ones to break the monotony and test the golfer at all points. The situation of these short holes in the round will naturally be decided to a large extent by the land and other circumstances, but when the power of selection is left to the designer, I incline to the belief that Nos. 3 and 7 are the best for these dainties. I like a short hole to come early in the round, as at No. 3, because then a golfer who has made a bad start is given a chance of recovering before he is hopelessly out of the hunt. He has a better prospect of making such a recovery (or thinks he has, which is much the same thing) at a short hole than at a long one, and, being put in a good temper again, he will very likely go on very well for the next two or three, when he will be favoured with another short one. The plight of the player who has discovered at the beginning of a medal round that he is off his drive and brassy, and that six or seven holes have to be played before a little one is reached, is certainly not pleasant. I call a good short hole one that can be reached by good play at any time with an iron club, because it fails to be a short hole when it is necessary to take wood upon the tee in order to get to the green. In an eighteen-hole course you might have three or four short holes—I think three are sufficient—and it would be well to vary their length so as to test the capacity of the golfer with different clubs, and to bring out all his qualities of resource. For a fourth hole on the short side plenty of sporting chance would constantly be afforded by one of 200 yards length. This could not be called a short hole, because under ordinary circumstances and on most days it would be too far for even a good driver to reach from the tee, but he would often be tempted to nerve himself to a superior effort, and an occasional strain of this kind is advantageous in the long run. Besides, when the wind was at his back he would frequently be successful, and on such occasions he would experience more pleasure and satisfaction from this particular tee shot than from any other of the whole round.

The remainder of the course should be made up of a variety of two-shot and three-shot holes. The lengths should be varied as much as possible, and with limits of 370 yards, and, say, 530 to work between, it should surely not be so difficult as it appears to have been in so many cases of inland links to get fourteen or fifteen quite different holes. Those of from 230 to 330 yards, with which so many courses abound, are not good holes in my opinion, because they give an almost equal chance to the man who has driven well and the man who has driven badly. Take a common sort of hole, 280 yards in length. A player misses his drive, and his ball travels only for, say, 100 or 120 yards. He may still reach the green with his brassy, and should be able to do so. Now the man who drove well at this hole would need to make a second stroke with an iron club to reach the green, and would thus gain nothing from his better play. This is unfair, and what is unfair is bad. The good two-shot hole is one of the nicest and best holes on a course when it is really good. Its length is about 370 to 380 yards. Thus it will be perceived that a first-class drive from the tee must be followed up by a fine second, as straight as it is long, if the green is to be reached. The good player who has done all that he ought is thus rewarded by the clear gain of a stroke and the capture of a hole in 4, whilst the man who is a trifle weak with either his drive or his second, or has faltered to the slightest extent at either stroke, has for a certainty to use his mashie before he can call for the putter. When a two-shot hole is to be adjusted to this nicety of perfection, there is plainly not much margin for the variation of its length; but it is not necessary, nor is it even desirable, to demand continually such unerring skill from the golfer. My idea of a good three-shot hole is one that stretches for 500 to 530 yards, three fine shots being wanted. For holes of much greater length than this I have no fancy. Perhaps no serious objection can be laid against an occasional hole of 550 yards length, but what is really gained by such long journeys? Certainly the true skill of the golfer is not being more severely tested. When we come to such monstrosities as holes of 600 yards in length, it is time to call out "Enough!" for by this time we have descended to slogging pure and simple, and the hard field work at which an agricultural labourer would have the right to grumble. So I repeat that the best hole for golfing is that good two-shotter which takes the ball from the tee to the green in two well-played strokes without any actual pressing. As for total length, it should be borne in mind that a links over 6000 yards long is considered a long one, and that there are championship greens, Prestwick and Muirfield, which are (or were until quite recently; there is a tendency to stretch everywhere since the rubber-cored ball became predominant) shorter than 6000 yards.

In making the plan of the course, a point of interest and

importance to decide upon is the direction in which the holes shall be played. Some golfers prefer that the first and succeeding holes shall lie to the right of the starting-point, while others like best to go out on the left-hand side, that is, to play round the course in the same direction as that pursued by the hands of a clock. It is largely a matter of fancy, but personally my choice is for going out to the left because I think in this case the holes are generally more difficult, and the boundary usually being near to the left, constant precautions must be taken against pulling. Another matter particularly to be remembered is that the first tee and the last green should be close together, and neither of them more distant from the club-house than is necessary. A wide separation of these points always seems to be contrary to the proper order of things.

And now we come to the perplexing problem of bunkers and where to place them, and in this connection I would remark that it would be well not to regard the lengths of the holes, as so far arranged, as final and irrevocable, and not to establish permanent teeing grounds accordingly, for it must necessarily happen, as the bunkers come to be formed on the course, and more trial rounds are played, that one's ideas will undergo considerable change, and it is easier to lengthen a hole at this stage of the proceedings, by simply placing the tee further back, than it will be afterwards.

It has been a great question with some committees of newly-established clubs or of older ones in search of new courses, as to whether, in laying out their greens and settling upon the location of all their nice new bunkers, they should keep more particularly in mind the excellences of the scratch player or the trials and troubles of the 12 to 18 handicap men. On the one hand, the scratch player is the experienced golfer, the man who plays the true game as it should be played, and who finds no real enjoyment in so-called golf wherein he is never called upon to do more than tap the ball over an obstacle ninety or a hundred yards in front. Such links never put up a fight against him, and he finishes his listless round with something as near to the sense of weariness as it is possible for the golfer ever to experience. But these scratch players, in common with the men with all handicaps up to 5 or 6, are in a very heavy and hopeless minority in most clubs to-day. The bulk of the membership is made up of players of from 6 to 24, with a concentration of forces between 12 and 18. These men say, or at all events think, that as they run the club they have a right to be considered, and in their hearts the committee believe that they are justified. These men with long handicaps—some of whom have not even a desire to reduce them to any considerable extent, deriving the utmost pleasure in playing the game in their own way—can find no fun in being always and inevitably in the same bunkers, and regard driving from a tee, when they are either obliged to play short deliberately with an iron or be bunkered for a certainty with their driver, as the most dismal occupation with which a Saturday or Sunday sportsman could ever be afflicted. Therefore they cry loudly for shorter carries. They say the others are not fair, and from their particular point of view the remark is possibly justified. Even the young golfer who is determined to be a scratch man some day, though he is eighteen strokes from that pinnacle of excellence as yet, becomes rather tired in the long run of finding constant punishment waiting upon his valiant attempts to drive his longest ball, and thinks the committee should be reminded that there are others in the world besides the immediately coming champions. Amidst these conflicting desires, committees and course designers appear frequently to have attempted a compromise with no particular satisfaction to anybody. It is impossible to lay out a course to suit all the different players in a club, and my own most decided opinion is that the bunkers and other hazards should always be placed to test the game of the scratch player, and not that of the handicap man. A course that is laid out for the latter very often inflicts severe punishment on the scratch player, and it is surely hard that the man who has spent many years in the most patient and painstaking practice should be deliberately treated in this manner when the comparative novice is allowed to go scot free. Moreover, when a bunker is so placed that a long carry is needed from the tee, the handicap man will find his game much improved by playing on the course. At first he finds he cannot carry the hazard, and for a little while contents himself with playing short. But he soon tires of this timidity, takes more pains with his strokes, braces himself up to bigger efforts, and at last the day comes when his ball goes sailing over the obstruction. Afterwards the performance is repeated quite easily, and the views of one man as to the unfairness of that particular carry have undergone a radical change. It is better for the beginner that he should have a hard course to play over than an easy one, and, much as he may grumble at the beginning, he will in the end be thankful to those who imposed a severe experience upon him in his early days as a golfer.

Therefore, if it is decided that there must be a bunker in the centre of the course in the line of the drive, I suggest that it should be placed at a distance of about 130 to 145 yards from the tee. The second bunker, if there is to be another stretching across the course with a view to imposing difficulties on second shots or guarding the green, should be rather less than this distance from the first, so that the man who has topped his drive and is short of the first hazard should still have a chance of clearing the next one with his second shot. Recovery ought never to be impossible. But really I am no believer at all in bunkers placed across the course. Certainly let there be one in front of the tee to catch the bad drive, and another to guard the green; but, generally speaking, the merely short ball carries its own punishment with it in the distance that has been lost and has to be made good again. The straight driver is not the man to be punished. It is the player who slices and pulls and has obviously little command over his club and the ball, and who has taken no pains to master the intricate technique of the drive, for whose careless shots traps should be laid. As often as not the bunker in the centre of the course lets off the ball with a bad slice or pull on it. So I say that bunkers should be placed down both sides of the course, and they may be as numerous and as difficult as the controlling authority likes to make them. But hazards of any description should be amongst the last features to be added to a newly-made golf links. Not until the course has been played over many times under different conditions, and particularly in different winds, can anyone properly determine which is the true place for a hazard to be made. At the beginning it may have been placed elsewhere in a hurry, and it may have seemed on a few trials to answer its purpose admirably, but another day under different conditions it may be made clear that it is in the very place where it will catch a thoroughly good shot and allow only a bad one to escape. I would not have insisted so much on this need for deliberation and patience, if it did not so often happen that as the result of placing the hazards on a new course in too much haste, they are found afterwards to be altogether wrong and have to be moved, with the waste of much time and money.

There is little to the point that I can say about the making of the putting greens, as so much depends upon the natural conditions and opportunities. Sometimes there is nothing to do but to cut the grass short and pass the roller over it a few times and the green is made, and a first-class green too. At other times there is need for much digging, and the turf with which the carpet is to be relaid may have to be carried to the spot from a considerable distance. Particularly when so much trouble is being taken over the laying of the greens, do I beg the makers of courses to see that they are not made dead level and as much like a billiard table as possible, which often seems to be the chief desire. To say that a putting green is like a billiard table is one of the worst compliments that you can pay to it. By all means let it be true in the sense of being smooth and even, and presenting no lumps or inequalities of surface that are not plainly visible to the eye, and the effect of which cannot be accurately gauged by the golfer who has taught himself how to make allowances. But on far too many greens the man with the putter has nothing to do but gauge the strength of his stroke and aim dead straight at the hole. He derives infinitely less satisfaction from getting down a fifteen-yards putt of this sort than does the man who has holed out at ten feet, and has estimated the rise and fall and the sideway slope of an intervening hillock to begin with and a winding valley to follow, his ball first of all running far away to the right, then trickling across to the left, and finally wheeling round again and rolling into the tin. Only when there is so much calculation to be done and it is so precisely accomplished does the golfer practise the real art of putting, and taste the delights of this delicate part of the game. The other is dull and insipid in comparison. There is the less excuse for making the flat and level greens, inasmuch as even the beginners can appreciate the sporting quality of the others and enjoy practice upon them from the first day of their play. Let there be plenty of undulations, and then with the changing positions of the hole a player can practically never come to any particular green upon which he may have putted hundreds of times without having a problem set him entirely different from any that he has had to work out before. Greens, of course, are of all sizes, from fifteen to fifty yards square, and I beg leave to remark that large size is a fault in them, inasmuch as the bigger they are the less is the skill required in the approach shot.

It is perhaps unnecessary for me to point out as a final word, that when tees have to be specially prepared and turfed, it is a decided improvement to a course to have two at different points for each hole, one nearer and more to one side than the other. Not only do these alternative tees enable each of them to be given a periodical rest for recovery from wear and tear, but they afford an interesting variation of the play, make it possible to impose a more severe test than usual upon the players when it is felt desirable to do so, as on competition days, and also in some measure to counteract the effects of winds. Of course when tees have not to be specially made there is endless variety open.

It is obvious that the greater part of the foregoing remarks applies chiefly to the construction of inland courses. Seaside links laid over the dunes are made by Nature herself, and generally as regards their chief features they must be taken or left as the golfer decides. A new hazard may be thrown up here and there, but usually the part of the constructor of a seaside course is to make proper use of those that are there ready made for him, and which are frequently better than any that could be designed by man.

CHAPTER XX

LINKS I HAVE PLAYED ON

Many first-class links—The best of all—Sandwich—Merits of the Royal St. George's course—Punishments for faults and rewards for skill—Not a short course—The best hole—The Maiden—Other good holes—Prestwick an excellent course—The third and the ninth holes—The finest hole anywhere—Hoylake—Two or three tame holes—A means of improvement —Good hazards and a premium on straight play—St. Andrews—Badly-placed bunkers—A good second hole—The finest one-shot hole to be found anywhere—An unfair hole—The best holes at Muirfield—Troon—North Berwick—Cruden Bay—Dornoch—Machrihanish—A splendid course at Islay—The most difficult hole I know—Gullane—Kilspindie—Luffness— Links in Ireland — Portrush — Portmarnock — Dollymount — Lahinch— Newcastle—Welsh courses—Ashburnham—Harlech—On the south and south-west coasts—The rushes at Westward Ho !—Newquay—Good holes at Deal—Littlestone—Rye—The advantage of Cromer—Brancaster— Hunstanton—Sheringham—Redcar—Seaton Carew—St. Anne's—Formby —Wallasey—Inland courses—Sunningdale—A splendid course—Another at Walton Heath—Huntercombe—London links—Courses in the country— Sheffield—Manchester—Huddersfield—"Inland" courses at the seaside— A warning.

OF all the golf courses that have any pretensions to being considered first class, or even good second class, I can call to mind very few over which I have not played a round, and at a time when the reputations of so many of them are being severely overhauled, and their merits and demerits criticised, some expression of my own opinions may prove interesting alike to the golfers who know them well and to others who are looking forward with eagerness to the enjoyment of games upon them at future holiday times. Recent championships and big matches have resulted in such wonderful scores, that some golfers are inclined to ask despairingly whether we have any really first-class course at all; and links which in the past have been considered perfect are spoken of contemptuously as fit only for handicap men who want their golf made easy. If they attach any importance to my opinion, then let them be assured that we still have many links which come near to being perfect, and that, notwithstanding the advent of the rubber-cored ball, there is no reason to complain about them or agitate for great alterations. We have them in England, Scotland, and Ireland—perhaps more in Scotland than elsewhere, but that is chiefly due to accidental circumstances.

I am constantly asked, when the discussions to which I have referred are taking place, which in my opinion is the best course in the world. Many considerations enter into such a reckoning; but, after making it carefully, and with full knowledge of the fact that my answer is at variance with many of the best authorities on the game, I say Sandwich. Then let me tell you why I consider the links of the Royal St. George's Club to be the best that are to be found anywhere. There is, in the first place, not a single tee shot in the round where good play must not be shown by the golfer if he wants to achieve success. There is scarcely a hole at which a player who only half hits his ball from the tee does not find himself in grave difficulties, demanding an unusually brilliant recovery and sterling play until he has holed out, if he is to have any chance of getting on level terms with his opponent again, assuming that the latter is playing the proper game. The bunkers are so placed that a good shot has to be made every time to carry them. On the other hand, you are always satisfied that virtue is properly rewarded at Sandwich, and that if your tee shot is hit truly and well you are certain to be nicely situated for your second. Elementary considerations as these may appear to be, there are many courses having the reputation of being first-class where this reward is not always so sure as it is at Sandwich. The greens on that course

are in all cases well protected, and they abound in
character and variety. Some critics say that the carries
over the first bunkers from the tees are too long; but I do
not agree with them. Without being a particularly long
driver, anybody who hits his ball truly can carry any
bunker at Sandwich that ought to be carried from the tee.
Then at the Championships in 1904 everybody was declaring,
with much knowledge that had come after the event, that
the course was on the short side, as was proved, they said,
by the phenomenal scores that were made in the Open
competition. I do not agree. The scores made by two
or three players were certainly low, but that was because
they played exceptional golf. If I admit that the course is
the merest trifle on the short side in going out, I hasten to
add that a man must be playing perfect golf to get to the
turn with a low score, while, unless his play does come
within these narrow limits of perfection, he may find, grand
player though he be, that he may easily run up a total for
his nine holes that would look foolishly large. Coming in,
there is certainly no shortness about the holes, and there
is plenty of scope for the man who wants to open out his
shoulders with his driver and his brassy, while there are
hazards everywhere for the punishment of the balls that are
not kept in the fairway. These are the chief considerations
which lead me to give an emphatic vote in favour of
Sandwich when I am asked which is the best course—that
is to say, the best test of golf—that is to be found in the
British Isles, or elsewhere so far as I know, and I ask to be
given no more favourable opportunity of studying a golfer's
points, than to see him play a round or two over the St.
George's links.

I should say that the third hole at Sandwich, although
a short one, is in golfing quality one of the best of the
eighteen, because it is so splendidly protected with bunkers
and rushes everywhere, so that the player who would get on
to the green from the tee does indeed need to be bold, and

as accurate as he is bold. No faintness of heart, no doubtful stroke, will ever in the result be flattered by this third
hole. The sixth or Maiden, famous everywhere, is very fine
indeed, though it is not nearly so difficult as it used to be.
The eighth is another beauty, well guarded by bunkers; a
trifle on the short side if the wind is following, but a terror
in length if the breeze is coming from the green. The ninth
is good. The tenth calls for a perfect drive straight down
the middle of the course, in default of which the second shot
will abound with difficulty; and at the fifteenth another very
straight tee shot is wanted. If there is a breath of wind to
help the ball from the tee, a plucky player may then come
to the conclusion that he has a chance of reaching the green
with his second, and a fine shot will take him over the
treacherous little bunker that guards it, giving him a 4 of
which he may be proud in the best of company. These are
the gems of Sandwich.

Next to this course, I think that Prestwick with its
Himalayas and its Alps is the finest that we have. It
is an excellent test to apply to a would - be champion,
although there have been complaints that this course also is
short. Yet it is longer than it used to be, and it is merely
the rubber-filled ball that makes it seem short. The third
hole at Prestwick is one that stirs the soul of the dare-devil
golfer, for, after he has despatched the ball safely and well
from the tee, he finds a big, gaping bunker, the famous
"Cardinal," ahead of him for his second—an ugly brute
that gives a sickening feeling to the man who is off his
game. Defy this bunker, be on the green with your brassy,
put a 4 on your card, and you have done something which
should make you happy for the morning. The ninth again
is an excellent hole at which the straight driver is rewarded
all the way, and, if he does his duty, is given a 5. I have
no hesitation in giving my judgment that the seventeenth is
the finest hole to be found on any links. I say so because it
is the best specimen of a really perfect two-shot hole. If

there is the slightest flaw in either the drive or the second stroke, all prospect of reaching the green in two vanishes into thin air.   Mr. Laidlay once lost a match and an amateur championship because his second shot here was not quite good enough.   A good tee shot well into the middle of the course, a second that is as clean as a shot can be and as straight as a bullet from a gun, with the gods of golf smiling approval all the way and particularly when your second is nearing the green—with all these you may ask for your putter for the third stroke.   But there is a bunker before the green, a bunker just beyond the green, and rushes to the right and left, so that the second shot has indeed to be a beauty for its maker to be wholly satisfied.   This is the sort of hole that all good golfers best like to play, because they know that the good shots are certain of their reward, and that not merely the bad shots but the indifferent ones are met with just penalties every time.   It is said that no two golf strokes are ever alike, but there is just enough similarity about them to prevent individual strokes from living very long in history except in a few striking cases. Perhaps the most memorable shot ever played in golf was that made at this hole by the late Mr. Fred Tait when he was engaging with Mr. John Ball, jun., in the final tie of the Amateur Championship in 1899.   The Scottish favourite was in the bunker guarding the green with his second, and it so happened that the bunker on this occasion was filled with rain water, in which the ball was floating.   Mr. Tait chipped the ball out beautifully on to the green, and saved a hole which seemed a certain loss.   It is hard to find many holes that are worthy of being put in the same class as this. Man cannot make such holes.   They are there when he seeks out the land for the first time with his golf clubs.

Hoylake is a good course.   There are one or two holes on it that must be admitted to be very tame.   If the land in the middle of the course which is at present out of bounds were taken in and made playable, these holes could be **much** improved. The hazards are good and plentiful, and a satisfactory premium is put upon straight play. The ninth is a nice hole, a really good drive helping the player considerably. The eleventh is another pretty one, neither long nor short, but just that length which a fine shot from the tee will reach, and accuracy is demanded by the rushes which seem all over the course as you stand to drive.

I call St. Andrews a good course generally; but its bunkers are badly placed. They punish the man who is driving well more than the man who is driving badly, for they are generally the length of a good long drive. If this defect could be remedied, and if there were a few more bunkers at the sides to catch the pulled and sliced balls, then St. Andrews would be a fine links indeed. As it is, there are some excellent holes. The second is beautiful— beautiful if the flag is put in the centre of the green—because then a good second shot is rewarded as it ought to be. But it generally happens when big matches are being played there that the hole is placed in a corner, which frequently spoils the prospects of these good second shots. The seventh is good, calling for a most accurate second, and the eleventh is the finest one-shot hole to be found anywhere. The green is on a plateau with bunkers all about it, and if you overpitch it your ball will be in the rushes beyond. Many golfers swear by the seventeenth; but I am not one of them. I declare that it is a very unfair hole, and there is no encouragement here to be plucky. The player must be pawky all the way, for it is fully two to one against there being anything but punishment as the result of bold tactics. The man who tries to place his long shot on the green may try again and again, and he will be convinced that it is next to impossible to stop there when he reaches it.

For some reasons I like Muirfield; but it does not enjoy so many advantages as the other championship courses. There are not so many sandhills. It is on the flat side, and at the first glance you might take it to be an inland course ; but after a single round you are greatly impressed by the good golf that is to be obtained upon it.   The turf is capital, some of the hazards are very fine, and on the whole I think it may fairly be regarded as a very good championship test of golf.   The fourth, twelfth, and eighteenth holes all call for first-class seconds if the greens are to be reached.

There are so many other good links in the north that a further selection becomes increasingly difficult.   Troon, abounding in sandhills, is very fine, and the player needs to be very skilful to get round it in a low score.   North Berwick is also good, and it is surprising to see how well the links are preserved considering the enormous amount of play to which they are subjected.   There are many good holes at popular Carnoustie, with a fine length about them which calls for good brassy play, and which is calculated to bring out all the good points that a golfer has in him. Cruden Bay and Dornoch are enjoyable ; but those who want to get the best golf in Scotland need not always go to those places that revel in reputation and where an inconvenient crowd may at most times be depended upon.   Some of the gems of North Britain are hidden away in inaccessible corners, and the golfers who would reach them must make tedious journeys by land and sea.   But he who is worthy of the game is in my opinion amply rewarded for these travelling labours, by the quality of the golf that is vouchsafed to him at his journey's end, and he is spared the annoyance of being obliged to book his starting time overnight and of having a couple of hours to wait upon the tee if he is a minute late in the morning.   I believe that Machrihanish is one of these very fine but out-of-the-way courses, but it happens to be one over which I have not hitherto played.   I can tell of another where the most glorious golf is to be obtained, and which I can strongly recommend to those on the lookout for a place at which to spend a golfing holiday.   It is at Islay.   There the air is grand, there is excellent accommodation to be obtained at the combined hotel and club-house, and as for the quality of the golf I do not hesitate to say that the course is in every respect fit for the championships to be decided upon it. There is one hole here, the third, which is the most difficult anyone can imagine. If I were asked to select one from all the thousands of holes that I have played in my time, I should pick this one out for difficulty. They call it Mount Zion, and I think it is a good name for it. You must make three very good shots to reach the green, and in the matter of accuracy the third needs to be a gem if any satisfaction whatever is to be got out of the whole business. The green is on a plateau, and it is protected by every contrivance that ingenious Nature has vouchsafed to the makers of courses. If you are short you are in a running stream; if you pull you go out of bounds; and if your ball trickles over the green, away it goes into the sea—tortures the most terrible for the erring ball. Yes, decidedly I think this is the hardest hole I have ever seen. The first time I played it I took 10 to hole out, and yet won it from a very fine professional player who is an ex-champion! I have never done a hole better in my life than when I once halved this with Taylor in 4 in the course of a match which Taylor won at the twenty-fourth hole. The seventh is also a very fine hole with a bunker in front of the tee, which is very similar to the Maiden at Sandwich. An old golfer who lives there told me he can remember the time when it was a rabbit scrape. Like all golfers who know them, I sing the praises of Gullane, Kilspindie, and Luffness.

There is a variety of good golf to be obtained in Ireland also. Portrush, Portmarnock, Dollymount, Lahinch, and Newcastle (co. Down)—all these are fine links. For a place to visit for an enjoyable golfing holiday, when health is a governing consideration also, I should select Portrush as one of the very best, while golfers who wish to play at Portmarnock and elect to put up in a Dublin hotel have an experience of pleasant variety which I at all events have found very agreeable, for you have first the train, then the car, and last of all the boat to take in order to reach the course, and not an inch of the journey is wearisome. Of course this proceeding cannot be recommended to those golfers who prefer to sleep in close proximity to the first tee, regardless of all other pleasures that are to be obtained without any sacrifice of the game. The course I like best in Wales is that at Ashburnham, over which the Welsh Championship was last played for. It is one of those excellent natural links which require very little attention. The Royal St. David's course at Harlech is also very good.

Coming back to England again, I agree with all others that splendid golf is to be obtained at Westward Ho! although there is one quite unique feature of this course of which some golfers, myself among the number, do not bear the pleasantest recollections. I refer, of course, to the rushes of a peculiar growth which are to be found there in such abundance. I can conceive no nightmare more horrible to a player than one in which during his hours of troubled sleep he is in imagination vainly trying to rescue his unhappy ball from the clutches of these famous rushes. They stand full five feet high, strong and stiff like stout twigs, and they have sharp and dangerous points which seem as if they might be made of tempered steel. A kind of blossom appears on them in the season as if to disguise their evil features. Any player who is unlucky enough to put his ball into them (and there are one or two holes at which even a good shot may find its way there) must always encounter a considerable risk of breaking his club in the endeavour to play out again. I believe that attempts have been made to grow these rushes elsewhere, but the seeds that have been carried away from their native Westward Ho! have never prospered. Perhaps some golfers may reflect that this is just as well, though with all their faults and dangers I certainly do not condemn them as a hazard. They are a novelty, and all things that come from Nature must be admitted without question into the game of golf. On the south coast there are several fine links. Newquay is excellent for a holiday, and the course of the Cinque Ports Club at Deal, now that it is eighteen holes, is very fine. I have not enjoyed recent acquaintance with it, but the short fourth hole which they call the Sandy Parlour struck me when I was last down there as being a very sporting little piece of golf. Both Littlestone and Rye are admirable, and I have pleasant memories of the latter, particularly in connection with a match I once played there with Mr. Fred Tait.

Again, on the east coast of England there are courses in number which afford the best opportunities for enjoyable and skilful golf. Cromer is a mixture of inland and seaside. It is one of those seaside courses which don't look what they are, but some parts of it are good, especially those which lie through the sand dunes. The lower part is tame. However the air is beautiful, and the golfer who makes his headquarters at this place enjoys the material advantage of having three or four other first-class links within easy reach. For example, there is Brancaster, which, though a long distance from any railway station, is worth any amount of trouble that may be expended on the journey. The turf is excellent, the hazards well placed, and the golfer who does not keep straight is penalised as he ought to be. It is a fine course. Then there is Hunstanton, which is also very good, and Sheringham too. Higher up there is golf at Redcar and Seaton Carew which none need despise. On the north-west coast there is more golf to be had that is well worthy of the name. St. Anne's and Formby are both capital, and fine golf is necessary to get round these courses at all well. Wallasey is highly satisfactory. Both my space and my memory are unequal to giving a complete list of all the seaside courses that should be commended, and the absence of any particular one from my little list does not imply that I rank it as inferior, although I have tried to mention all those that I consider the very best

So far I have said nothing about inland links, because the golfer who is going away from his own for a brief period for pleasure and improvement usually elects to play at the seaside, and wisely so, for, apart from the superior hygienic properties of atmosphere, there is no getting rid of the fact, however much we may be attached to some inland courses, that seaside golf, when it is the real thing, is entirely different from any other. It is better in every respect; in fact it is usually ideal. It gives more benefit to the mind and body of the overworked player, it pulls out his game and makes a golfer of him as nothing else can ever do, and it affords such variety of a true sporting character as nothing but Nature can provide. But in thus extolling the seaside game, I do not wish for a moment to be considered as disparaging the golf that is to be had almost everywhere throughout the country in these days. Inland golf is a necessity to all except the leisured people who have no occupation which chains them to cities and towns, and there is now so much of it that it has taken a dominant place in the golfing world. And if the inland turf does not possess those glorious qualities that distinguish the seaside article, and if the bunkers constantly bear evidence of having been carted to the place where they are situated, and if, moreover, the evenness of many green fields becomes somewhat monotonous, nevertheless the golf which is to be obtained at many of these places is thoroughly enjoyable, and at the same time as severe a test of skill as the most conceited player could ever wish for. Take Sunningdale, for instance. This course, in my opinion, is the best of all the inland links with which I am familiar, and it requires the very finest golf to get round it in anything like a decent score. Unless the golfer plays with his head as well as with his club, he will find himself in difficulties all the way. Walton Heath is another good example. Here also a capital player must be on the top of his game to get round in anything like bogey. Those who made this course have mastered the undesirable eccentricities of the rubber-cored ball as few others have done. This ball is too apt to despise the average inland bunker, particularly in the summer-time, and goes skipping over it as if there were no obstruction in sight. But it does not do that at Walton Heath, where they have made the bunkers so deep that the ball inevitably stops in, and there is nothing for it but to ask the caddie for the niblick and resign yourself to losing a stroke. I should like to see the managers of other courses take a leaf out of the Walton Heath book. Bunkers that were once quite deep in the old days of the gutty are in too many cases shallow and useless under the new conditions. I do think that the splendid state of the Walton Heath links is marvellous considering the short time that has elapsed since the club was formed. I have never played at Huntercombe, over which my old friend and opponent, Willie Park, has spent so much care and time and money, but I believe that it is similarly good, and I have heard golfers, for whose opinion I have the highest respect, declare enthusiastically that it is one of the best inland courses to be found anywhere, while the high hill air is splendid.

Considering the many disadvantages under which they labour, particularly in the matter of soil, which is mostly of the clay variety, the links round about London may be considered good, and though the metropolitan golfer may not always appreciate the fact, during one period of the year he scores over all others. This is in the summer-time, when the hot sun has at last dried and burnt up the grass on many seaside links and made them slippery and difficult even to walk upon. At such time the grass on the London links is still usually quite fresh and green, and not until some weeks later does it yield to the scorching rays. For the most part, too, the London links are exceedingly well kept. Lees, the greenkeeper at the Mid-Surrey course at Richmond, is the best man for that duty that I know.

I cannot attempt to give any adequate information about

the hundreds of links that are now dotted about all over the shires. It must suffice to say, in confining myself to large centres, that I have pleasant memories of good golf that I have had on the fine course at Lindrick in the Sheffield district, and at Trafford Park near Manchester. This is indeed a very nice inland course, with gravelly soil and a capacity for keeping dry during the winter. At Timperley there is another good links. The Huddersfield course is a splendid one to play upon, and very tricky too. Its merits are indicated by the quality of golfers that it breeds. It has made several men who have won the Yorkshire championships, and in club matches the Huddersfield team is a very hard one to beat.

There is one class of course of which I have not yet made any mention, and which I do not think it is necessary to do more than refer to. It is that mongrel kind which is both seaside and inland, but which is in the full sense neither, situated, that is, at a seaside resort, and may be in the very closest proximity to the sea, but with none of the properties of the real seaside course—no seaside turf, no sand dunes, no wild natural golf. These courses are usually elevated on cliffs. In many cases the golf that is to be obtained upon them is excellent, and I only wish to point out to unpractised golfers who are about to start for a holiday and have taken no advice, that if they are making for a seaside place and want that kind of golf which they have heard is to be had at Deal, Sandwich, Rye, Westward Ho! Littlestone, St. Andrews, North Berwick, and scores of other places, they should make quite certain that they are taking their railway tickets in the proper direction. Otherwise, when they arrive upon the links that they have chosen, they may fail to discover any difference between the course visited and that on which they are in the habit of playing when at home. I only mention the matter because I have known so many cases of severe disappointment arise through mistakes of this kind.

CHAPTER XXI

GOLF IN AMERICA

I HAVE a higher opinion of both the present and the future of golf in America than that which seems to be entertained by a large number of eminent players in this country. I think that American golf is very good at the present time—much better than it is given credit for being —and I am convinced that it will be still better in the future. I made a long golfing tour through the United States in 1900, when Englishmen for the most part regarded the game in that country with as much seriousness as they would have bestowed upon golf in Timbuctoo if they had heard that it was being played there. At that time it seemed to be taking a firm grip of our cousins, and I saw enough to convince me that America was coming on quickly, and that before long the old country would have reason to fear her. Everything that has happened since then has strengthened my belief, and the eyes of the British were at last fairly opened when

the Championship was played for at Sandwich in June of last
year, when, to the chagrin of our own leading amateurs, an
American, in the person of Mr. Walter J. Travis, became the
victor, and took back with him across the Atlantic the
Amateur Championship Cup. So far from surprising me,
that event was exactly what I expected. When I was in
America I played against Mr. Travis once or twice, and
though he was then in the improving stage and evidently
not at the top of his career, I felt that he was a man who
might very likely do great things in the future. Afterwards
I followed his play with some curiosity and interest. I saw
that in course of time he beat many good men whose form
I understood precisely. I knew that he was one of the
steadiest golfers I had ever seen—a man of fine judgment
and marvellous exactness, who always played with his head,
and was constantly giving the closest possible study to the
game. I felt that when he came to play for our Championship he would make a very bold bid for it. When I heard
that he was going to Sandwich last year, I made him my
"tip" for premier honours, and before the first round was
played I said to many friends, "Mark my words; if Travis
gets anything like a fairly easy draw to start with he will go
right through." And so he did. I saw him play on this
memorable occasion, which will never be forgotten as long as
any of the events of golfing history are remembered, and, in
opposition to the opinions of other British critics expressed
in many columns of print during the weeks following, it was
and is my absolute conviction that his was the best golf
played in that tournament, and that he thoroughly deserved
to win. He played with his head the whole way through,
and his golf was really excellent. It was only natural that
our people should be very downhearted when they saw
what had happened, for it seemed nothing else than a great
disaster. I do not think that in the long run it will prove to
have been so, for the inevitable effect of it was to wake up
our British golf, which stood sadly in need of arousing. I

think that amateur golf in this country has been steadily depreciating for some time, and at the present moment I think that the standard of merit of our best players is lower than in the days when Mr. Harold Hilton, Mr. John Ball, jun., and the late Mr. Freddy Tait were at their best. And despite the American shock, I cannot profess that the outlook at the present moment is particularly encouraging. There are other good golfers in the States besides Mr. Travis, and, frankly, I think that unless we wake up in this country the Cup will go there again. For the moment our numerical strength in the Championship tournament is in our favour. When there are only half a dozen Americans entered out of a total number of over a hundred, the odds are evidently against them, but an "American invasion" is threatened, and then we shall see what we shall see.

The chief reason why it is difficult to feel optimistic about the prospects of amateur golf in this country is because the rising generation, upon whom we must depend for our future champions, do not take sufficient pains to make themselves masters of the game. They are too haphazard in learning it. The beginners on our side are too apt to say to themselves, "I will go and teach myself to hit a ball first, and then I will take a lesson," which is, of course, entirely wrong. Then one of their friends tells them to do a certain stroke in one way, and another tells them the opposite, and thus at the end of six months they have got into such a thoroughly bad style that it is the most difficult task in the world for a professional to set them right. Those who have the future of British golf at heart cannot afford to disregard or wink at these vagaries on the part of beginners, on whom we depend to constitute the national system in coming years. Now the national system of America is altogether different. They are not haphazard there. They seem to take a deeper interest in the game and its science, and they never think of trying to learn it by the chance methods which are so much in favour with us. They take the game with the utmost seriousness from the very beginning, and obtain the very best advice that they can. The professionals never have a minute to spare, and their engagement-books are constantly filled up for three weeks in advance, so that without that length of notice nobody stands a chance of getting a lesson for love or money. That is the way in which the people of America are learning to play golf, and it is the proper way. It is slow but it is very sure; and unless I am very much mistaken, there will in the future be other players coming across the Atlantic to take part in our championships who will be as great as Travis if not greater, and if we on our part do not forthwith begin to take our golf more seriously it may be a sad day for us when they do come.

As I have said, American golf was only just budding when I made my tour through the country in 1900; but nevertheless I found that tour extremely interesting and enjoyable, and everywhere I was given the heartiest and most enthusiastic reception. Nobody even begrudged me the American Championship which I brought back with me, and nobody made any unkind criticisms of my play, or suggested that I did not in any way deserve the victory. My tour began in March and did not finish until the end of the year, but was interrupted for a short period at the beginning of the summer, when I made a flying trip home in order to take part in our own Open Championship. As it happened, the best that I could do was to finish second to Taylor, but I may add that this result was better than I expected, considering the sudden change of golf and climate that I experienced. I had to cover several thousands of miles in order to play the matches in which I took part in America. Of these matches I only lost two when playing against a single opponent, and each time it was Bernard Nicholls who beat me, first at Ormonde and then at Brae Burn. There was not a blade of grass on the course on which Nicholls won his first match from me, and I leave my readers to imagine what playing on a links consisting of nothing but

loose sand was like. Altogether I suffered only thirteen
defeats, but in eleven of them I was playing the best ball of
two or more opponents, which was the task that was generally set me. I won over fifty matches and halved two.
Some of my victories were somewhat substantial. At Point
Comfort I beat Willie Dunn by sixteen up and fifteen to
play, and at Scarsdale I got the better of the same opponent
to the extent of fifteen and fourteen. Such wide margins
naturally suggest opponents of inferior ability; but if I may
modestly say so, I do not think that was wholly the case. I
consider that at that time I was playing better golf than I
had ever played before or have done since. As was the
custom there, I used to go out on the links in the very
thinnest and airiest costume. In Florida it was too warm to
play with either coat or vest, so both were discarded and
shirt sleeves rolled up. Generally, like my opponents, I
wore no jacket, but a neat waistcoat with sleeves which
helped to keep the arms together. In such attire one was
afforded a delightful sense of ease and freedom which considerably helped one's golf. Then again, whether it was due
to the fine dry atmosphere—as I think it was—or not, the
ball certainly seemed to fly through the air with less resistance offered to it than I had ever experienced before. Never
have I driven so well as I did with the old gutty in America
in that year. Many of the professionals whom I met were
men who were taught their golf in this country, and were
players who would usually hold their own in the best of
professional company. The American papers gave very
lengthy reports of all the matches in which I took part, the
headlines and what followed them being frequently very
flattering. There was " The Golf King," and many such as
that, in type nearly an inch deep. Perhaps I may, without
offence, be permitted to quote from the account given in a
leading daily newspaper of the second match in which I
defeated Willie Dunn—at Scarsdale—which I only do for
the purpose of showing that the conditions of play were

sometimes really trying, and not at all conducive to big victories or record breaking. This paper said: "If it were necessary to dwell upon the extraordinary consistency of the champion's game, one has only to refer to his card for the four rounds (it was a nine-hole course) in yesterday's match, as his worst nine holes totalled forty-one and his best thirty-seven. If the turf could only unearth a thoroughbred as reliable as Vardon, poolrooms in Greater New York would be past history in very short order. Vardon's skill probably never underwent a severer test than in the match yesterday. Everything was against his exhibiting anything approaching championship form. He had not only to contend against a biting north-west wind, which temporarily got mixed up with a flurry of snow, but the course itself, from the character of the land, is about as difficult to score over as any in the country. The ground is one succession of 'kopjes,' while seven of the nine holes are 'on the collar' all the time, and at an angle of from twenty to thirty degrees. The course is only 2677 yards in playing distance. On paper this gives the impression of being nothing out of the ordinary, but confronted with it in actuality, it is about as hard a proposition as any victim of the golf habit could tackle. The only course one can compare with it here is Oakland, and the latter is a billiard table by the side of it. At the finish of the thirty-six holes Vardon said, 'I never felt so fagged out in my life. In fact I could play seventy-two holes on the other side every day for a week and not have been fatigued half so much.'" I do not remember that I ever committed myself to such an extravagant statement as this, but the course was certainly a very trying one that day. Yet on that occasion I lowered the eighteen holes record for the course. Altogether I beat most of the records of the courses during my tour. The first time I ever took my clubs out on American soil, on the course of the Lawrence Harbour Country Club, I reduced the record for the nine holes (held by Willie Dunn) from forty-one to forty. Yet the weather was so bad just then, and the clay greens were in such a state of puddle, that temporary greens had to be made on the fairway. I won my first match by nine up with eight to play. On one or two occasions I was obliged to beat the record in order to win my game. Thus, when playing on the Wheaton links at Chicago, Will Smith was three up on me at one time, but by beating the links record I won at the finish by two up with one to play. This was one of the very toughest struggles I had over there.

There was no mistaking the enthusiasm of the American spectators. They came to the matches in great crowds—always a large proportion of ladies—and they seemed bent on learning all that they could from the play. Everybody seemed to be trying to practise my grip. All kinds of theories were invented to account for the manner in which my shots came off. On one occasion, after I had got in a good one with a cleek, an excited spectator jumped the ropes, ran up to a friend of mine and screamed, " Say, which arm did he do that with?" I looked to see if all my arms and legs were intact, or if there was anything that appeared unusual about them. I discovered afterwards that by " arm " he meant " club." Many places of business were closed for the afternoon when I was playing in certain districts, and on one occasion the Stock Exchange did so. A letter to one of the papers, concerning the extraordinary manner in which America was taking the golf fever, contained these sentences: —" I went into a leading business house to-day and found the three partners of the firm in a violent discussion. As I thought they were talking business I concluded that my presence was unnecessary, and started to edge away. Suddenly I noticed the head of the firm rush into his office and rush out again with a cane. As the words were heated I was just about to interfere when I saw a weapon appear on the scene, but the head partner wasn't looking for blood. Instead of hitting anyone he swiped the cane along the ground, and then I heard the words—' This is how Vardon holds it.' I wanted to make an appointment with one of the partners, but he told me that he wouldn't be in. However, I guess I'll meet him, because I'm going out to Dixie myself." The professionals and the golf shops suddenly began to do an enormous trade in sticks, and Bernard Nicholls, the only man who defeated me single-handed, preferred not to play me again for a long time. He said his victory had done an enormous amount of good to his business, and he did not want to spoil it. From numerous quarters I received all kinds of offers to "star" in one way or another, some very big fees being suggested. Would I become a store manager at a huge salary? Would I make an exhibition for so many hours daily of driving golf balls in a padded room in the city? And so on. I actually did accept an offer one day to do exhibition swings in a room in a Boston store. I was to start at 9.30 and continue until 5 each day, doing tee and other shots into a net for half an hour at a time, and then resting for an hour before taking the next turn. There was a fresh "house" of about two hundred people every time, and it was part of the bargain that my manager should stand by and explain everything. But he had had enough of it after one or two turns. Then I found it became terribly monotonous, and to interest myself I kept trying to hit a particular spot on the wall near the ceiling, until the stores manager came forward in a state of great excitement, declaring that only six inches from that spot was the tap of a patent fire extinguishing arrangement, and that if I hit it the room would be flooded by a series of waterspouts in less time than I could imagine! By four o'clock my hands were blistered badly, and at that stage I had had enough and went out. In the meantime I was the constant recipient of numerous presents of all kinds, and the invitations that I received to dinners were far too many for any professional golfer to accept. I do not mention these things with any desire for self-glorification. They are ancient history now, and nobody cares about them. But they serve to show the whole-hearted manner in which America was going in for golf, and the tremendous hold that it took on the people. We talk on this side of the "golfing fever" and of people "going mad" about the game. Believe me, the Britisher is a mere dallier in comparison with his American golfing cousin.

An interesting incident happened when the American Championship was played for on the Wheaton course, when, as I was informed, the game of golf achieved the most notable victory that it had ever achieved in the United States. This was the complete surrender to it of the veteran champion and overlord of baseball, the American national game. How that came about I will leave one of the Chicago newspapers to relate:—"Cap. Anson surrendered to golf yesterday. The capitulation of the veteran of America's national game took place on the links at Wheaton during the race between Harry Vardon and J. H. Taylor. 'Cap.' says the game of golf is a go. He has stood out against it and ridiculed it ever since it began to get the people. Anson knows Charles S. Cox, Vardon's manager, and accepted an invitation yesterday morning to look in on the game. On the links he balked at the proposition of walking four miles in one trip around the course, but he lined up with the crowd to see Vardon drive off. The ball went higher than any fly 'Pop' ever saw in his life. It sailed 220 yards. Anson was first to start the applause with a 'Good boy. She's a homer.' Then he led the gallery to the first green. He was puffing when he pulled up at the eighteenth hole, but he felt better than if he had stolen second base. 'I'd like to take a crack at that golf ball,' he said. 'You can put me down for a trial the first chance I get. Wouldn't mind togging up in kilts just to give the Prince of Wales a run for his money.'" For the sake of giving prominence to it, this paragraph was put in a fancy border and let into the middle of the sheet of newspaper, so the Chicago people evidently attached some im-

portance to the capitulation of the worthy captain, and I
hope that by this time he has had many thousands of cracks
at the golf ball and that his handicap is low.

I was intent on making a bold bid for this American
Open Championship. Victory in it seemed to be the one
thing essential to make my trip the greatest possible success.
My friend Taylor, who had just beaten me for the Open
Championship at St. Andrews, had himself come over to the
States, and was also a candidate for the premier honours of
American golf. As it turned out, we had practically the
whole contest at Wheaton to ourselves, and a rare good
duel it was, at the end of which I was at the top of the list,
but only two strokes in front of my English opponent, while
he was eight in front of the next man. The system of deciding the championship was the same as on this side, that
is to say, four medal rounds were played, two on one day
and two on the next. At the end of the first day's play I
was just one stroke better than Taylor, my score for the two
rounds bring 157 to his 158, and on the second day I did
156 to his 157, so that on the whole event I was 313 to his
315. Taylor waited on the edge of the green while I holed
out my last putt, and was the first to grasp my hand in
sincere congratulation. Beautiful weather, the biggest golfing crowd ever seen in America up to that time, and a good
links, made the tournament a great success. The partner
who went round with me during this championship competition was Will Smith, the holder, who finished fifth.

I had some curious experiences in the course of my
journeyings about the country, and I am not sure that they
were all good for my game. During the early months I was
down in Florida away from the cold and the snow. I met
some good golfers there. It was necessary to play an entirely different game from that to which we are accustomed in
this country. There was no grass on the putting "greens."
They were simply made of loose sand, sprinkled on the
baked ground and watered and rolled. When there was a

shortage of water and there was wind about, the fine part of
the sand was blown away, and the surface of the "greens"
then consisted of nothing but little pebbles. It was not
easy to putt over this kind of thing, but I must not convey
the impression that these sand "greens" were wholly bad.
When properly attended to they are really nice to putt upon
after you have become accustomed to them. It was impossible to pitch on to them, and one had to cultivate the
habit of running up from a very long distance. Thus I got
into the way of playing a kind of stab shot. The tees consisted not of grass but of hard soil, and one had to tee up
much higher than usual in order to avoid damaging the sole
of the driver. This provoked the habit of cocking the ball up,
and as a corrective all the teeing grounds in Florida sloped
upwards in front. Locusts were responsible for eating all
the grass away from some courses, and I had a unique
experience when I played Findlay at Portland. When we
were on the putting greens, men had constantly to be beating sticks to keep the locusts off the lines of our putts. If
it struck a locust the ball would come to a sudden stop.
Acres and acres of land about there were without a single
blade of grass. The locusts had eaten it all away. After
we left Florida we reached some good courses, and resumed
the old kind of play. It has often been suggested that the
peculiar conditions of play in America, to which I was subjected for a long period, resulted in a permanent injury to
my game as played at home, and in the light of reflection
and experience I am persuaded to think that this is so. I have
played well since then, have felt equal to doing anything
that I ever did before, and have indeed won the Championship, but I think I left a very small fraction of my game in
the United States.

In the way of other novel experiences I might mention
that on one occasion I played as "Mr. Jones." I wanted a
quiet day, and did not wish a too attentive public to know
where I was. Three friends joined me in a foursome, but

when we went into the club-house after our game, another anxious golfer went up to my partner when I was standing by, and inquired of him whether he had heard that Vardon was playing on the links. My friend declared that he knew nothing of such a rumour, and I could hardly refrain from laughter as the anxious one went to pursue his inquiries in other quarters. Another time two other professionals and myself visited a course where we were unknown, and, hiding our identity, pretended that we were novices at the game, and begged of our caddies to advise us as to the best manner of playing each shot, which they did accordingly. We deliberately duffed most of our strokes at several holes, but this course of procedure tired us immensely, and so at last we abandoned it and began to play our natural game.   Imagine the consternation and the indignation of those caddies! Each one of them threw down his bag of clubs, and, declining to carry them for another hole, walked sulkily off the course. On one occasion we camped out for the night on the links on which we were playing, and a very pleasant variation from the ordinary routine we found it.

The American newspapers, to which I have frequently referred, do their golf reporting very well.   Their journalism may be " sensational " or whatever you like to call it, but the golfing section of it was usually interesting, ingenious, and very intelligent and reliable. On the occasion of one match in which I played, a paper gave up nearly the whole of one of its pages to a large panoramic view of the links. The flight of my ball and that of my opponent, and the places where they stopped after every stroke, from the first to the last, were accurately marked. Thus the whole game was illustrated in a single picture in a very effective manner. As was inevitable, I was sometimes victimised by interviewers who wrote " interviews " with me which I had never accorded, containing most amazing particulars about my methods and habits. Occasionally a reporter was turned on to describe a game when he knew nothing about golf, and then the results were sometimes amusing. One of these writers had it that I " carried away the green with my drive." Another said I " dropped dead at the hole." When playing at Washington against two opponents, I happened to beat bogey at the first hole. One of the reporters was told of this achievement, but did not quite understand it. Going to the next hole, we were walking through a bunker when he came up to me and politely inquired if that—the bunker —was the kind of bogey that I had beaten. I was told a very good story of American golf reporting. A match was arranged between two well-known amateurs, one of whom happened to be a very rich banker. One reporter, who admitted that he " knew nothing about the darned game," arrived rather late on the course, and borrowed the " copy " of an experienced golfing journalist for information of what had already happened. When this " copy " was duly returned with thanks, the late-comer remarked to his obliging friend, " Say, you made a bad mistake in one part." " What was it ? " the other asked. " Waal, you say that So-and-so 'lipped the hole for a half.'" " Yes, that is right." " Oh, go away; you don't mean to tell me that a rich man like that would be playing for a paltry fifty cents. I've altered it to 'lipped the hole for a hundred dollars.'" And I remember that once when I was playing the best ball of two amateurs, one of the reporters had been instructed by his chief to keep the best ball score. I happened to lose the match on the last green, but on looking through the paper the next morning I was surprised to see it stated that I was beaten by not one but many holes, making this defeat in fact the biggest inflicted on me during my tour. The paper said that it was. I could not make anything out of it for some time, until at last I discovered that the reporter had reckoned my score also in the best ball figures! Obviously I could not beat myself. The best I could do was to get a half, and that was how it came about that I never won a single hole in the " Harry Vardon v. Harry Vardon and two others" match.

CONCERNING CADDIES

THE caddie is an indispensable adjunct to the game of
golf, and for the most part he fulfils his functions very
capably ; but there are caddies of every imaginable variety,
and their vagaries are such as to cause wonderment on the
part of their employers sometimes, amusement at others, and
not infrequently exasperation. Some of them know too
much about the game, and others far too little, and I hardly
know which of these classes is in the long run the worse for
the golfers who engage them to carry their clubs.

An incident of which I heard that happened to a well-
known player on the North Berwick links, must have been
very trying to him. On a busy day all the regular caddies
had been engaged, and the fishermen were drafted into the
club-carrying service. The player, having asked one of
these fishermen if he knew anything about the game, and
having been informed that he had only a little knowledge
of it, resigned himself calmly to the inevitable, and told
the man complacently that he would do. This player

happened to be left-handed, and took up his stance on the first tee accordingly, whereupon the son of the sea at once adopted the part of tutor, and with some warmth and show of contempt exclaimed loudly, "I dinna ken much aboot the game, but ye dinna ken a wee bit. Mon, ye're standing on the wrong side of the baw! Awa' to the other side!" Golfers at the beginning of a round are proverbially susceptible to small influences, and when a player is accustomed to lean somewhat upon his caddie, as even some of the best occasionally do, I can well imagine that such a trivial matter as this is enough to mar a tee shot.

There were some strange specimens of the caddie species at Ganton when I was there. "Make a tee, boy," said a golfer to one of them, evidently a novice, one day. The player had been waiting about for something under a minute, while his servant showed no sign of making the usual preparations for the tee shot. The boy did not seem to understand. "Make a tee, boy," exclaimed the player a second time sharply, but still there was no response, and then the man called for some sand, bent down and made the tee himself. At this the boy attributed the failure of his understanding to the player's limited powers of expression, and somewhat scornfully exclaimed, "Why, if you had told me it was a cock-shot that was wanted, I should have known what you meant!" On competition days at Ganton we had often to secure a number of lads who had never seen the game played before, and very interesting specimens of the youth of Yorkshire they often were. One day, I remember, a competitor pulled his ball very badly, and his caddie, who had gone on a little way in front, received it hard on a very tender part of his head. He was not seriously hurt, but much pained, and forthwith, excusably perhaps, he gave way to tears. To soothe him his employer presented him with half a sovereign. The tears suddenly ceased, the boy's face broke into a happy smile, and a moment later, when the two were trudging away

towards the hole, the youngster ingenuously inquired, "Will
you be coming out again this week, sir?"

There is a kinship between this story and that of the
caddie at North Berwick, son of the greenkeeper there, some
years ago, when first he began to carry clubs. He was
a very precocious little fellow, and the player for whom he
had been engaged to carry for the day was a well-known
golfer from the south. When the day's play was far
advanced, and the time of reckoning was drawing nigh,
the boy seized an opportunity of sidling close up to his
patron and asking him, "D'ye ken Bob S——?" the said
Bob being one of the notabilities of the links. The player
answered that he had not the pleasure of Mr. Robert's
acquaintance so far, and inquired of the boy why he asked
such a question. "Weel," was the answer, "it's a peety ye
dinna ken Bob S——. He's a rale fine gentleman, for he aye
gies twa shillin' a roond for carryin' till 'm; no like some
that ca' themsels gentlemen, an' only gie a shillin'."

But lest it should be imagined from the recital of these
incidents that the caddie is invariably over-greedy, and that
he has no soul for anything but the pecuniary reward of
his service, let there by way of contrast be told the story of
the boy who was willing to carry clubs for nothing—the one
solitary instance of such a disposition to self-sacrifice that
there is on record. This time the golfer was not a great
one. He had his faults, and they were numerous, and for
their conquest and suppression he came to the conclusion
that it would be better if he went out alone over the links
and wrestled with them determinedly. A caddie watched
him going out thus solitary, and felt sorry, so he said to him,
"I will carry your clubs for a shilling, sir." But the golfer
replied, "No, my boy, not to-day, thanks; I will carry them
myself." The golfer missed his drive, foozled his second,
put his third into a bunker, and endured other agonies. The
caddie had been following at a respectful distance, and when
the ball had been duly picked up out of the bunker, he made

a further appeal. " I will carry for ninepence, sir." " No, I do not want a caddie," was the answer again. " I will carry for sixpence, then." " No, go away." On the next tee the player, overcome by conflicting emotions, missed the ball altogether two or three times, and then was the caddie's opportunity, which he seized without hesitation. " I will carry for the fun of the thing, sir ! "

This is a digression, but I fear that digressions are inevitable when one enters upon the subject of caddies, and is persuaded to dip into one's recollection of caddie stories. The ignorant caddie is trying, but not less is the one who knows too much about the game, or thinks he does, and insists upon inflicting his superior knowledge upon you during the whole course of the round. Once when I was playing for the Championship, my clubs were carried by a caddie who swore horribly at me all the time, notwithstanding that from the beginning I was going strongly for the first place. That boy got on my nerves. I was approaching well, but my putting was certainly not so sure and confident as it might have been. " What the —— is the good of shooting at the flag if you can't putt worth a d——!" he exclaimed in great disgust on one occasion when I had the misfortune to miss holing out a somewhat short putt. He has begged to be allowed to carry for me many times since then, but I have steadfastly refused his offer, for I would not be handicapped with him upon any consideration. The caddie I like best of all, and he who I am convinced is the best servant for the average golfer, is he who thoroughly understands the game, has a deep knowledge of the course that is being played over, knows exactly what club to give you upon any and every occasion, and limits his functions to giving you that club without being asked for it. This caddie is a silent caddie, who knows that words of his are out of place, and that they would only tend to upset his master's game. It will generally be found that he, above all others, is the one who takes a deep and sympathetic interest

in that game.   He never upon any consideration gives
advice without being asked for it.   On the other hand,
he takes care that no act or omission of his shall ever cause
his man the most momentary irritation, for he has sufficient
knowledge of the golfer's temperament to know that these
trifles are a constant source of bad holes.   When the player
is preparing for his shot, and his eye is wandering anxiously
between the ball and the hole, he puts out his hand whilst
still continuing his survey of the ground, and as he puts it
out he feels it grasp the handle of the exact club that is
wanted.   There is little need to look at it.   The caddie knew
and acted.   The stance is taken while the player is still in
his thoughtful mood, the shot is made while his mind is still
concentrated to the utmost extent on the difficult task in
hand, and then, after a happy result, the player and this
faithful, truly sympathetic caddie go quietly on their way.
When you are on the green he never needs to be told to go
to the pin.   He is always there, standing at the hole as soon
as the time has come to putt; and while, if the putt is a poor
thing, he has nothing to say (for silence is more than ever
welcome at such a time of sorrow and disappointment), he
permits himself a few courteous words of congratulation if
a great success has been achieved at the last stroke at the
hole, and the crown been placed upon an effort that has
been truly praiseworthy throughout.   This is my ideal
caddie, and I am prepared to make some concessions to
have him always at my side during the most trying rounds
that I have to play.   If he always performs the duties I have
named, promptly and quietly, I do not care whether he
really knows much about the game or not.   If a caddie does
the round of a course often enough in the company of good
golfers, he knows the club to use for every particular stroke,
even though he may have no practical knowledge of the game,
and I ask nothing more of him than that he should always
hand that club to me without keeping me waiting for a single
moment.   These caddies are a rarer species than the others.

I am no advocate of female labour, but I have often, after an experience of the girl caddie, been tempted to wish that there were more of them in the land, for they are uncommonly good. The little girl of humble lot seems, nine times out of ten, to possess all those qualities which go to the making of a good caddie—according to my standard of a good caddie—in a remarkable degree. Unlike some of her elder sisters, she never talks; but she always watches the game very closely and takes a deep interest in it. She is most anxious—if anything too anxious—to do her service properly and well, and to the most complete satisfaction of the gentleman who will reward her for it at the finish. She never keeps you waiting for your bag. The clubs are always there at your hand. If it is obvious to this little girl's simple intelligence that you want your brassy, she has it ready for you. If there is a doubt about the club, she does not make the mistake of offering you one on chance, as it were. She is too timid for that. She holds the bag before you and lets you choose yourself and carry all the responsibility on your own shoulders. The good boy caddie, whom I have referred to as my ideal, does that also. I said he was always waiting with the club ready, but if it is evident to him, as to the player, that it is a difficult question of judgment as to which particular club should be taken in somewhat puzzling circumstances, he allows the golfer to make his choice from the whole collection in the bag, making no suggestion of his own either by word or movement, unless invited to do so. Cannot every golfer recall numberless instances of bad shots and holes lost because in one of these moments of doubt, when his own inclination was leaning to the employment of one particular club, his caddie thrust another before him? Feeling that there must be something good in the caddie's recommendation, he has been tempted in spite of himself to use it. How frequently are the consequences disastrous in such circumstances as these, and how unenviable are the golfer's after reflections upon his own weakness! Yes,

decidedly the girl caddie excels. I have seen her on many
links up and down the country, and she is always good. In
one of my last matches last season—at Luton—I had one to
carry for me, and she was as good as any. Perhaps it may
be urged by some players that it is not a good thing for
girls to do this work. About that I have nothing to say. I
only know that they do their duty well.

A peculiarly caustic but half-unconscious humour is the
characteristic of caddies everywhere, but particularly in the
north, and while golfers continue to lack absolute perfection,
and their ministering attendants to expect it from them
every time, it will probably remain a characteristic. A fair
specimen was the remark of his caddie to a player whose
handicap was several strokes removed from scratch, and who,
having become badly bunkered on one occasion, tried nearly
every iron club in his bag in a vain endeavour to get out.
The case was heartbreaking, and he turned despairingly to
his caddie with the question, "What on earth shall I take
now?" There was little encouragement in the answer,
"Take the 4.5 train." There is a good story also of a
certain Welshman of title who became enthusiastic over the
game, though he did not excel at it. He conceived that it
would be a good thing to make a tour of the famous Scottish
courses with the object of improving his play, and in due
season he arrived at a certain famous green, where he employed as his caddie an individual who had a considerable
reputation for blunt candour. The turf suffered severely
every time this player made use of his irons, and the caddie
shook his head gloomily and sadly as he witnessed the
destructive work that went on daily. At last there came a
day when he could stand it no longer, and when the Welshman had taken a mighty swipe at the ball with a heavy iron
and made a deep excavation for several inches behind it, the
club carrier moaned painfully, "O lord, man, hae mercy on
puir auld Scotland!" It is said that the golfer played no
more on those links. It was on this same course that two

players went out one morning to play, and found a friend
waiting alone on the first tee, who said that he had fixed
up a match with a certain Captain Blank, who would be
coming along presently. The possibility of a foursome was
considered, and a question was asked as to what kind of a
player the Captain was, his partner replying, "Oh, he is
excellent. He drives a good ball, plays his irons well, and
is exceedingly useful at the short game; in fact, he is a
first-rate all-round man." Expecting confirmation of this
eulogium, he turned to his caddie and said, "You know the
Captain's play well enough. Now, what sort of a player
would you say he is?" The caddie replied scornfully,
"Captain Blank! He canna play a shot worth a d——.
He's nae better than yoursel'!"

The fact is that no player is great in the eyes of his
caddie, for on one occasion when two gentlemen who were
very fair hands at the game were doing a round and being
closely pressed by a couple behind, who seemed to be
driving inordinately long balls, one of them observed that
perhaps they had better let them go through as they seemed
to be playing both well and quickly. "Na, na, naething o'
the kind," interposed one of the caddies. "They're just twa
duffers like yersels!" And great eminence in other fields
counts for nothing with the caddie if his man cannot golf in
good style. There is the story told by Mr. Balfour of the
distinguished general, hero of many battles, who, having duly
found his way into his twentieth bunker, was startled by a
cry of irritation from his caddie, "Come, come, old gentleman, this will never do!" This great statesman - golfer
relates another anecdote showing that caddies are much the
same the whole world over. An English golfer was playing
at Pau and had a French caddie attending upon him. He
made one particularly fine approach shot, and, as golfers will
at such times, he turned round to the boy with excusable
vanity for applause. But the boy's English vocabulary so
far comprised only two words which he had heard uttered

on several occasions, but the sense of which he did not understand. Feeling sure, however, that they must be appropriate to this occasion, and desiring to be appreciative, he smiled pleasantly into the golfer's face and murmured, "Beastly fluke!" Mr. Balfour, by the way, has a particular and decided taste in caddies, for he has written that he can gladly endure severe or even contemptuous criticism from them ; can bear to have it pointed out to him that all his misfortunes are the direct and inevitable result of his own folly; can listen with equanimity when failure is prophesied of some stroke he is attempting, and can note unmoved the self-satisfied smile with which the fulfilment of the prophecy is accentuated; but ignorant and stupid indifference is intolerable to him. The caddie, in the statesman's opinion, is not, and ought not, to be regarded as a machine for carrying clubs at a shilling a round, but rather occupies, or ought to occupy, the position of competent adviser or interested spectator. The caddie ought to be as anxious for the success of his side as if he were one of the players, and should watch each move in the game with benevolent if critical interest, being always ready with the appropriate club, and, if need be, with the appropriate comment.

But I don't like to see this anxiety for the success of one's fortunes upon the links carried to excess. It is then a disturbing factor, and its humorous aspect does not always appeal to one as it should. Some golfers might be flattered when they come to know that their caddies have backed them to the extent of half the remuneration they will receive for carrying the clubs for the round. It is a touching expression of the caddie's belief in them. But after all this kind of thing does not help to make a good caddie. Apart from other considerations, it does not make the boy carry any the better because he is over-anxious about the result of the match, and, though some golfers might be inclined to ridicule the suggestion, it nevertheless is a disturbing element in one's game if one knows that even the caddie will be very deeply concerned if every stroke does not come off just as well as it ought to do. The caddie is not above letting you know of his wager ; sometimes he will even tell you of it. Two golfers of some Highland celebrity were playing a match one day at Luffness, and after a hard round they came to the eighteenth tee all square and but this one hole to play. At this critical stage of the game the caddie of one of them approached his master and nervously whispered to him, " Please, sir, wad ye do your very best here, for there's money on this match." And the golfer did try to do his very best indeed, but he pressed and he foozled, and he lost the hole and the match. Sympathetically he turned to his caddie to ask him what was the amount of the lost wager that he might pay it for him and soften his disappointment. " It was a penny, sir," said the boy.

But despite his constant sarcasm and his utter inability to tolerate anything except the very best in golf, there is after all much good human kindness in your caddie if he is worthy of the name. " Big Crawford " will always be remembered as a fine specimen. On the day when Mr. A. J. Balfour played himself into the captaincy of the Royal and Ancient club, a gentleman who was looking on, and who was well acquainted with the fact that when Mr. Balfour was in Ireland as Chief Secretary he never played a round of any of the Irish links without having plain-clothes detectives walking fore and aft, inquired very audibly, " Is there no one looking after Mr. Balfour now?" " Big Crawford " was carrying for him that day, and he heard the question. He turned with a look of severe pride towards the quarter whence it came, and answered it as loudly, " Aw'm lookin' aifter Maister Balfour." There was nothing more to be said. The chief of the Conservatives has certainly an enormous popularity with the caddies. He so evidently loves his golf so much, and he has great sympathy with them. He bears amiably with their weaknesses. He was one day playing a match with Tom Dunn, who was his tutor, at North

Berwick, and by a mixture of skill and luck was enabled
to hole out at "Pointgarry out" in two. It happened that
he received a stroke from Dunn at this hole, and the caddie
ingeniously pointed out to him that he was thus entitled to
consider that he had done the hole in one. "How excellent!" he said. But in the same breath the caddie begged
leave to remind him that it was customary for all good
golfers to celebrate the performance of this particular feat by
the bestowal of some special token upon their caddies. Mr.
Balfour was amused. He tantalised the boy by observing
that rather than that he should have to pay anyone for
watching him do these great things, he surely ought to
receive remuneration from all spectators for doing them.
The boy felt that there was truth in this new view of things,
and a sad look was stealing over his face, when the right
honourable gentleman handed over to him the customary
fee. Another time on the links, two officers, a Colonel and a
Major, were playing in front of Mr. Balfour and his partner,
when the latter were courteously invited to go through so
that their enjoyment of the round would not be interfered
with by any waiting. At the moment when Mr. Balfour
was passing the others, he was surprised to hear a word of
command called out by the Colonel's caddie, who happened to
be a Lucknow veteran. "Attention! Eyes front! Shoulder
arms! Present arms!" And thereupon each of the caddies
took from his bag a driver and with it presented arms in
proper soldierly style, Mr. Balfour, who was Chief Secretary
at the time, smiling with pleasure at the interesting compliment and acknowledging the salute. He has a remarkable memory for the caddies who have served him, and once,
when on the tee, just about to engage in a foursome, he
recognised one of his opponents' caddies as a boy who on
a former occasion had carried his own clubs, and he nodded
to him kindly. Naturally the caddie was immensely pleased,
and turning to one of his colleagues he remarked, "Ye see
hoo we Conservatives ken ane anither!"

Another instance of the deep humanity of "Big Craw-ford," whom I have just mentioned, occurred on one occasion when he was carrying for an Edinburgh clergyman, who, in going for the Redan, had the misfortune to be badly bunkered, his ball, in addition to the other difficulties of the situation, lying in a deep heel mark. He was palpably in great agony of mind, all the greater in that he never uttered a word. Crawford crept quietly to his side and whispered gently, "What a peety! What a peety! But gin an aith wad relieve ye, sir, dinna mind me, dinna mind me!" and thereupon he discreetly retired for some little distance. Sandy Smith, another famous caddie, was one day carrying for a player who had the good fortune to be no fewer than six holes up on his opponent by the time the eighth hole was reached. At this green, something having gone wrong with the reckoning of the strokes, there was a mild dispute as to whether the hole had been won by Sandy's man or whether it had been halved. Eventually it was agreed that it was halved, but as the players moved away to the next tee, he who was six down being out of earshot in front, his opponent remarked to Sandy, "You know, Sandy, I still think I won that hole after all." Sandy seemed shocked at such a cold-blooded greed for holes, and reprovingly, very seriously, and sharply said to his employer, "Haud yer tongue, sir; haud yer tongue. Wad ye break the man's heart?" Sandy used to remark that "the finest gowffer on the green was Maister Edward Blyth," and it was not until he had expressed this opinion with an almost wearying frequency that his hearers suspected that there was some connection between his choice and the fact, which he ad-mitted one day, that "his auld claes fits me best." Ap-parently he had the measure of every player on the course. "I'm wantin' a word wi' ye, Mr. Blyth," he said to his favourite one day. "What is it, Sandy?" "It's no' muckle, sir; it's jist this, ye ken. I'm wantin' an auld suit o' claes frae ye; ye're the only man hereaboot that'll fit me." But apparently there were others, for one day when a player for whom he was carrying asked him if he knew the Lord Justice-Clerk, who happened just then to be passing in a foursome, Sandy replied, "That's Lord Kingsbury, ye mean. O ay, he's a great freen' o' mine. Naebody kens his lordship better nor me. Thae's his breeks I've on."

Golfers should, I think, sometimes be on their guard lest a too kind-hearted caddie, in an excess of zeal for his employer, should be tempted to transgress the laws of the game, or depart from strict truthfulness in his behalf. Sometimes it is done with a wonderful air of innocence and simplicity. Caddies have been known, when their employers have been in doubt as to exactly how many strokes they have played at certain holes, to give an emphatic, but none the less untruthful declaration, on the side of fewness. They mean well, but mistakenly, and it is better for everybody concerned, but particularly for the caddies, that they should be severely reprimanded when there is reason to doubt their good faith.

And who shall say that another, and for our purposes the final characteristic of the average caddie of experience, is not a wonderful amount of solid worldly common-sense of a variety specially adapted to golf? And what golfer is there who has not at one time or another had the advantage of it? But he may at the time have been unconscious of the assistance. There is the historic case of the caddie on the Scottish links who warned a beginner, dallying too much on the tee, that he "maunna address the ba' sae muckle." Forthwith the southern tyro, greatly exasperated at his own failures, burst out, "So far as I know I haven't said a word to the infernal thing, but the irritation of this beastly game is enough, and if I have any more of your confounded tongue you may repent it!" Then the caddie murmured to himself, "I dinna like 'is look. I'll better get 'm roond as pleesant as possible." Could any advice have been more delicately worded than that of the caddie to the stout clergyman who with all his strength made a most mighty swing at his ball on the tee with the usual result—a foozle? "It'll nae do, sir; ye ken ye canna drive as far as that." "Wha—wha— what do you mean by such a remark? As far as what?" gasped the reverend but irate gentleman. "I jist mean, sir, that ye canna drive as far as ye wad like."

Perhaps we shall never hear the best caddie stories, for is it not likely that a great abundance of them are made and told in the sheds after the day's play is over, and when the golfer's tools are being wiped and cleaned, and his irons burnished to a beautiful brightness? It is then that the caddie is in his happiest vein, his tongue and disposition un-trammelled by the presence of the club members. "What 're ye doin' cleanin' them clubs so grand?" asked one caddie of another, who was evidently bestowing unusual pains on the polishing of the set that were in his keeping. The caddie was in a thoughtful mood. He was the regular attendant of an old golfer who had had a most disastrous day. "I'm to clean 'em better than ever," he answered. "And when I've cleaned 'em I've got to break 'em across my knee. And then I've got to chuck 'em in the bloomin' river." Sometimes, we see, if he is a simple-hearted, faithful caddie, his lot is not a happy one.

CHAPTER XXIII

REFLECTIONS AND RECOLLECTIONS

Good golf to come—Giants of the past—The amateurs of to-day—The greatness of "Freddy" Tait — Modern professionals — Good sportsmen and good friends—A misconception—The constant strain—How we always play our best — Difficult tasks—No "close season" in golf—Spectators at big matches — Certain anecdotes—Putting for applause — Shovelling from a bunker—The greatest match I have ever played in—A curious incident—A record in halves—A coincidence—The exasperation of Andrew—The coming of spring—The joyful golfer.

I THINK that every good golfer of experience reflects upon his past history with mingled pleasure and sorrow —pleasure when he calls to mind all the many glorious matches in which he has taken part, and sorrow when the thought arises that all that golf has been played and done with, and can never be played again. But we have all this abiding consolation, that even if we cannot retain our very best form to the end of our days, we can hope still to play a good game to the finish, and there is the heroic example of rare old Tom Morris to stimulate us in this hope. Much is given to golfers,—perhaps more than to the participators in any other sport,—but they are rarely satisfied. The wonderful fascination of golf is indicated in this eternal longing for more. Sometimes when I glance over the records of the history of the game, I feel a twinge of regret that it was not possible for me to play with, or even to see, such giants of the past as Allan Robertson, David Strath, the Dunns, Willie Campbell, Willie Park, senior, or the famous young Tom Morris. Golf is great to-day, but it must have been great in those days also, even if there was less of it than there is now.

But I have had the good fortune to play with all the well-known amateurs and professionals of my own time, and it is pleasant to think that they are nearly all still alive, and that therefore I may sometime or another play with them again. There is one great exception—Mr. Fred Tait, who was killed in South Africa. I don't think anyone could ever have the smallest doubt about the reason for his enormous popularity. I had the delight of playing against him two or three times, and I thought that he was not only a very fine golfer indeed, but one of the very finest gentlemen that I could imagine. It is something for me to remember that I played in the last important match in which he figured before he went out to the war—an international foursome, England *v.* Scotland, that was played at Ganton, Willie Park and Mr. Tait representing Scotland, while Mr. John Ball, junior, and I were for England. From all the amateurs with whom I have ever come in contact I have always received the very greatest kindness and encouragement, and I do not know a single one with whom I would not like to play again some day or other. It has always seemed to me that there is something about golf that makes a man a good fellow whether he is amateur or professional.

I wish to speak in the same way about my professional brothers as I have done about the amateurs. I have always found them all first-class sportsmen in the strictest and best sense of the word, and some of the best friends I have in the world are among them. There are some very fine players among the professionals of to-day. I have often watched and greatly admired the splendid skill of such friends and constant opponents as J. H. Taylor, James Braid, Alexander Herd, Jack White, and many others whose names would fill a page, not forgetting my own brother Tom. I have from time to time been indebted to many of them for various acts of kindness. There is a fine spirit of freemasonry amongst us professionals. Whenever we play against each other each of us does his level best to win, and gives no quarter with a single stroke, but it has been my invariable experience that when the match is over the loser is always the first to congratulate the winner, and to do it not as a mere matter of form but with the very utmost sincerity.

And here I should like to say a few words with the object of removing a misconception which still seems to linger in the minds of followers of the game. " Dear me, Vardon, what a grand time you fellows have, travelling all over the country in this manner, and doing nothing but playing golf on the very best courses," is the kind of remark that often greets me when I have just returned from playing in one match or tournament, and am due to start for another in a day or two. But I am not sure that we have such a grand time as those who say these things seem to think. We enjoy it just because we enjoy everything connected with golf, and particularly the playing of it; but playing these exhibition matches is not quite the same thing as going away for the week-end and having a quiet round or two with a friend, however hard you may try to beat him. Some people entertain a fancy that we do not need to strain ourselves to the utmost in these engagements, and that therefore we take things easily. I can answer for myself, and I am sure for all my brother professionals, that we never take things easily, that we always play the very best golf of which we are capable, and that if a championship rested on each match we could not play any better. It must be remembered that when we are invited by any club to play an exhibition match, that club expects to see some golf, and thus it happens that the fear of a great responsibility is always overhanging us. We dare not play tricks with such reputations as we may have had the good fortune to obtain. We are always well aware that there are very good golfers in the crowd, who are watching and criticising every stroke that we make. Therefore we keep ourselves in the very best of condition, and do our utmost always to play our best. How difficult is our task when sometimes we are not feeling as well as we might wish—as must occasionally happen—I will leave the charitable reader to imagine. Has he ever felt like playing his best game when a little below par in either mind or body? This is where the really hard work of the professional's life comes in. There is no "close season" in golf, as in cricket, football, and other sports. When a cricketer plays indifferently, after two months of the game, his admirers cry out that he is stale and needs a rest. But there are eleven players on each side in a cricket match, and constant rests for all of them, so that to my mind their work is very light in comparison with that of the golfer, who enjoys no "close season," and has all the work of each match on his own shoulders. Surely he also must become stale, but such a state on his part is not tolerated. Again, one often hears that a certain match between professional players has been halved purposely—that is to say, that it was an arranged thing from start to finish. Such things may have happened in other sports, but take it from me that it never, never happens in golf. One man never plays down to another, whatever disparity there may be in their respective degrees of skill. It does not matter how many holes one is up on one's opponent; there is never any slackening until the game has been won. It makes no difference if the man you are playing against is your very best friend or your brother, and one has sometimes to pass through the trying ordeal of straining his every nerve to win a match when in his heart of hearts, for some particular reason, he would like the other man to win. I intrude these affairs of our own in these concluding reflections only for the purpose of indicating that, though we love our game and always enjoy it, professional golf is not quite the same thing as that played by amateurs, and must not be judged from the same standpoint. I think it is because of this continual sense of a great responsibility, and the custom and necessity of always—absolutely always—trying to play our very best game, that the leading professionals are constantly a stroke or two better than the most skilful amateurs, even though the latter practise the game quite as much, and have apparently just as much opportunity, or even more, of making themselves perfect.

I have mentioned the spectators.   I have generally found the crowds who follow a big professional match round the links both highly intelligent and exceedingly considerate. But sometimes we overhear some strange things said. Taylor and I were once fulfilling an important engagement together, and when my opponent had a particularly difficult shot to play, two ladies came up quite close to him and persisted in talking in a loud tone of voice.   Taylor waited for a little while in the hope that their chatter would cease, but it did not.   Then, in a feeling of desperation, he attempted to address his ball ; but the task was hopeless.   The conversation went on more loudly than ever, and he was doomed to certain failure if he attempted his stroke in these circumstances. So he stood up again, and looked round in the direction whence the voices came.   "Oh," said one of the ladies then, "you can go on now.   We've quite finished."   We must be thankful for small mercies.   James Braid and I were once playing down at Beckenham.   At one of the putting greens we were both a long way from the hole.   My ball was a trifle the more distant of the two, and so I played the odd, and managed to get down a wonderfully fine putt.   Then Braid played the like and holed out also.   These were two rather creditable achievements with our putters.   When his ball had trickled safely into the hole, and the spectators were moving towards the next tee, Braid and I were amused, but not flattered, by the words of a man who was speaking to a friend in such a loud voice that we could all hear.   "Oh," he exclaimed deprecatingly, "those fellows only do that sort of thing for the sake of the applause!"   How happy we should be if we could always make certain of those long putts without any applause at all! It was with Braid also that I was playing in a match at Luton towards the close of last year, when I overheard a singular remark. I happened to be bunkered at the fourteenth, and took my niblick to get out, but lost the hole. We walked on together to the next tee, and Braid was taking his stance when we heard two gentlemen eagerly discussing and explaining the recent bunker incident. Evidently one of them was supposed to know something of golf and the other nothing at all. "You see," said the former to his friend, "there is really no rule in the matter at all. Vardon or any other player could have used a shovel in that bunker and have simply shovelled the ball over on to the other side." I was surprised that Braid got his next tee shot in so well as he did. And how very often have I heard the question asked in the crowd, "Why do those fellows chalk the faces of their clubs?" and how invariably has the answer been, "So that they can see afterwards where they hit the ball!" When I write my recollection of these things, I do not wish it to be imagined that I am making any sort of accusation against golf crowds generally. They are excellent from all points of view; but it must inevitably happen that there are some people among them who know little of the game, and others who do not appreciate what a trying ordeal a hard-fought match usually is.

Such questions are often put to me as, "Vardon, what was the greatest match in which you ever played?" or, "What was the most extraordinary occurrence you have ever seen on the links?" and so forth. They are questions which it is difficult to answer, for is not nearly every match that we play brimful of incident and interest, and at the time do we not regard many of the incidents as most extraordinary? It would, then, be too serious a task to attempt a selection from such a huge mass. But, looking back over the last few years, it seems that my £100 match with Willie Park is that which remains uppermost in my mind, and the one that I am least likely to forget. There was more talking and writing about it than about any other match in which I have played. The "gallery" that followed this match was the greatest I have ever seen or heard of. And as I am questioned also about the curious and the singular in golf, I may say that there was a coincidence in this game that struck me at the time as being quite unusual. In a closely-fought match it is often interesting to notice how nearly each player's ball often follows the other. Frequently they are side by side within one or two clubs' length after the drives from the tee. But in the first stage of this match against Park, after he had driven a long ball from the tee at the eleventh hole, I drove and my ball pitched exactly on the top of his! The Messrs. Hunter were kindly serving in the capacity of forecaddies, and they were both positive upon this incident. My ball after striking his rebounded slightly, and then stopped dead about two feet behind. Its position rather affected my follow-through, so that I duffed my stroke and lost the hole. This record—if it was a record—was also the means of eclipsing what I believe was another record in first-class golf. The first ten holes in this match were halved, and it was the incident of which I have just been speaking and the duffed stroke that followed it that led to the breaking of the sequence.

"Now, Vardon, how often have you holed out in one?" they ask me also, regardless of the fact that this event demands not only a perfect shot but a perfect fluke, and that the professional player is no more likely to accomplish it than anyone else. Well, I have only been guilty of this fluke on one occasion—and that was not so very long ago—and when it happened it was at a hole a little over two hundred yards in length. On one occasion, also, I have enjoyed the coincidence of holing out with my mashie approach at the same hole twice in one day. That was in the course of a tournament at Elie, in which I had the good fortune to finish first. As it happened, Andrew Kirkaldy, who hoped to end high up in the list, was my partner for the first round, and it came about also that he was watching me play when the holing-out process was accomplished for the second time. Then he lifted up his hands in horror and delivered himself of his famous remark, "Ye're enough to break the heart of an iron ox!" During the last round of this same tournament Andrew, who was playing some holes behind me, and was then himself in the running for the first place, was kept posted up by a friend as to my score for each hole. He did not seem to derive much encouragement from the reports, for when the last one was carried to him he asked the friend who brought it if he thought that there was nobody who could play golf besides Vardon, and intimated at the same time that if anyone else brought him any more of those tales he would strike him with his niblick! Of course we all know what a really fine fellow is Andrew Kirkaldy, and how much poorer the golf world would be without his presence and his constant humour.

And now I think I have holed out on the last green and this long match is finished. After all it is better to play golf than to write or read about it. What anticipation is more gloriously joyful than that of the man who handles his driver on the first tee on a bright morning of the spring-time! He has all the round, and all the day, and all the spring and summer and autumn before him. And at this moment another spring is breaking brightly, and the golf that is before each of us promises to be as momentous and soul-satisfying as any that has gone before.

APPENDIX

THE RULES OF THE GAME OF GOLF

As approved by the Royal and Ancient Golf Club of St. Andrews, September 1908, *and first becoming operative on* 1st *January* 1909; *together with Recommendations, Form and Make of Golf Clubs, Etiquette, Special Rules for Match Play Competitions, Rules for Three-ball, Best Ball, and Four-ball Matches, and Special Rules for Stroke Competitions.*

THE RULES

DEFINITIONS

(1) A "side" consists either of one player or of two players. If one player play against another, the match is called "a single." If two play against two, each side playing one ball, the match is called "a foursome." If one play against two playing one ball between them, the match is called "a threesome."

(2) "Advice" is any counsel or suggestion which could influence a player in determining the line of play, in the choice of a club, or in the method of making a stroke.

(3) The "Course" is the whole area within which play is permitted ; more particularly, it is the ground between the holes which is specially prepared for play.

(4) The "teeing-ground" is the starting place for a hole. The front of each teeing-ground shall be indicated by two marks placed in a line as nearly as possible at right angles to the line of play, and the teeing-ground shall include a rectangular space of the depth of two club lengths directly behind the line indicated by the two marks.

(5) "Through the green" is all ground on which play is permitted, except hazards and the putting-green of the hole that is being played.

(6) A "hazard" is any bunker, water (except casual water), sand, path, road, ditch, bush, or rushes. Sand blown on to the grass, or sprinkled on the course for its preservation, bare patches, sheep-tracks, snow, and ice are not hazards.

(7) "Casual water" is any temporary accumulation of water (whether caused by rainfall, flooding, or otherwise) which is not one of the ordinary and recognised hazards of the course.

(8) "Out of bounds" is all ground on which play is prohibited.

(9) A ball is "out of bounds" when the greater part of it lies within a prohibited area.

(10) The "putting-green is all ground, except hazards, within twenty yards of the hole.

(11) The hole shall be 4¼ inches in diameter, and at least 4 inches deep. If a metal lining be used, it shall be sunk below the lip of the hole and its outer diameter shall not exceed 4¼ inches.

(12) The term "loose impediments" denotes any obstructions not fixed or growing, and includes dung, worm-casts, mole-hills, snow, and ice.

(13) A "stroke" is the forward movement of the club made with the intention of striking the ball, or any contact between the head of the club and the ball resulting in movement of the ball, except in the case of a ball accidentally knocked off a tee (Rule 2 (1)).

(14) A "penalty stroke" is a stroke added to the score of a side under certain rules, and does not affect the rotation of play.

(15) The side which plays off first from a teeing-ground is said to have the "honour."

(16) In "teeing," the ball may be placed on the ground, or on sand or other substance in order to raise it off the ground.

(17) A player has "addressed the ball" when he has taken his stance and grounded his club, or, if in a hazard, when he has taken his stance preparatory to striking at the ball.

(18) A ball is "in play" as soon as the player has made a stroke at a teeing-ground, and it remains in play until holed out, except when lifted in accordance with the rules.

(19) A ball is deemed to "move" if it leave its original position in the least degree ; but it is not considered to "move" if it merely oscillate and come to rest in its original position.

(20) A ball is "lost" if it be not found within five minutes after the search for it has begun.

(21) The reckoning of strokes is kept by the terms—"the odd," "two more," "three more," etc., and "one off three," "one off two," "the like." The reckoning of holes is kept by the terms—so many "holes up," or "all even," and so many "to play."

A side is said to be "dormie" when it is as many holes up as there are holes remaining to be played.

General and through the Green

Rule 1.—(1) The game of golf is played by two sides, each playing its own ball.

The game consists in each side playing a ball from a teeing-ground into a hole by successive strokes. The hole is won by the side which holes its ball in fewer strokes than the opposing side, except as otherwise provided for in the **Rules.**

The hole is halved if both sides hole out in the same number of strokes.

(2) A match consists of one round of the course unless it be otherwise agreed. A match is won by the side which is leading by a number of holes greater than the number of holes remaining to be played.

A match is halved if each side win the same number of holes.

Matches constituted of singles, threesomes, or foursomes shall have precedence of and be entitled to pass any other kind of match.

A single player has no standing, and shall always give way to a match of any kind.

Any match playing a whole round shall be entitled to pass a match playing a shorter round.

If a match fail to keep its place on the green, and lose in distance more than one clear hole on the players on front, it may be passed, on request being made.

Rule 2.—(1) A match begins by each side playing a ball from the first teeing-ground.

A ball played from outside the limits of the teeing-ground, or played by a player when his opponent should have had the honour, may be at once recalled by the opposing side, and may be re-teed without penalty.

If a ball fall or be knocked off a tee by the player in addressing it, it may be re-teed without penalty ; if the ball be struck when so moving, no penalty shall be incurred.

(2) The option of taking the honour at the first teeing-ground shall, if necessary, be decided by lot.

The side which wins a hole shall take the honour at the next teeing-ground. If a hole has been halved, the side which had the honour at the previous teeing-ground shall retain it.

On beginning a new match, the winner of the long match in the previous round shall take the honour ; if the previous long match was halved, the side which last won a hole shall take the honour.

Rule 3.—In a threesome or foursome the partners shall strike off alternately from the teeing-grounds, and shall strike alternately during the play of each hole.

If a player play when his partner should have played, his side shall lose the hole.

Rule 4.—(1) A player may not ask for nor willingly receive advice from any one except his own caddie, his partner, or his partner's caddie.

(2) A player may employ a forecaddie, but may not receive advice from him.

(3) When playing through the green, or from a hazard, a player may have the line to the hole indicated to him, but no mark shall be placed nor shall any one stand on the proposed line, in order to indicate it, while the stroke is being made.

The penalty for a breach of this Rule shall be the loss of the hole.

Rule 5.—The ball must be fairly struck at with the head of the club, not pushed, scraped, nor spooned.

The penalty for a breach of this Rule shall be the loss of the hole.

Rule 6.—A ball must be played wherever it lies or the hole be given up, except as otherwise provided for in the Rules and Local Rules.

Rule 7.—When the balls are in play, the ball farther from the hole shall be played first. Through the green, or in a hazard, if a player play when his opponent should have played, the opponent may at once recall the stroke. A ball so recalled shall be dropped as near as possible to the place where it lay, without penalty.

Rule 8.—A ball shall be dropped in the following manner : The player himself shall drop it. He shall face the hole, stand erect, and drop the ball behind him over his shoulder.

The penalty for a breach of this Rule shall be the loss of the hole.

If, in the act of dropping, the ball touch the player, he shall incur no penalty, and if it roll into a hazard the player may re-drop the ball without penalty.

Rule 9.—(1) A ball in play may not be touched before the hole is played out, except as provided for in the Rules.

The penalty for a breach of this Rule shall be one stroke.

The player may, without penalty, touch his ball with his club in the act of addressing it, provided he does not move it.

A ball in play may, with the opponent's consent, be lifted for the purpose of identification, but it must be carefully replaced.

(2) If the player's ball move the opponent's ball through the green or in a hazard, the opponent, if he choose, may drop a ball, without penalty, as near as possible to the place where his ball lay, but this must be done before another stroke is played by either side.

Rule 10.—In playing through the green, irregularities of surface which could in any way affect the player's stroke shall not be removed nor pressed down by the player, his partner, or either of their caddies : a player is, however, always entitled to place his feet firmly on the ground when taking his stance.

The penalty for a breach of this Rule shall be the loss of the hole.

Rule 11.—Any flag-stick, guide-flag, movable guide-post, wheel-barrow, tool, roller, grass-cutter, box, vehicle, or similar obstruction may be removed. A ball moved in removing such an obstruction shall be replaced without penalty. A ball lying on or touching such an obstruction, or lying on or touching clothes, or nets, or ground under repair or covered up or opened for the purpose of the upkeep of the course, or lying in one of the holes, or in a guide-flag hole, or in a hole made by the greenkeeper, may be lifted and dropped without penalty as near as possible to the place where it lay, but not nearer to the hole. A ball lifted in a hazard, under such circumstances, shall be dropped in the hazard.

Rule 12.—(1) Any loose impediment lying within a club length of the ball and not being in or touching a hazard, may be removed without penalty ; if the ball move after any such loose impediment has been touched by the player, his partner, or either of their caddies, the player shall be deemed to have caused the ball to move and the penalty shall be one stroke.

(2) A loose impediment lying more than a club length from the ball may not be moved under penalty of the loss of the hole, unless the loose impediment lie on the putting-green (see Rule 28 (1)).

(3) When a ball is in play, if a player, or his partner, or either of their caddies accidentally move his or their ball, or by touching anything cause it to move, the penalty shall be one stroke.

(4) If a ball in play move after the player has grounded his club in the act of addressing it, or if a ball in play being in a hazard move after the player has taken his stance to play it, he shall be deemed to have caused it to move, and the penalty shall be one stroke.

NOTE.—If the player has lifted a loose impediment (see Rules 12 (1) and 28 (1)) and the ball has not moved until the player has grounded his club, he shall only be deemed to have caused the ball to move under Section (4) of this Rule, and the penalty shall be one stroke.

Rule 13.—A player shall not play while his ball is moving, under the penalty of the loss of the hole, except in the case of a teed ball (Rule 2), or a ball struck twice (Rule 14), or a ball in water (Rule 26). When the ball only begins to move while the player is making his backward or forward swing, he shall incur no penalty under this Rule, but he is not exempted from the provisions of Rule 12 (1) or Rule 28 (1) and of Rule 12 (3) and (4).

Rule 14.—If a player, when making a stroke, strike the ball twice, the penalty shall be one stroke, but he shall incur no further penalty by reason of his having played while his ball was moving.

Rule 15.—Before striking at a ball in play, a player shall not move, bend, nor break anything fixed or growing, except so far as is necessary to enable him fairly to take his stance in addressing the ball, or in making his backward or forward swing. The club may only be grounded lightly, and not pressed on the ground.

The penalty for a breach of this Rule shall be the loss of the hole.

Rule 16.—When the balls lie within a club length of each other through the green or in a hazard, the ball lying nearer to the hole may, at the option of either the player or the opponent, be lifted until the other ball is played, and shall then be replaced as near as possible to the place where it lay.

If either ball be accidentally moved in complying with this Rule, no penalty shall be incurred, and the ball so moved shall be replaced.

If the lie of the lifted ball be altered in playing the other ball, the lifted ball may be placed as near as possible to the place where it lay and in a lie similar to that which it originally occupied.

Rule 17.—(1) If a ball *in motion* be stopped or deflected by any agency outside the match, or by a forecaddie, it is a rub of the green and the ball shall be played from the spot where it lies.

(2) If a ball lodge in *anything moving*, a ball shall be dropped, or if on the putting-green, placed, as near as possible to the place where the object was when the ball lodged in it, without penalty.

(3) If a ball *at rest* be displaced by any agency outside the match, except wind, the player shall drop a ball as near as possible to the place where it lay, without penalty ; and if the ball be displaced on the putting-green, it shall be replaced without penalty.

Rule 18.—If a player's ball strike, or be stopped, or be moved by an opponent or an opponent's caddie or clubs, the opponent shall lose the hole, except as provided for in Rule 22 (3) and Rule 33.

Rule 19.—If a player's ball strike or be stopped by himself, or his partner, or either of their caddies, or their clubs, his side shall lose the hole.

Rule 20.—(1) If a player play the opponent's ball, his side shall lose the hole, unless—

(*a*) The opponent then play the player's ball, in which case the penalty is cancelled, and the hole shall be played out with the balls thus exchanged ;

(*b*) The mistake occur through wrong information given by an opponent or his caddie, in which case there shall be no penalty ; if the mistake be discovered before the opponent has played, it shall be rectified by dropping a ball as near as possible to the place where the opponent's ball lay.

On the putting-green the ball shall be replaced.

(2) If a player play a stroke with the ball of any one not engaged in the match, and the mistake be discovered and intimated to his opponent before his opponent has played his next stroke, there shall be no penalty ; if the mistake be not discovered and so intimated until after the opponent has played his next stroke, the player's side shall lose the hole.

Rule 21.—If a ball be "lost," except in water, casual water, or out of bounds, the player's side shall lose the hole, unless it is afterwards discovered that the opponent's ball is also lost, when the hole shall be halved.

Rule 22.—(1) If a ball lie in fog, bent, bushes, long grass, or the like, only so much thereof shall be touched as will enable the player to find his ball.

(2) If a ball be completely covered by sand, only so much thereof may be removed as will enable the player to see the top of the ball ; if the ball be touched in removing the sand, no penalty shall be incurred.

(3) If a player or his caddie when searching for an opponent's ball accidentally touch or move it, no penalty shall be incurred, and the ball, if moved, shall be replaced.

The penalty for a breach of this Rule shall be the loss of the hole.

Rule 23.—(1) If a ball lie out of bounds, the player shall play his next stroke as nearly as possible at the spot from which the ball which is out of bounds was played. If the ball was played out of bounds from the teeing-ground, the player may tee a ball for his next stroke; in every other case the ball shall be dropped.

(2) If a player after making a stroke be doubtful whether his ball ,s out of bounds or not, he may play another ball as provided for in par. (1) of this Rule, but if it be discovered that the first ball is not out of bounds, it shall continue in play without penalty.

On reaching the place where the first ball is likely to be, if the player or his opponent be still in doubt, the player is not entitled to presume that the first ball is out of bounds till he has made a search of five minutes.

(3) A player has the right at any time of ascertaining whether his opponent's ball is out of bounds or not, before his opponent can compel him to continue his play.

(4) A player may stand out of bounds to play a ball lying within bounds.

Rule 24.—If a ball split into separate pieces, another ball may be dropped where any piece lies. If a ball crack or become unfit for play, the player may change it on intimating to his apponent his intention to do so. Mud adhering to a ball shall not be considered as making it unfit for play.

HAZARDS AND CASUAL WATER

Rule 25.—When a ball lies in or touches a hazard, nothing shall be done which can in any way improve its lie ; the club shall not touch the ground, nor shall anything be touched or moved, before the player strikes at the ball, subject to the following exceptions : (1) The player may place his feet firmly on the ground for the purpose of taking his stance ; (2) in addressing the ball, or in the backward or forward swing, any grass, bent, bush, or other growing substance, or the side of a bunker, wall, paling, or other immovable obstacle may be touched ; (3) steps or planks placed in a hazard by the Green Committee for access to or egress from such hazard may be removed, and if a ball be moved in so doing, it shall be replaced without penalty ; (4) any loose impediment may be lifted from the putting-green ; (5) the player shall be entitled to find his ball as provided for by Rule 22.

The penalty for a breach of this Rule shall be the loss of the hole.

Rule 26.—When a ball is in water a player may, without penalty, strike at it while it is moving, but he must not delay to make his stroke in order to allow the wind or current to better the position of the ball, under penalty of the loss of the hole.

Rule 27.—(1) If a ball lie or be lost in a recognised water hazard (whether the ball lie in water or not) or in casual water in a hazard, the player may drop a ball, under penalty of one stroke, either (*a*) behind the hazard, keeping the spot at which the ball crossed the margin of the hazard between himself and the hole, or (*b*) in the hazard, keeping the spot at which the ball entered the water between himself and the hole.

(2) If a ball lie or be lost in casual water through the green, the player may drop a ball, without penalty, within two club lengths of the margin, as near as possible to the spot where the ball lay, but not nearer to the hole.

If a ball when dropped roll into the water, it may be re-dropped without penalty.

(3) If a ball on the putting-green lie in casual water, or if casual water intervene between a ball lying on the putting-green and the hole, the ball may be played where it lies, or it may be lifted without penalty and placed by hand, either within two club lengths directly behind the spot from which the ball was lifted, or in the nearest position to that spot which is not nearer to the hole and which affords a putt to the hole without casual water intervening.

(4) A ball lying so near to casual water that the water interferes with the player's stance may be treated as if it lay in casual water, under the preceding Sections of this Rule.

(5) If it be impossible from want of space in which to play, or from any other cause, for a player to drop a ball in conformity with Sections (1) and (2) of this Rule, or to place it in conformity with Section (3), he shall "drop" or "place" as nearly as possible within the limits laid down in these sections, but not nearer to the hole.

The penalty for a breach of this Rule shall be the loss of the hole.

PUTTING-GREEN

Rule 28.—(1) Any loose impediment may be lifted from the putting-green, irrespective of the position of the player's ball. If the player's ball, when on the putting-green, move after any loose impediment lying within six inches of it has been touched by the player, his partner, or either of their caddies, the player shall be deemed to have caused it to move and the penalty shall be one stroke.

(2) Dung, worm-casts, snow, and ice may be scraped aside with a club, but the club must not be laid with more than its own weight upon the ground, nor must anything be pressed down either with the club or in any other way.

(3) The line of the putt must not be touched, except by placing the club immediately in front of the ball in the act of addressing it, and as above authorised.

The penalty for a breach of this Rule shall be the loss of the hole.

Rule 29.—(1) When the player's ball is on the putting-green, the player's caddie, his partner, or his partner's caddie may, before the stroke is played, point out a direction for putting, but in doing this they shall not touch the ground on the proposed line of the putt. No mark shall be placed anywhere on the putting-green.

(2) Any player or caddie engaged in the match may stand at the hole, but no player or caddie shall endeavour, by moving or otherwise, to influence the action of the wind upon the ball.

A player is, however, always entitled to send his own caddie to stand at the hole while he plays his stroke.

Either side may refuse to allow a person who is not engaged in the match to stand at the hole.

The penalty for a breach of this Rule shall be the loss of the hole.

Rule 30.—When the player's ball lies on the putting-green, he shall not play until the opponent's ball is at rest.

The penalty for a breach of this Rule shall be the loss of the hole.

Rule 31.—(1) When the balls lie within six inches of each other on the putting-green (the distance to be measured from their nearest points), the ball lying nearer to the hole may, at the option of either the player or the opponent, be lifted until the other ball is played, and the lifted ball shall then be replaced as near as possible to the place where it lay.

If either ball be accidentally moved in complying with this Rule, no penalty shall be incurred, and the ball so moved shall be replaced.

(2) On the putting-green, if a player play when his opponent should have played, the stroke may be at once recalled by the opponent, and the ball replaced.

NOTE.—For a ball which is displaced on a putting-green, see Rule 17 (2) and (3).

For a player playing the opponent's ball on the putting-green, see Rule 20 (1).

For casual water on a putting-green, see Rule 27 (3).

Rule 32.—(1) Either side is entitled to have the flag-stick removed when approaching the hole; if a player's ball strike the flag-stick, which has been so removed by himself, or his partner, or either of their caddies, his side shall lose the hole.

If the ball rest against the flag-stick which is in the hole, the player shall be entitled to remove the flag-stick, and if the ball fall into the hole, the player shall be deemed to have holed out at his last stroke.

(2) If the player's ball knock the opponent's ball into the hole, the opponent shall be deemed to have holed out at his last stroke.

If the player's ball move the opponent's ball, the opponent, if he choose, may replace it, but this must be done before another stroke is played by either side.

If the player's ball stop on the spot formerly occupied by the opponent's ball, and the opponent declare his intention to replace his ball, the player shall first play another stroke, after which the opponent shall replace and play his ball.

(3) If the player has holed out and the opponent then plays to the lip of the hole, the player may not knock the ball away, but the opponent, if asked, shall play his next stroke without delay.

If the opponent's ball lie on the lip of the hole, the player, after holing out, may knock the ball away, claiming the hole if holing at the like, and the half if holing at the odd, provided that the player's ball does not strike the opponent's ball and set it in motion ; if the player neglect to knock away the opponent's ball, and it fall into the hole, the opponent shall be deemed to have holed out at his last stroke.

Rule 33.—When a player has holed out and his opponent has been left with a stroke for the half, nothing that the player who has holed out can do shall deprive him of the half which he has already gained.

General Penalty

Rule 34.—Where no penalty for the breach of a Rule is stated, the penalty shall be the loss of the hole.

Disputes

Rule 35.—An umpire or referee, when appointed, shall take cognisance of any breach of Rule that he may observe, whether he be appealed to on the point or not.

Rule 36.—If a dispute arise on any point, a claim must be made before the players strike off from the next teeing-ground, or, in the case of the last hole of the round, before they leave the putting-green. The players have the right of determining to whom the point shall be referred, but should they not agree, either side may have it referred officially through the Secretary of the Club to the Rules of Golf Committee, whose decision shall be final. If the point in dispute be not covered by the Rules of Golf, the arbiters shall decide it by equity.

Recommendations for Local Rules

When necessary, local Rules should be made for such obstructions as trees, hedges, fixed seats, fences, gates, railways, and walls, for such difficulties as rabbit scrapes, hoof marks, and other damage caused to the course by animals, and for such local conditions as the existence of mud, which may be held to interfere with the proper playing of the game.

When a ball is lifted under a Local Rule, as in the case of a ball lifted from a putting-green other than that of the hole which is being played, the Rules of Golf Committee recommends that if it is to be played from "through the green," it should be *dropped*; if it is to be played on the putting-green of the hole that is being played, it should be *placed*.

Form and Make of Golf Clubs

The Rules of Golf Committee intimates that it will not sanction any substantial departure from the traditional and accepted form and make of golf clubs, which, in its opinion, consist of a plain shaft and a head which does not contain any mechanical contrivance, such as springs.

Etiquette of Golf

1. No one should stand close to or directly behind the ball, move, or talk, when a player is making a stroke.

On the putting-green no one should stand beyond the hole in the line of a player's stroke.

2. The player who has the honour should be allowed to play before his opponent tees his ball.

3. No player should play from the tee until the party in front have played their second strokes and are out of range, nor play up to the putting-green till the party in front have holed out and moved away.

4. Players who have holed out should not try their putts over again when other players are following them.

5. Players looking for a lost ball should allow other matches coming up to pass them ; they should signal to the players following them to pass, and, having given such a signal, they should not continue their play until these players have passed and are out of reach.

6. Turf cut or displaced by a player should be at once replaced and pressed down with the foot.

7. A player should carefully fill up all holes made by himself in a bunker.

8. Players should see that their caddies do not injure the holes by standing close to them when the ground is soft.

9. A player who has incurred a penalty stroke should intimate the fact to his opponent as soon as possible.

Special Rules for Match Play Competitions

Rule 1.—On the putting-green, if the competitor whose ball is the nearer to the hole play first, his ball shall be at once replaced.

The penalty for a breach of this Rule shall be the disqualification of both competitors.

Rule 2.—A competitor shall not waive any penalty incurred by his opponent, under penalty of disqualification.

Rule 3. Competitors shall not agree to exclude the operation of any Rule or Local Rule, under penalty of disqualification.

The Rules of Golf Committee recommends that players should not concede putts to their opponents.

RULES FOR THREE-BALL, BEST BALL, AND FOUR-BALL MATCHES

Definitions

(1) When three players play against each other, each playing his own ball, the match is called a three-ball match.

(2) When one player plays his ball against the best ball of two or more players, the match is called a best ball match.

(3) When two players play their better ball against the better ball of two other players, the match is called a four-ball match.

General

Rule 1.—Any player may have any ball in the match lifted or played, at the option of its owner, if he consider that it might interfere with or be of assistance to a player or side.

Rule 2.—If a player's ball move any other ball in the match, the moved ball must be replaced as near as possible to the spot where it lay, without penalty.

Rule 3.—Through the green a player shall incur no penalty for playing when an opponent should have done so, and the stroke shall not be recalled.

On the putting-green the stroke may be recalled by an opponent, but no penalty shall be incurred.

Three-Ball Matches

Rule 4.—During a three-ball match, if no player is entitled at a teeing-ground to claim the honour from both opponents, the same order of striking shall be followed as at the last teeing-ground.

Rule 5.—In a three-ball match, if a player's ball strike, or be stopped, or moved by an opponent or an opponent's caddie or clubs, that opponent shall lose the hole to the player. As regards the other opponent the occurence shall be treated as a rub of the green.

Best-Ball and Four-Ball Matches

Rule 6.—Balls belonging to the same side may be played in the order the side deems best.

Rule 7.—If a player's ball strike, or be stopped, or moved by an opponent, or an opponent's caddie or clubs, the opponent's side shall lose the hole.

Rule 8.—If a player's ball (the player being one of a side) strike, or be stopped by himself, or his partner, or either of their caddies or clubs, only that player shall be disqualified for that hole.

Rule 9.—If a player play a stroke with his partner's ball, and the mistake be discovered and intimated to the other side before an opponent has played another stroke, the player shall be disqualified for that hole, and his partner shall drop a ball as near as possible to the spot from which his ball was played, without penalty. If the mistake be not discovered till after the opponent has played a stroke, the player's side shall lose the hole.

Rule 10.—In all other cases where a player would by the Rules of Golf incur the loss of the hole, he shall be disqualified for that hole, but the disqualification shall not apply to his partner.

SPECIAL RULES FOR STROKE COMPETITIONS

Rules for the Conduct of Stroke Competitions

Wherever the word Committee is used in these Rules, it refers to the Committee in charge of the Competition.

Rule 1.—(1) In Stroke Competitions the competitor who holes the stipulated round or rounds in the fewest strokes shall be the winner.

(2) Competitors shall play in couples; if from any cause there be a single competitor, the Committee shall either provide him with a player, or select a marker for him and allow him to compete alone.

The order and times of starting should, when possible, be determined by ballot.

Competitors should strike off from the first tee in the order in which their names appear upon the starting list. Thereafter the honour should be taken as in match play, but if a competitor by mistake play out of turn, no penalty shall be incurred, and the stroke cannot be recalled.

Rule 2.—(1) Competitors shall start in the order and at the times arranged by the Committee. They shall not discontinue play nor delay to start on account of bad weather or for any other reason whatever, except such as the Committee may consider satisfactory.

The penalty for a breach of this Rule shall be disqualification.

(2) If the Committee consider that the course is not in a playable condition, or that insufficient light renders the proper playing of the game impossible, it shall at any time have power to declare the day's play null and void.

Rule 3.—If the lowest scores be made by two or more competitors, the tie or ties shall be decided by another round to be played on the same day; but if the Committee determine that this is inexpedient or impossible, it shall appoint a day and time for the decision of the tie or ties.

Should an uneven number of competitors tie, their names shall be drawn by ballot and placed upon a list; the competitors shall then play in couples in the order in which their names appear. The single competitor shall be provided for by the Committee either under Rule 1 (2), or by allowing three competitors to play together if their unanimous consent has been obtained.

Rule 4.—(1) New holes should be made on the day on which Stroke Competitions begin.

(2) On the day of the Competition, before starting, no competitor shall play on, or on to, any of the putting-greens, nor shall he intentionally play at any hole of the stipulated round which is within his reach, under penalty of disqualification.

Rule 5.—(1) The score for each hole shall be kept by a marker or by each competitor noting the other's score. Should more than one marker keep a score, each shall sign the part of the score for which he is responsible. The scores should be called out after each hole. On completion of the stipulated round the card shall be signed by the person who has marked it, and the competitor shall see that it is handed in as soon as reasonably possible. The penalty for a breach of this Rule shall be disqualification.

Scoring cards should be issued with the date and the player's name entered on the card.

(2) Competitors must satisfy themselves before the cards are handed in that the scores for each hole are correctly marked, as no alteration can be made on any card after it has been returned. If it be found that a competitor has returned a score lower than that actually played he shall be disqualified. For the additions of the scores marked the Committee shall be responsible.

(3) If, on the completion of the stipulated round, a player is doubtful whether he has incurred a penalty at any hole, he may enclose his scoring card with a written statement of the circumstances to the Committee, who shall decide what penalty, if any, has been incurred.

Rules for Play in Stroke Competitions

Rule 6.—A competitor shall not ask for nor willingly receive advice from any one except his caddie.

The penalty for a breach of this Rule shall be disqualification.

Rule 7.—If at any hole a competitor play his first stroke from outside the limits of the teeing-ground, he shall count that stroke, tee a ball, and play his second stroke from within these limits.

The penalty for a breach of this Rule shall be disqualification.

Rule 8.—(1) A competitor shall hole out with his own ball at every hole. The penalty for a breach of this Rule shall be disqualification.

(2) If a competitor play a stroke with a ball other than his own, he shall incur no penalty provided he then play his own ball ; but if he play two consecutive strokes with a wrong ball, he shall be disqualified.

(3) In a hazard, if a competitor play more than one stroke with a ball other than his own, and the mistake be discovered before he has played a stroke with the wrong ball from outside the limits of the hazard, he shall incur no penalty provided he then play his own ball.

The penalty for a breach of this Rule shall be disqualification.

Rule 9.—If a competitor's ball strike or be stopped by himself, his clubs, or his caddie, the penalty shall be one stroke, except as provided for in Stroke Rule 13 (1).

Rule 10.—(1) If a competitor's ball strike or be stopped by another competitor, or his clubs, or his caddie, it is a rub of the green, and the ball shall be played from where it lies, except as provided for in Stroke Rule 13 (1). If a competitor's ball which is at rest be accidentally moved by another competitor, or his caddie, or his clubs, or his ball, or any outside agency except wind, it shall be replaced as near as possible to the spot where it lay. The penalty for a breach of this Rule shall be disqualification.

(2) A competitor may have any other player's ball played or lifted, at the option of its owner, if he find that it interferes with his stroke.

Rule 11.—(1) A ball may be lifted from any place on the course under penalty of two strokes. A ball so lifted shall be teed and played behind the place where it lay ; if this be impossible, it shall be teed and played as near as possible to the place where it lay, but not nearer to the hole.

In preparing a tee as above authorised, the player is exempted from the restrictions imposed by Rule 15.

The penalty for a breach of this Section of the Rule shall be disqualification.

(2) For the purpose of identification, a competitor may at any time lift and carefully replace his ball in the presence of the player with whom he is competing.

The penalty for a breach of this Section of the Rule shall be one stroke.

Rule 12.—If a ball be " lost " (except in water, casual water, or out of bounds), the competitor shall, whether he has played from " through the green " or from a hazard, return as near as possible to the spot from which the ball was struck, and there tee a ball, under penalty of one stroke.

[Under this Rule a ball shall only be considered lost when it has not been found after a search of five minutes.]

Rule 13.—(1) When a competitor's ball lying within twenty yards of the hole is played and strikes either the flag-stick or the person standing at the hole, the penalty shall be two strokes.

(2) When both balls are on the putting-green, if a competitor's ball strike the ball of the player with whom he is competing, the competitor shall incur a penalty of one stroke, and the ball which was struck shall be at once replaced, see Stroke Rule 10 (1).

(3) The competitor whose ball is the farther from the hole may have the ball which is nearer to the hole lifted or played at the option of its

owner. If the latter refuse to comply with this Rule when requested to do so, he shall be disqualified.

(4) If the competitor whose ball is the nearer to the hole consider that his ball might be of assistance to the player with whom he is competing, he should lift it or play first.

(5) If the competitor whose ball is the nearer to the hole lift his ball while the player's ball is in motion, he shall incur a penalty of one stroke.

(6) If a competitor or his caddie pick up his ball from the putting-green before it is holed out (except as provided for above), he shall, before he has struck off from the next tee, or, in the case of the last hole of the round, before he has left the putting-green, be permitted to replace the ball under penalty of two strokes.

Rule 14.—Where in the Rules of Golf the penalty for the breach of any Rule is the loss of the hole, in Stroke Competitions the penalty shall be the loss of two strokes, except where otherwise provided for in these Special Rules.

Rule 15.—The Rules of Golf, so far as they are not at variance with these Special Rules, shall apply to Stroke Competitions.

Rule 16.—If a dispute arise on any point, it shall be decided by the Committee, whose decision shall be final, unless an appeal be made to the Rules of Golf Committee, as provided for in Rule 36.

INDEX